Tinsley E. Yarbrough

Location!

The Sphinx Rock in the Garden of the Gods at the Iverson Motion Picture Ranch,
Chatsworth, California–the most familiar location backdrop of them all.
Friends and Lovers (1931). Photo Bison Archives

Location!

John Wayne in Monument Valley, the most spectacular filming location of all, for She Wore a Yellow Ribbon (1949).

Location!

And the cucumber shaped Gene Autry Rock in the fabulous Alabama Hills of Lone Pine, most scenic of the California filming sites. Photo Bill Sasser

Those Great Western

Movie Locations

Tinsley E. Yarbrough

Tumbleweed Press

Those Great Western Movie Locations

Copyright 2008 by Tinsley E. Yarbrough

ISBN 978-1-60643-255-6

Manufactured in the United States

Published by Tumbleweed Press
337 Glenn Court
Greenville, North Carolina 27858
252-756-7642

To

Cole and Christine

Steve

and the memory of

Bill Witney

Table of Contents

Prologue

For nearly four decades beginning in the early 1930s—the "golden age" of motion pictures—western movies were a staple of the industry. Such stars as Gary Cooper, Randolph Scott, John Wayne, Clark Gable, Henry Fonda, Audie Murphy and Alan Ladd regularly appeared in western productions. Until the mid-fifties, kids of all ages also thrilled to a steady diet of B-western Saturday matinee series, programmers featuring Tom Mix, Buck Jones, Ken Maynard, Tim McCoy, Gene Autry, Roy Rogers, "Wild Bill" Elliott, Allan "Rocky" Lane, Rex Allen, Charles ("The Durango Kid") Starrett, Johnny Mack Brown and a host of other stars, as well as Bob Livingston, Ray "Crash" Corrigan and other leads of such trio series as "The Three Mesquiteers," "The Rough Riders," "The Range Busters," "The Trail Blazers" and "The Texas Rangers"—topped off, of course, by weekly episodes of such cliffhanger serials as *Spy Smasher*, *Perils of Nyoka*, *The Adventures of Captain Marvel*, *Batman* and *Superman*.

When I was a boy in the mid-forties and early fifties, Decatur, my Alabama hometown, boasted three movie palaces—the Princess, the Capital and the Roxy. On Friday afternoons after school, my brother Steve and I rushed down town to the Capital—by then a rundown house that mainly featured re-releases of A- and B-westerns and serials. On Saturday, we went to the Princess, Decatur's major theater, for a newly released B-western, serial chapter, cartoon and, if we were lucky, a comedy (The Three Stooges, naturally, were our favorites)—plus, in later years, a second feature. Some weekends, we even took in a third matinee at the Roxy across town. During the week, we often attended newly released A-westerns, with Randolph Scott, Audie Murphy and Gary Cooper my favorites.

By sight if not name, western feature, cliffhanger and, later, TV filming locations became almost as familiar to me as the stars. Early in my movie-going days, I began to recognize the same landscapes appearing in title after title. The same chase roads, the same cliffs, the same vistas, the same western streets and ranches, the same lakes. Gradually, I began to attach names to many of those sites. I learned, for example, that most A- and B-westerns utilized a few locations close to Hollywood—especially the great Iverson Motion Picture Ranch of Chatsworth, in the northwest corner of Los Angeles' San Fernando Valley; western star Ray "Crash" Corrigan's Simi Valley ranch, called Corriganville when it also became a weekend tourist attraction in the late forties; Newhall's Monogram Ranch, renamed Melody Ranch when acquired by Gene Autry in 1952, and other Newhall area ranches, including the Jauregui and Walker spreads, as well as the Vasquez Rocks north of Newhall, with their distinctive formations jutting upward at an angle into the sky—rocks seen frequently even today in television commercials advertising everything from Taco Bell to automobiles.

Later, I was able to identify more distant filming sites, among them the massive Alabama Hills rock formations of Lone Pine, two hundred miles north of Los Angeles, and the Big Bear Lake area, southeast of L. A. Western sets on studio back lots and ranches also became increasingly recognizable, especially those at the grand old Republic lot in North Hollywood (now CBS Studio Center), the Columbia Ranch in

Burbank, featured in *High Noon* as well as countless other westerns, and Universal Studio's Six-Points western street. So, too, did sites beyond California, including those of Kanab, Utah; Gallup, New Mexico; Monument Valley and Moab; Sedona and Old Tucson, Arizona.

Finally, in 1985 I began making periodic location trips west, first to various California sites, then to Utah, Arizona, Nevada, New Mexico, Wyoming, Montana and other states. Occasionally, I was able to "discover" locations that had largely escaped notice since the filming days, including the beautiful, white, Spanish-style French Ranch in Hidden Valley near Thousand Oaks, California; Kentucky Park Farm (now Ventura Farms), the Hidden Valley thoroughbred ranch that appeared in *My Pal Trigger* (1946) and several other Roy Rogers titles, as well as Ronald Reagan's *Stallion Road* (1947); the Agoura-Albertson Ranch; the long "lost" Blue Canyon outside Tuba City, Arizona, put to such splendid use in the Hopalong Cassidy title *Texas Trail* (1937); and the equally obscure Brandeis Ranch on the western border of the Iverson spread.

My location interest (obsession) could be a real distraction to my enjoyment of films. I found myself tending to look "behind" or "past" a scene to its background. Is that Iverson? Corriganville? Kanab? Ah, yes, the Jack Ingram Ranch. But I was hooked. Most of my leisure time was devoted to collecting information about film sites.

Wishing to share my research with others, I put together crude but, I hoped, helpful videos based on my travels. Next, I wrote a locations column that appeared for nine years in Boyd and Donna Magers' fine *Western Clippings* film magazine and I contributed columns to their excellent *Serial Report* for several years as well. Finally, I decided to organize that material, collect additional research and write this book. It is based not only on personal visits to most of the locations surveyed and comparisons of my video and photographic images with thousands of films and television episodes, but also on interviews with actors, directors, stunt people and persons connected with the sites covered; research in newspaper, library and film organization files; published memoirs and other film-related books and articles. Amply documented with numerous references to titles shot at the sites covered, the book traces the film history of most of the locations, highlights their most prominent landscape features and recounts colorful "on location" stories drawn from my sources.

Mercifully, I have spared the reader any effort to place western filming locations in some broader analytical framework–whether philosophical, cultural or sociological. The locales examined contributed significantly, however, to our largely mythical popular image of the American west and frontier expansion. I hope, therefore, that this book will make an important addition to the ever-growing body of literature on western cinema.

Responsibility for what follows, of course, is entirely mine. This book would not have been possible, however, without the assistance of many individuals and institutions, including Patricia Russell Miller, Jack Garner, Richard Martin, Pat Distal, Jean Stimolo, Rosemary Couch, Jean Forsythe, Camille Jauregui, Noureen Jauregui Baer, Brent Davis, Richard Angullo, Bob Ayers, Dr. Robert Hertz, Joan Cooper, Whitey Hughes, Alice Allen, Pierce Lyden, Neil Summers, Edwin Iverson, Marc Lawrence, Sigurd Furubotten, Virginia Watson, Merrill McCord, Harry Carey, Jr., Bear Hudkins, Mildred Walker Fisher, Alex Gordon, Tom Frew, Gary Gray, Tommy Ivo, Teresa Rogers, Marc Wanamaker, Earl Bellamy, Steve Sligh, Chellis Hurdle, Renaud Veluzat, Jim Clark, Bill Couch, John Wofford, Tom Slaback, Melanie Sturgeon, Al Ellena, Jack Mathis, Rex Allen, Sue Birmingham, Richard J. Schmidt, Cheryl Rogers-Barnett, Adrian Booth Brian, Kay Aldridge, Linda Stirling, Monte Hale, Ben Johnson, Harry Carey, Jr., Charlie Aldrich, Jerry Vance, Tom Goldrup, Jim Goldrup, George Starbuck, Lee Mace, Keith Foster, Glenn Hughes, Dave Holland, Henry

Donovan, Hoyt Johnson, Bob Bradshaw, Dick Farnsworth, Ben Cooper, Debra Paget, Morgan Woodward, Ace Hudkins, Jack Williams, Roydon Clark, Jock Mahoney, James Drury, Michael Fitzgerald, Packy Smith, Robert S. Birchard, Barry Martin, Leith Adams, Vince Guerriero, Brian Dalrymple, Will Hutchins, Peggy Stewart, Jackie Hamblin Rife, Steve Browning, Dick Jones and Robert J. Thompson, as well as the staffs of Rocketdyne, the Margaret Herrick Library, Sharlot Hall Museum, Jamestown Railtown Park, Arizona state archives, New Mexico film commission, Imperial County Film Commission, and the public libraries of Los Angeles, Valencia, Newhall, Chatsworth, Thousand Oaks, Agoura, Calabasas, Indio, and Palmdale, California; Kanab and St. George, Utah; Missoula and Billings, Montana; and Gallup, New Mexico.

I am especially indebted to several people. As a certified computer "illiterate," I owe a tremendous debt of thanks to Sheila Ellis and my colleagues Bonnie Mani, Jody Baumgartner and Jalil Roshandel. Don Key, former publisher of *The Big Reel*, gave me my earliest opportunity to write a location article. Through his 1994 invitation to do a regular column for *Western Clippings*, Boyd Magers provided me with an incentive to build on my initial research–and deadlines to assure that I completed my assignments. Boyd also gave me the opportunity to obtain electronic images from his huge collection of stills and he and his wife Donna carefully reviewed the manuscript, offering this novice numerous helpful suggestions to vastly improve the book's layout and overall appearance. Of "fellow travelers" whom I was privileged to join on early location treks, I am particularly grateful to Sherman and Carolyn Pippen, who graciously invited me to join them and others on my first location trips, and to their friend Evelyn Finley, that wonderful stunt woman and B-western heroine, who proved to be the perfect location guide. Sherman and Evelyn are no longer with us but they are always in my thoughts.

I also appreciate the many other friends I have made through my interest in locations and western films–the late Ed Wyatt, Nick Ellerbe, "Buddy" Bryant, Jerry Campbell, James Howard, Norman Foster, Wayne Short, Clay Satcher, Jim Hamby, Bill Sasser, Gene Blottner, George Coan and Phil Loy, to mention only a few. To one degree or another, each of them assisted me with my research.

Of all my location friends and traveling companions, I am most grateful to John Leonard, the foremost authority on the life and films of William "Wild Bill" Elliott. John graciously shared with me terrific photographs taken during his visits in the 1970s to the Iverson ranch, Corriganville, the old Republic lot and the Columbia Ranch. He also accompanied me on several California trips, following without complaint as I merrily ignored "No Trespassing" signs and more ominous warnings in my quest for yet another "lost" filming site. Once, he even watched dubiously as I drove "our" rental car down the steep spillway of the Lake Sherwood dam, then through a posh riding academy, after a construction crew locked us in. John's close eye for locations was a tremendous help; so, too, have been our weekly telephone conversations and all-too-infrequent visits at western film festivals in the years since our California trips.

Although this book is based largely on primary research, I also drew, of course, on the work of others. Carlo Gaberscek is without doubt the foremost authority on A-western locations. His several books were of tremendous help to me; it is very unfortunate that they are available only in Italian. Kenny Stier published a very thorough listing of locations for thousands of titles, as well as brief profiles of most filming sites. David Rothel's *Ambush of Ghosts* (1991), written with the assistance of Ken Taylor, provided fans with an excellent and visually stunning introduction to major filming sites. Boyd Magers' *So You Wanna See Cowboy Stuff* (2003) includes excerpts from many of my *Western Clippings* location columns and much more of interest to western fans.

Various memoirs also include location information. Stuntman Chuck Roberson's colorful account of his life as *The Fall Guy* (1980) is highly recommended. So, also, is Harry Carey, Jr.'s *Company of Heroes*

(1994). Biographies of stars, including Randy Roberts and James S. Olson, *John Wayne: American* (1995), and Marc Elliot, *Jimmy Stewart* (2006), were also helpful.

Certain location researchers have focused primarily on a particular site or region. The late Dave Holland's *On Location in Lone Pine* (1990) is superb and his two videos on various filming sites were an important addition to location research. Dave is sorely missed. Also recommended are Richard J. Schmidt's excellent guide to filming at Red Rock Canyon, California, John A. Murray's *Cinema Southwest: An Illustrated Guide to the Movies and their Locations* (2000) and Betty L. Stanton's *"Where God Put the West"–Movie Making in the Desert* (1994), about filming in Moab and Monument Valley, Utah. W. Lee Cozad's *Those Magnificent Mountain Movies* (2002) contains relatively little specific location material but does include a filmography and stills of motion pictures made at Big Bear and other sites in the San Bernardino mountains. Although not very useful as an accurate or thorough account of filming at the Iverson ranch, Bob Sherman's *Quiet on the Set* (1984) provides interesting information on the history of the Iverson family. Bob Bradshaw's pamphlet on *Westerns of the Red Rock Country* (1991) contains photographs from 43 films shot in Sedona, Arizona. Jackson Hole resident Walt Farmer has produced excellent CD-ROMS on film-making in Wyoming–packing more into his CDs than many, many books could possibly have provided. Frederic B. Wildfang's *Hollywood of the Rockies* (1997) includes many interesting anecdotes on filming in Durango, Colorado.

Particularly because of the importance of trains to western plots, Larry Jensen's definitive *Movie Railroads* (1981) was another invaluable source. So, too, was the ongoing work of Jerry Schneider. Jerry is not only the author of excellent books on Corriganville and other film topics; his Movie Making Locations website is the most thorough online source of information about filming sites. On his website, Jerry acknowledges his indebtedness to Carlo Gaberscek and me. I am absolutely certain, however, that I have obtained at least as much from Jerry as he has derived from my efforts. Victor Medina's Visiting the Movie Sites website was also helpful, as were online sites covering filming in Arizona, New Mexico and other states.

Finally, I am forever indebted to the late William Witney, superb director of classic cliffhanger serials, exciting Roy Rogers and Rex Allen features, outstanding A-westerns and many television episodes. When Witney's name appeared on theater or TV screens, fans knew immediately that they were in for a treat. He gave me and other front-row kids hundreds of hours of unparalleled cinematic and video pleasure and his memoir of his serial-directing days, *In a Door, Into a Fight, Out a Door, Into a Chase: Moviemaking Remembered by the Guy at the Door* (1995), is a superb insider's look into that wonderful chapter in filmdom's golden age. Most important from my perspective, he had a wonderful memory and was an excellent source of directions to many of the locations used in his films. This book is dedicated to Bill Witney's memory.

Chapter 1

Studio Facilities, Ranches and other L. A. Locations

With the exception of the tiniest independents, the movie studios maintained western streets and other permanent sets on their back lots. Some also operated their own film ranches, either in Los Angeles or close by, and several rental studios had western streets for lease. Finally, a number of other L.A. ranches and sites sometimes appeared in films.

The Paramount Ranch

Paramount Studios had a western street in downtown Hollywood. Set against a huge horizon screen backdrop on which was painted an obviously fake mountain top, that street hosted, among other productions, *The Gunfight at the O. K. Corral* (1957) and many "Bonanza" episodes. During the golden era, however, Paramount's ranch at Agoura housed the most impressive of the studio's standing sets. Located originally along what is now the Ventura Freeway, about a forty minute drive northwest of L.A., the Paramount Ranch boasted some of the most elaborate exterior sets ever. When Jesse Lasky and New York theater owner and film distributor W. W. Hawkinson first formed Paramount Pictures, Lasky bought 2,000 acres of land in Burbank on which the studio first built standing sets. By 1921, the Burbank sets had become unduly familiar to moviegoers and Paramount acquired its Agoura property. "Rancho Paramount," as it was called, was situated along what is now the Ventura Freeway, near the Kanan Road exit. Originally part of the old Rancho Las Virgenes Spanish land grant, the parcel had also belonged to the grandfather of Agoura native Jack Dalmeyer, then to Frank T. Davis, and finally to "Jigs" Waring, who sold the land to Paramount. Certain sources claim the ranch comprised 4,000 acres and the National Park Service had found documentation for about 2,700 by the mid-1990s.

Whatever figure is correct, the Paramount Ranch was a huge operation that included not only an impressive western street set but others as well, including a colonial New England town built for Claudette

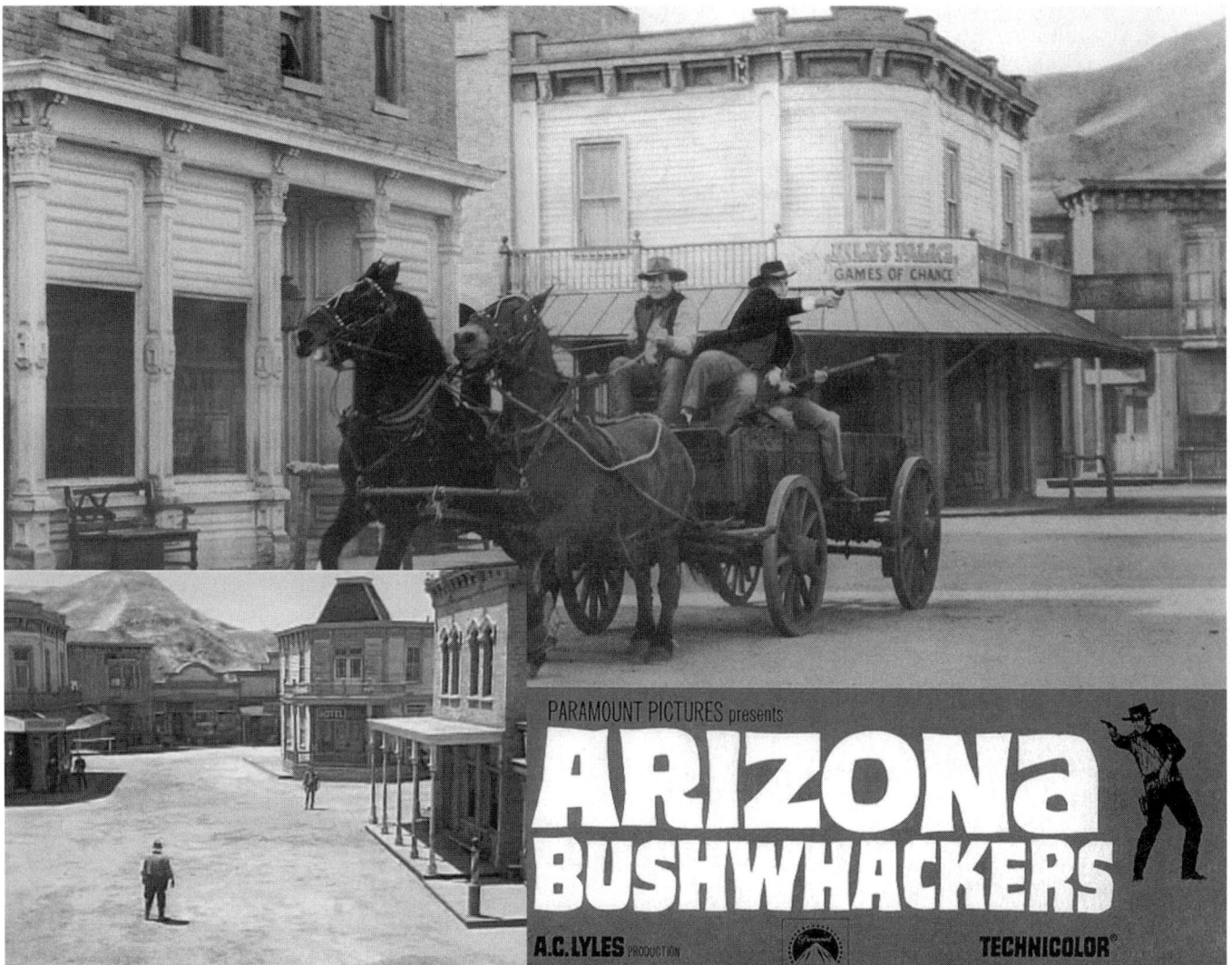

The Paramount Studio western street; the inset provides a fuller picture of the street.

Colbert's *Maid of Salem* (1937) and a massive fortress seen in Gary Cooper's *Adventures of Marco Polo* (1937). The ranch also boasted an entire supporting community of barns, stables, production craft shops and a commissary that reportedly could accommodate 4,500. The scenery was spectacular–grassy plains, rolling hills with scattered trees, woodlands, streams and a backdrop of mountains.

The ranch's large western street set had one feature in particular that distinguished it from other studio and location ranch western streets–a church with a high peaked roof and steeple at the end of one street and, camera right of the church, a similar smaller building with peaked roof but no steeple. The street set was probably first put to use in Gary Cooper's early sound title *The Virginian* (1929) and appeared in other A-westerns as well. It also appeared not only in some of the studio's Hoppy B-westerns (*Cassidy of Bar 20*, 1938, *Bar 20 Justice*, 1938, *Pride of the West*, 1938) but in the B-western productions of other companies, including early Buck Jones (*Deadline*,1931), Ken Maynard (*Phantom Thunderbolt*, 1933) and Tim McCoy (*Prescott Kid*,1934) titles. Interestingly, in fact, Hoppy's Paramount titles used the western streets at Monogram and Kernville more than the Agoura facilities.

The original western set also saw service in non-western rustics, such as early and late thirties versions of the Tom Sawyer and Huckleberry Finn sagas. Buck Jones' *The Avenger* (1931) gave prominent play to

The Paramount Ranch street made one of its most impressive appearances in a non-western title, The Adventures of Tom Sawyer (1938). *Photo Bison Archives*

Star Richard Arlen with ranch manager Roger Bothell on the street during production of Caught (1931). *Photo Bison Archives*

the picket fences and residences built for *Tom Sawyer* (1930) and *Huckleberry Finn* (1931). The western streets were even paved for *Miracle of Morgan's Creek* (1944).

Miracle of Morgan's Creek, however, was one of the last films using the ranch under the Paramount banner. A November 24, 1943, *Variety* item indicated that the ranch was auctioned that month to a contractor with no immediate plans for the site. The studio reserved the right to use the facilities for the next five years at a nominal annual rental rate of $500. Paramount, *Variety* reported, had bought the ranch for about $425,000 and had recently spent $60,000 rebuilding its western street. The property brought only $39,500 at auction. Paramount was left only with its Hollywood back lot western street.

But the Agoura site's filming days were hardly over. In 1952, William Bernhardt Hertz purchased a portion of the ranch. A New Jersey native with a romantic vision of the Old West, Bill Hertz had amassed sufficient wealth in various business ventures by the end of World War II to retire at 49 and realize his long-time dream of moving with his family to California. Hertz first bought a North Hollywood home with a riding ring, three horses and a stable. Later, with his brother-in-law as a silent partner, he purchased a 326-acre parcel on the southern portion of the old Paramount Agoura Hills property for $52,000.

Hertz Paramount Ranch.

By that point, the original ranch sets, which were a considerable distance north of the Hertz parcel, had been dismantled. But several large, corrugated metal buildings remained on the Hertz property. Hertz and his teenaged son, Robert, set to work facing the buildings with western facades. Once that was completed, Hertz placed an ad in the *Hollywood Reporter*, offering the property for rental to film and TV companies.

The Hertz Paramount Ranch's first client was Reelistic, which paid $50 to film a short at the ranch on how to draw pictures of horses. But soon, "Have Gun Will Travel," "The Cisco Kid," "Gunsmoke," "Bat Masterson," "Zane Grey Theater" and other TV series were filming at the ranch and, more frequently, at the old Ingram ranch in Woodland Hills, which Hertz had also purchased. Years later, Robert Hertz, who sometimes rode his pinto, Reno, as an extra in series shot there, still had vivid memories of the amazing speed with which "The Cisco Kid" company filmed two shows at once, often in a day or two, on the spreads.

As business grew, Bill Hertz added buckboards and other rolling stock, built a fort set on the site where the church often seen in "Dr Quinn, Medicine Woman" TV episodes later stood, and acquired western buildings and props from RKO's Encino ranch, which had been in operation since 1929-30, but was dismantled following its 1953 sale to developers.

Hertz also played host to social and political gatherings as well as hayrides, with his son Robert and other area teenagers staging holdups to "terrorize" the visitors. Hertz had planned to building a home near Ronald Reagan's Lake Malibu ranch, on the Hertz Ranch's southern boundary. But ill health obliged him and his brother-in law to sell the parcel for $200,000 in the late fifties.

The ranch next became the Paramount Sportsman's Ranch, offering a variety of recreational opportunities and a midget-auto race track. In 1962, Dee Cooper–slit-eyed veteran of Lash LaRue, Whip Wilson, Eddie Dean, Johnny Mack Brown and other latter-day B-western epics–began leasing the property from its current owners, including Arthur Whizzin, for rental to movie and television companies, as well as producers of TV commercials. Cooper's ramshackle "ghost town" set even impersonated Chatsworth's Spahn Movie Ranch for "Helter Skelter" (1976), the TV dramatization of the Charles Manson case. Portions of the ranch also appeared in Warren Beatty's *Reds* (1981) as well as other features and such TV series as "CHIPS" and "BJ and the Bear."

A 45-year member of the Screen Actors Guild, Cooper often appeared in entries for friend Lee Majors' "Fall Guy" series and other titles shot at the ranch but was perhaps best known in later years for his role as a prospector type in commercials. The last western feature shot at the ranch during Cooper's tenure was apparently the little-seen 1978 independent production *Shame, Shame on the Bixby Boys*, starring Monte Markham, Don Barry, Marshall Reed and Cooper.

For a time, the area seemed doomed to the developers' bulldozers. But in 1980, the National Park Service rode to the rescue, taking permanent possession of the property but also continuing the ranch's long tradition as a filming site. With Ranger Alice Allen as film coordinator, the sets left from the Hertz and Cooper days, refurbished and augmented with new studio-constructed sets, soon attracted a brisk business, including the long-running "Dr. Quinn" series.

Although no longer connected with the ranch's operations, Dee Cooper and his wife Joan continued to serve as location brokers for other area ranches. Cooper died in 1989, at 69. But his wife still arranged filming sites for TV and movie producers through Paramount Ranch Locations, the company they formed during Dee Cooper's tenure at the ranch.

Directions: To reach the only working movie ranch open free to the public, take the Ventura Freeway west from L.A. to Agoura's Kanan Road exit, Kanan Road south to Cornell Road, left on Cornell to the ranch entrance on the right.

Universal Studios

Carl Laemmle, founder of Universal studios, began his motion picture career as a Chicago theater owner in 1906 but soon became a film-maker. Laemmle's Independent Motion Picture (Imp) Company released his first feature, *Hiawatha,* in 1909 and in 1912 he consolidated Imp, Bison 101 and several other companies to form Universal Pictures.

Two years later, Laemmle acquired a Hollywood studio at Sunset and Gower. But in 1915, he bought a 410-acre chicken ranch in what was to become North Hollywood and built Universal City. At that point, his studio was so remote the 15,000 who attended its opening had to hike seven miles through the Caheunga Pass to reach the site. But Universal quickly became a film-making Mecca, producing the silent classics of Lon Chaney, Mary Pickford and Rudolph Valentino, among others, and making sound-era box office cash registers jingle with the features of such stars as Abbott and Costello, Deanna Durbin, Tony Curtis and Rock Hudson, as well as its Dracula, Frankenstein and Wolf Man horror titles. But western stars, both A and B, would also be a Universal staple–from the Duke, Randolph Scott, Jimmy Stewart and Jock Mahoney, to Hoot Gibson, Tom Mix, Buck Jones and Maynard, to Bob Baker, Johnny Mack Brown and Tex Ritter, to Rod Cameron, Eddie Dew and Kirby Grant. In fact, the first filming on the lot apparently took place at what was to become the elaborate "Six Points, Texas" streets, the core of the studio's western sets.

Especially in the early days, production crews sometimes used location town sets, such as Kernville's western street. But most Universal titles used Six Points and other production units sometimes rented those sets as well. Town scenes for Hoppy's *Riders of the Timberline* (1941), a Paramount release, were filmed on Six Points, for example. In fact, even such independent cheapies as Wally Wales' *Breed of the West*

The large livery stable on the main Six Points Street, in Riders of Death Valley (1941).

(1930) and Reb Russell's *Cheyenne Tornado* (1935) sometimes made brief use of the Universal street.

As its name suggests, the Six Points set consisted of six streets running out from a square roughly like the spokes on a wheel. The first developed and most widely used of those streets, especially in the early years, ran southeast down a hill into the square and featured a large livery stable, perhaps the most recognizable Six Points set. Tom Mix's *The Fourth Horseman* (1932), like many other titles, made prominent use of that street.

Around the right corner from that street on the square was a second, less frequently used thoroughfare that ran southwest away from the square. On its southeast corner in later years was a large hotel/saloon set with a covered balcony. Running southeast along the side of the hotel and away from the square was a third street that ended at Park Lake, a large pool that served as the Western Street Dock.

Audie Murphy and his sons at the studio dock set.

On the opposite, northeast side of the square from those three streets were three others. One ran southeast to the dock, where a large riverboat set, first built for *The Mississippi Gambler* (1953) and later featured in Darrin McGavin's "Riverboat" TV series, was anchored. Along that street on the square was another prominent Six Points set, a large building usually featured as a bank. A little used second street ran northeast from the square. Camera left of that street was a third street that ran northwest from the square up a hill into a Mexican village set–the site initially, I believe, for a walled fort occasionally seen in the studio's B-western titles (e.g., *Deep in the Heart of Texas*, 1942), but frequently used as a village set in later features

Audie Murphy in action on Universal's Mexican set.

(e.g., Audie Murphy's *Ride Clear of Diablo*, 1954) and especially in the "Laredo" TV series.

Nor were those the only western streets on that part of the lot. Running southeast from the Mexican set was a narrow thoroughfare identified on studio maps as Denver Street. It played Medicine Bow, Wyoming, on "The Virginian," with the Six Points sets generally used as out-of-town locales on that fine series. The studio's locomotive, railroad station set and a short stretch of track were also located in that area.

Occasionally, of course, each street set would be enlarged or modified to fit a particular plot line. For Audie Murphy's *The Kid from Texas* (1950), for example, an upscale, walled facade used as the residence for heavy Albert Dekker was constructed in the Six Points square (then later moved, I believe, to the Mexican section and modified in appearance). In the early days, the studio also maintained a ranch set with a main house that featured a railed front porch and several barns. That set was seen in Buck Jones and Ken Maynard features, as well as later Johnny Mack Brown and Tex Ritter titles (e.g., *Cheyenne Roundup*, 1943).

West of Denver Street and the railroad set was yet another filming area, Falls Lake. In later years that lake would play host to part of the "Jaws" attraction on Universal's famed studio tours and its New England waterfront set would be featured regularly in the "Murder, She Wrote" TV series. But during the western feature and TV era, a fake mountain with dirt-filled roads sturdy enough for horseback riding served as a backdrop to the lake and also included a waterfall that could be activated at the call of a plot line.

By that point, however, the studio's character and principal product had changed considerably. In a 1946 merger, Universal had become Universal-International and dismantled its B-western, B-feature and serial units, choosing to focus its assets instead entirely on higher budget titles. Financially, that move proved a near-disaster. But MCA (Music Corporation of America) eventually rode to the rescue. In 1950, the talent agency giant formed its television arm Revue Productions and acquired space at Republic Studios (now CBS Studio Center) on Radford Avenue in North Hollywood, where Revue began churning out dozens of video series, including "Tales of Wells Fargo," "The Deputy," "State Trooper," "Alfred Hitchcock Presents" and "Leave It to Beaver."

In 1959, MCA moved its productions to Universal, purchasing the lot and dubbing it Revue Studios. In 1964, Revue was renamed Universal City Studios and its TV production arm became Universal Television. From 1950 to 1980, according to Jeb H. Perry's authoritative history, the company produced more than 200 series, among them such favorites as "The Virginian," "Wagon Train" and "Laramie."

For "The Virginian," star James Drury recalled, the impressive Shiloh Ranch set was developed east of the Hollywood Freeway. In an effort to keep the freeway out of camera range and cut down on traffic noise, the studio built a 150-200-foot high berm or hill about a hundred yards from the freeway. The hill served its purpose reasonably well. But the valley it created with adjacent hills on the lot also trapped smog and intense heat, making filming on the Shiloh spread, Drury remembered, uncomfortable at best. "The Virginian" spread was apparently used for no more shows. But a three-sided ranch set situated closer to the western streets appeared in "The Virginian" as well as other features and series (especially "Laramie").

The studio also planted small groves and rows of different strains of trees to fit varying plotlines. Prolific director Earl Bellamy, who worked on 1200 television shows, remembered, for example, supervising the planting of a row of pine trees along one of the chase roads running through the studio hills. That tree-lined road became a familiar sight to video kids and their parents. Unfortunately, such roads, settings for many western and serial chases, are now paved and used mainly by the trams carrying thousands of riders daily over the lot on the highly profitable studio tour, while the site of the Shiloh spread now hosts the tour parking lot.

A 1990 fire destroyed four acres of sets (about 20 percent of the studio's back lot facades), including portions of New York Street and Court House Square (*Back to the Future, To Kill a Mockingbird*). But the Little Europe sets, scene for Lon Chaney's *Hunchback of Notre Dame* and the "Frankenstein" entries, among many other titles, escaped damage, as did the hillside residences used in countless sit-coms and, most important, the western and Mexican sets. The lot still remains a busy site for feature and television productions, although its tours are probably its most profitable venture.

Republic Studios

Arguably, the 43-acre Republic Studio in North Hollywood produced the best B-westerns and was clearly "King of the Serials" during the movies' golden age. Located at 4024 Radford Avenue off Ventura Blvd. in Studio City, the San Fernando Valley thrill factory, which the major studios unjustly dubbed "Repulsive Pictures" (while privately envying and seeking to copy its super-streamlined technical facilities), produced 386 series westerns and 66 serials, many of them classics, as well as a host of A-westerns and many B and A non-westerns during its comparatively brief history. There were few "dogs" in the lot–not surprisingly, given the talents of such ace directors as Bill Witney, Joseph Kane and Spencer Bennet, the extraordinary skill of Reggie Lanning, Bud Thackery and other studio camera whizzes, the stirring agitatos of such composer-conductors as William Lava and Mort Glickman, and the special effects genius of the Lydecker brothers, Howard and Theodore.

But almost as responsible for the studio's success as its production crews, superb stunt people and immensely appealing company of players were Republic's physical facilities and sets–the focus of this profile. Bordered on the south by Ventura Blvd., west by Radford Avenue, east by Colfax Avenue and north by a tributary of the Los Angeles River (now long part of L.A.'s aqueduct system), the studio's facilities, first constructed in 1928, were originally home to comedy king Mack Sennett. Initially, they consisted primarily of an administration-writers building, two-story dressing rooms (with exterior porches) adjoining a large sound stage and, to the east, a second sound stage with a swimming pool beneath its floor–all located near the southwest boundary of the current studio property.

The Sennett studio produced not only the Keystone Cops series but ten musical shorts with then-unknown crooner Bing Crosby. When Sennett went into bankruptcy in 1933, Mascot Pictures became a major tenant for two years. Then, in 1935, Herbert J. Yates, owner of Republic Film Laboratories and the American Record Company, joined with Mascot, Monogram and Liberty Pictures to form the Republic Pictures Corporation. Its first two titles, *Westward Ho* (1935) and *Tumbling Tumbleweeds* (1935), starring John Wayne and Gene Autry, were instant hits and, in 1937, Yates assumed sole control of studio operations.

Over the years, Yates gradually added new sound stages, including a gigantic stage named for Sennett star Mabel Normand, reputedly for years the largest sound stage in Hollywood. By 1950, the lot comprised many sound stages, two dubbing and musical scoring stages, a large carpentry-miniature building, scene docks and a blacksmith shop, as well as other facilities and many permanent exterior sets.

Titles with a movie studio setting, such as Roy Rogers' *Bells of Rosarita* (1945), Monte Hale's *Out California Way* (1946) and the B-plus feature *Sons of Adventure* (1948), gave prominent play to Republic's production facilities. The administration-writers building and its well-manicured lawn, which resembled a college campus, often played an airport (*G-Men vs. the Black Dragon*, 1943) or scientific institute (*King of the Rocket Men*, 1949) in Republic features and serials.

The studio's lawn and outer walls doubled for the grounds of a country estate in *Drums of Fu Manchu* (1940). Sound stages and the carpentry-miniature shop often posed as warehouses and garages for exciting serial fight scenes, including one fight for *Dick Tracy vs. Crime, Inc.* (1941) that took place amid oil derrick miniatures constructed for *King of the Texas Rangers* (1941). The loading dock for a small storage building near the south end of the lot was the setting for several serial fights and shootouts (*Federal Agents vs.

Underworld, Inc., 1949). A main thoroughfare ran west to east from the administration-writers building to the studio's west (service) gate on Colfax Avenue. The carpentry-miniature building, with large, high windows running across its front, was located along that street near Colfax.

Across from the front of that building, the exterior of which was blown up (in miniature) in numerous Republic serials, was a horizon pool (for miniature shots, among others) that also served as a waterfront in many titles (*North of the Great Divide*,1950, *Zombies of the Stratosphere*, 1952), and an underwater filming tank. Providing a rare insider view of studio sets, the horizon pool and tank played part of the heavy's water company in Rex Allen's *The Last Musketeer* (1952). In the background of one scene in that title, a car can be seen driving along Colfax!

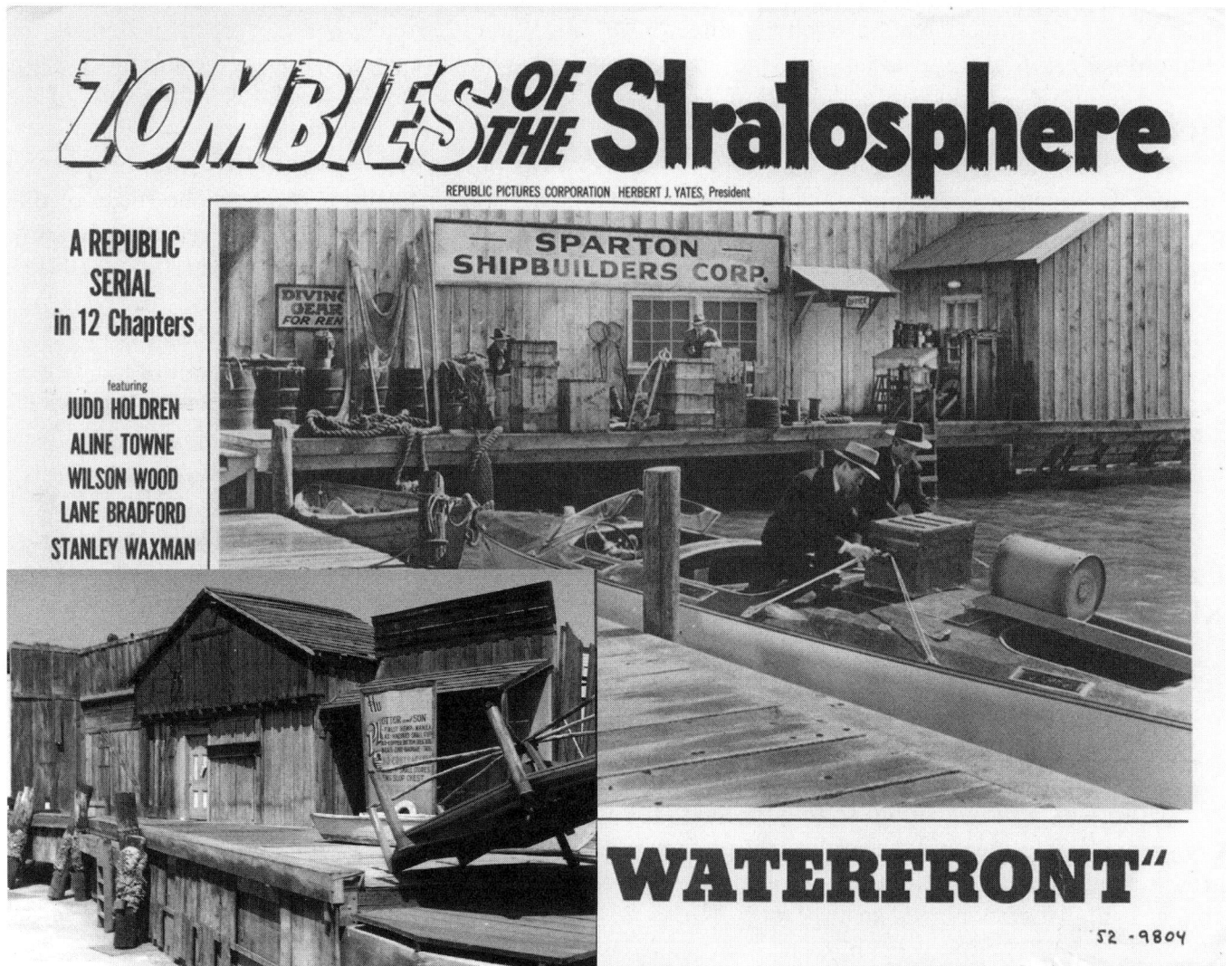

The Republic waterfront set as it appeared in a serial and (inset) in the 1970s.

East toward Colfax on a thoroughfare that ran from the studio's original Radford Avenue front gate (on property now occupied by the current studio administration building), the pavement ended and Republic's

Republic's principal western street, as it appeared through most of the studio's history.

The Republic cave set was the best in the business.

famed western street began, running east almost to Colfax. Over the years, the street underwent several changes in appearance. On the right near the east end of the street was the building that housed Republic's famed blacksmith shop set as well as its elaborate (and smelly, since horses were often corralled there in the cool between shots) cave set, put to such effective use in *Perils of Nyoka* (1942), *Daredevils of the West* (1943) and other titles.

Running left off that main street near its west entrance was an elaborate side street of upscale period residences and office buildings. Apparently first constructed for John Wayne's *Dakota* (1945) and known briefly as Dakota Street, although it did not appear in that film, that street was first used in the Bill Elliott/Vera Ralston starrer *Plainsman and the Lady* (1946) and was thereafter known as St. Joe Street, after the plot line of that movie. St. Joe Street was later seen in Elliott's *Savage Horde* (1950) and other A-westerns, as well as such Roy Rogers color titles as *Eyes of Texas* (1948), in which one St. Joe Street

Dakota/St. Joe Street.

building served as Andy "Cookie" Devine's medical office/home.

Near the north end of St. Joe Street at a slight angle was another area of building sets originally constructed for Republic's first big budget title *Man of Conquest* (1939) and labeled Brazos Street on studio maps based on its use in that film. Remembered as the "log cabin settlement" by Peggy Stewart and other Republic players, this street was largely a collection of log structures later used in Wayne's *Dark Command* (1940) and several Republic rustics (e.g., *Jeepers Creepers*, 1939), as well as an occasional B-westerns (as Harry Worth's outlaw town, for example, in the Three Mesquiteers entry *Riders of the Rio Grande*, 1943). It also served at times as a far-north community (*Dangers of the Canadian Mounted*, 1948, and *North of the Great Divide*, 1950).

A movable stockade fort entrance (*Sheriff of Wichita*, 1949) and church-schoolhouse set were also located in the same general area, as was a small suburban street, the residences of which were sometimes put to use in westerns. One served, for example, as the heavy's medical office in Rogers' *Bells of Coronado* (1950) and as villainess Nana Bryant's ranch/law office in *Eyes of Texas* (1948), although establishing shots

Brazos Street, recalled by cast and crew as the "Log Cabin Settlement."

Allan "Rocky" Lane on Brazos Street.

for the latter scenes were filmed on the Walker Ranch at Newhall.

The studio also maintained a New York Street seen mainly in serials. It was located south of the western street, across from the carpentry-miniature building and next to the horizon pool-waterfront set and underwater tank.

Farther east on the main western street was another side street running north to a Mexican cantina and village set (*Zorro's Fighting Legion*, 1939, Sunset Carson's *Santa Fe Saddlemates*, 1945, Monte Hale's *Pioneer Marshal*, 1949), parts of which dated back to the Sennett days. In that area, too, dating from Republic's early days, there was a fort set with adobe walls, seen in *Undersea Kingdom* (1936) and *Zorro's Fighting Legion*, among other titles.

When Roy Rogers introduced new studio star Rex Allen to movie audiences in a promotional short, Republic's Mexican set served as the backdrop.

The studio also maintained, of course, several ranch sets. A house located in a wooded area near the Los Angeles river appeared in a few early titles and was probably a carry-over from the Sennett days. But northwest of the log cabin settlement was a ranch set first constructed for Gene Autry's *Melody Ranch* (1940). It consisted of a two-story (later single-story) main house also seen in "Wild Bill" Elliott's *Mojave Firebrand* (1944), among other titles, as well as a smaller ranch/bunkhouse (*Calling "Wild Bill" Elliott*, 1943) and an oval-top barn (still referred to as the "Melody Barn" by studio personnel when I first visited the lot in 1985) that was frequently blown up in miniature for Republic titles (*Spy Smasher*, 1942, *Bandits of the West*,

Monte Hale on the Mexican set.

1953) and was later converted into a suburban home for the "My Three Sons" TV series. When friends and I first visited the lot, our guide identified the house as the home in that TV sit-com. Later, when I asked about the fate of the oval-top barn, he took us back to the "My Three Sons" set. In front, it was a suburban home. But on the sides and back, it was still "our" favorite Republic barn set.

Gene Autry and Ann Miller on the original Melody Ranch set for the film of that title.

The bunkhouse and familiar oval-top Melody Barn, in Brimstone (1950).

In later years, the barn played a suburban home.

But on the sides, it was still the Melody Barn.

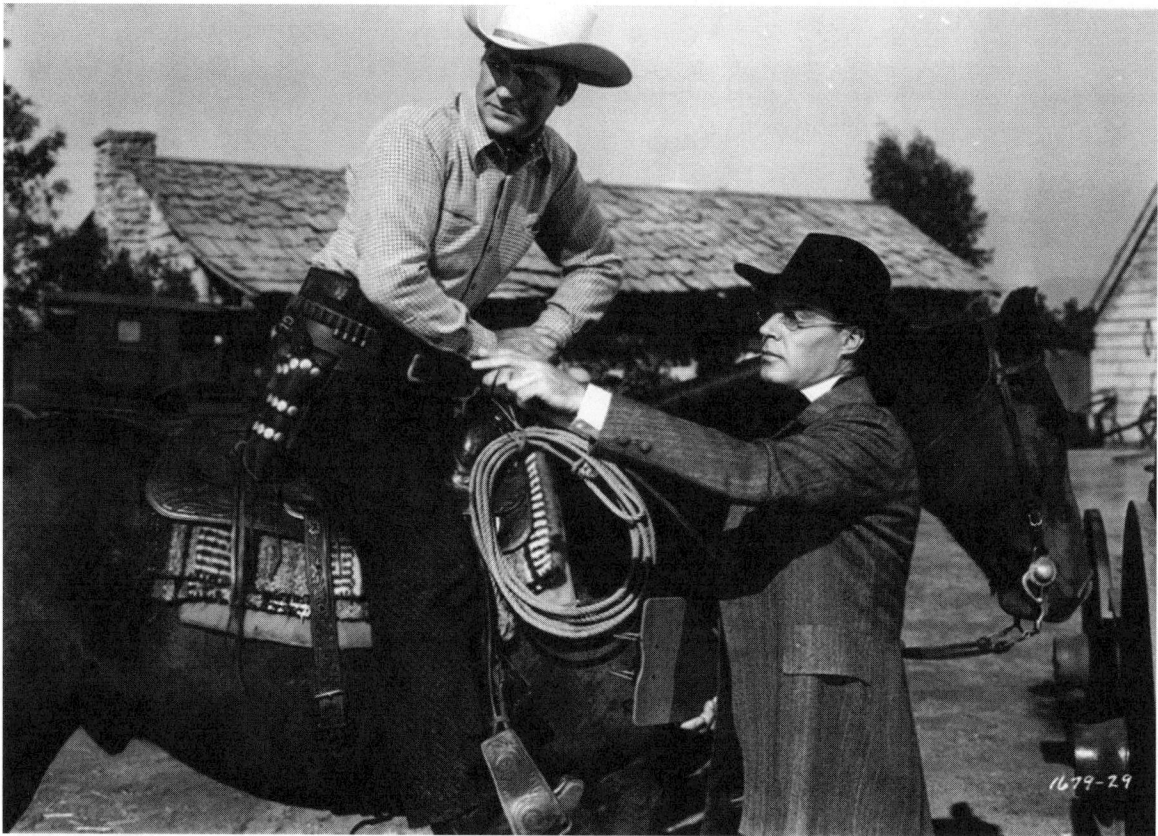

Monte Hale and veteran heavy Tris Coffin at Melody Ranch.

A road near the *Melody Ranch* set led down a hill to the lot's most used ranch set, the "Duchess Ranch," so named because it often played that role in the studio's Red Ryder titles. That set began appearing in films, however, at least as early as 1942, in Gene Autry's *Call of the Canyon*. First a one-story (*Tucson Raiders*, 1944), then a two-story spread (*Santa Fe Saddlemates*, 1945), the Duchess Ranch appeared in countless titles, as did its barn and a relay station set (that sometimes posed as a small ranch or general store) constructed on the east end of its main house (*Desperadoes of Dodge City*, 1948, *Bells of Coronado*, 1950). The Duchess spread also featured a bunkhouse southwest across from the front of the main house (*Sundown*

Republic heroine Ann Jeffreys sits by a fake tree in front of the Duchess Ranch's early, one-story main house, with the inset providing a fuller view.

Kid, *Santa Fe Saddlemates*) and a corral (*Phantom of the Plains*, 1945, *Out California Way*, 1946).

Allan "Rocky" Lane filmed more scenes on the Duchess Ranch than any other Republic star.
The larger image of the set's two-story facade is from his Desperadoes' Outpost (1952),
the inset from his Oklahoma Badlands (1948).

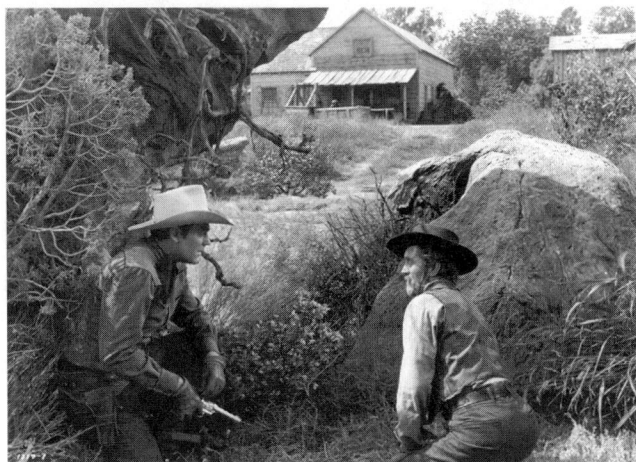

Republic relay station and barn on screen.

And in the 1970s.

West of the Duchess corral, briefly, was another ranch, first constructed for Bill Elliott's *Wyoming* (1947), which consisted of a main house and barn. It was luscious Stephanie Bachelor's ranch in Roy's *Springtime in the Sierras* (1947), a sanitarium in *G-Men Never Forget* (1948), hideout for Jack Holt's gang in "Rocky" Lane's *Wild Frontier* (1947) and spooky half-way house in his *Marshal of Amarillo* (1948).

After relatively limited use, however, that ranch set was replaced by a mansion set, apparently first constructed for Wayne's *The Fighting Kentuckian* (1949). The mansion was the chief heavy's lair in *Zombies of the Stratosphere* (1952) and the main house to the Barkley Ranch in TV's "Big Valley" series. In the first chapter of *Zombies of the Stratosphere*, heavies exit Valleyheart Drive, a side street running west off Radford Avenue, cross Radford onto the lot and the mansion driveway! The mansion's close proximity to the Duchess Ranch is clearly evident in a scene in one of the later Republic features, Mickey Rooney's *The Twinkle in God's Eye* (1955). As Rooney, or his stunt double, rode a bucking bronc around the Duchess corral, a quick shot of the mansion set was clearly visible in the background. Toward the end of the Fred MacMurray crime drama

The Wyoming *set.*

The Mansion set.

Borderline (1950)–a Universal release shot largely on the Republic lot with Republic crew–a car also can be seen driving down the hill leading to the Duchess Ranch, by the ranch set and over to the mansion set.

At one point, Republic's church-schoolhouse set was moved from the log cabin settlement to the mansion area (as evident in *Zombies of the Stratosphere*, for example). At the close of *Buckaroo Sheriff of Texas* (1951) in the studio's Rough Ridin' Kids series, for example, the church set can be seen in the distance to the west of the Duchess main house.

East of the Duchess Ranch was the studio's back lot lagoon, sometimes filled with water to form a pond (Sunset Carson's *Red River Renegades*, 1946), sometimes filmed as a dry wash ("Rocky" Lane's *Wyoming Bandit*, 1949). It later served as the lagoon for TV's "Gilligan's Island."

The Republic lagoon played a mine set in Bells of Coronado (1950).

Against a hillside adjacent to the lagoon area was a fake cliff and cave-mine entrance seen in numerous titles, such as *Bandits of Dark Canyon* (1947), *Night Time in Nevada* (1948) and *Sundown in Santa Fe* (1948). In the studio's earliest days, however, the entire Duchess Ranch area, from Radford Avenue to Colfax, consisted largely of a "jungle" seen in such serials as *Darkest Africa* (1936) and *Undersea Kingdom*.

A road running by the west side of the Duchess barn led down to the Los Angeles River bed, which provided the studio yet another filming site. A hideout shack in that area was used in several titles (Don "Red" Barry's *Fugitive from Sonora*, 1943), as was a small bridge set (*Oklahoma Badlands*, 1948). Shootouts and even chases were sometimes staged in that area (*Sun Valley Cyclone*, 1946) and it was also the site for the native village in *Jungle Girl* (1941). Scenes were sometimes shot, too, in the river itself

Republic players dreaded filming in the filthy L. A. riverbed. Beloved studio heavy Roy Barcroft took the plunge for "Wild Bill" Elliott and "Gabby" Hayes in Wagon Tracks West (1943).

(*Dead Man's Gulch*, 1943) or on the sand cliffs north of the river (*Bordertown Gunfighters*, 1944), which became part of L.A.'s aqueduct system in the 1950s. But after Republic built a parking lot north of the river and commercial and residential development became increasingly visible in that vicinity, the studio was obliged not only to cease filming in that area but also to provide protective backdrops for scenes shot on the Duchess Ranch.

The 1950s would witness Republic's decline and fall–a consequence of the rise of television, Herbert Yates' refusal to move aggressively into TV production and high-budget flops starring Yates' wife Vera Ralston, whom the mogul was obsessed with making a big star. The studio's B-western series era ended with the early 1954 release of Rex Allen's *The Phantom Stallion* and its serial output concluded with the lamentable *King of the Carnival* (1955). Although the studio's "Stories of the Century" series won an Emmy, Republic's other TV product was confined to Rex Allen's "Frontier Doctor" series, a very poorly produced "Dick Tracy" series and the "Adventures of Fu Manchu." In 1959, the studio released its last western feature, the forgettable *Plunderers of Painted Flats*. In May of that year, Yates called it quits, leasing the studio to Lippert Pictures. Even before that, other studios had released a number of features that used

Republic's facilities and personnel. For example, Jane Russell's *Montana Belle* (1952) and John Payne's *Silver Lode* (1954), both released through RKO, provided excellent views of Republic's back lot sets. Steve Cochran's *Quantrill's Raiders* (1958), released by Allied Artists, also used Republic's main western street.

CBS Television became the studio's principal lessee in 1963, renaming the lot CBS Studio Center. CBS purchased the property in April of 1967 and two years later built a four-story office building near the original Radford Avenue entrance. Independent television producers, especially 4-Star, had used the facilities for years and, as theatrical productions declined, CBS relied extensively on independent production companies, including Mary Tyler Moore's MTM Enterprises, to fill its sound stages.

In July 1982, CBS and 20th Century Fox entered a joint venture that included ownership and operation of the studio as CBS/Fox. MTM remained its principal tenant, producing such dramatic hits as "Hill Street Blues" and "St. Elsewhere," along with a host of popular sit-coms, on the lot. In the mid-1980s Fox sold its interest to MTM. Then, in 1992, CBS acquired MTM's interest and the CBS Studio Center sign went up at the main gate (now close to Ventura Blvd.) once again.

In 1995, the studio began construction of several new sound stages in the area north of the L.A. River occupied for years by the studio parking lot (seen in deep background in Episode 1 of *Zombies of the Stratosphere*). Western TV productions, including "Wanted Dead or Alive," "The Rifleman," "Tales of Wells Fargo" and color episodes of "Gunsmoke," figured prominently in studio production for many years. In 1967-68, many of the sets on the original western street were moved to a sound stage. A new, smaller, decidedly less impressive street was constructed roughly parallel to Colfax Avenue for the Stuart Whitman "Cimarron Strip" series.

The studio street during the later TV era. The first building with a balcony on the left was the only one left on the new set from the Republic days.

Opening scenes to early color "Gunsmoke" episodes gave viewers perhaps their last look at the western street of the Republic era. Otherwise, that series, as well as "Big Valley" and others, mainly used the sound stage street exteriors, the "Cimarron Strip" street set and some structures remaining from the old days. The "Gunsmoke" two-parter "Island in the Desert" (1974), with Strother Martin eating up the scenery as a deranged prospector/hermit, made use, for example, of the reconfigured western street, as well as the Johnson Canyon town set outside Kanab, Utah.

In addition to westerns, the new street also sometimes hosted non-westerns, including "Capricorn One" (1978) with James Brolin, about the faking of a manned flight to Mars. Scenes shot in 1985-86 for the nighttime soap opera "Falcon Crest" were among the last to use the "Cimarron Strip" set. But at least that episode gave prominent display to the new street's one building remaining from the main Republic western street–a two-story saloon with small side balcony seen in many studio oaters. Shortly thereafter, it fell victim to bulldozers, providing more space for production facilities.

And what of the great Duchess Ranch, relay station and barn, frequently seen on color "Gunsmoke" episodes but in later years tragically altered in appearance to satisfy whatever limited filming use they were expected to serve? The once proud main house became a storage shack for the studio's nursery or green department, then was torn down for more studio expansion. A sad end to the most wonderful thrill factory of them all.

Warner Bros. Studio and Ranch

The history of Warner Bros. studio began, in a sense, in early 1905, when Harry Warner established a 90-seat nickelodeon in Newcastle, Pennsylvania, and brought brothers Sam, Abe and Jack into the business. Soon the brothers Warner were involved in film distribution, with exchanges in Pennsylvania and Virginia. In 1913, they moved into film production with the formation of Warner Features.

After World War I, the brothers bought a ranch off Sunset Blvd. and built their first studio. Incorporated as Warner Bros. in 1923, the company released 14 pictures that year, including the first in the Rin-Tin-Tin series. Harry was company president, Abe its treasurer and Jack studio head. In 1925, the brothers acquired Vitagraph and began experimenting with sound. The next year, they released *Don Juan*, the first film with a synchronized musical score. Achieving instant success, they released *The Jazz Singer* in 1927 and, in July 1928, *Lights of New York*, the first all-talking motion picture.

That same year, the Warners acquired a theater circuit with 250 screens and bought First National Pictures, including its 135-acre Burbank studio and back lot, exchanges and theaters. In 1926, Warner Bros. had also purchased a studio ranch in Calabassas, about 20 miles northwest of L.A., on property now south of the Ventura Freeway, between Las Virgenes Road and Lake Calabasas and occupied largely by the Calabasas Country Club. Not to be confused with the Warner Ranch (often noted on road maps as situated near the intersection of Ventura Freeway and Topanga Canyon Blvd. in Woodland Hills), which was Harry Warner's personal estate, the 2,800 Warner studio ranch in Calabasas featured rolling hills and scattered trees. Its many permanent sets included a stockade fort, a walled Mexican hacienda seen in *The Lash* (1930) and *Ride Him Cowboy* (1932), the first entry in the John Wayne B-western series released by the studio, and a western street set seen in such big budget features as Errol Flynn's *Dodge City* (1939) and Gary Cooper's

Randolph Scott on the Warner Bros. Studio western street.

And on the Warner Bros. Ranch street.

Springfield Rifle (1952), which also featured the fort set. That street was used, too, for several entries in Dick Foran's short-lived B-series for the studio (*Cherokee Strip*, 1937, *Land Beyond the Law*, 1937).

The Burbank lot, of course, also included many permanent exterior sets, including New York and Midwestern streets, which were still there at this writing, a tenement street, English, Norwegian and Viennese streets and an ocean liner/pier set. In the mid-1930s, Warner Bros. constructed a Canadian/western street on the lot. Distinguishing that street from the one at Calabasas is not easy but occasionally the rolling hills of the Calabasas area can be spotted in the background of street scenes shot at the ranch (*Springfield Rifle*).

Warner Bros. sold its Calabasas property in the 1960s and a fire destroyed the studio's backlot movie western street set during the filming of *Gremlins* (1984), leaving only a livery stable, which still stands next to the Midwestern street set.

The back lot also included a Mexican set seen in the "Sugarfoot" TV episodes "Outlaw Island" and "Canary Kid," among others. That set was later used for construction of a castle set for *Camelot* (1967) and *Lost Horizon,* released through Columbia in 1967, and still later modified in appearance to serve as a temple for the "Kung Fu" (1972-73) TV series.

During production for Alan Ladd's *Santiago* (1956), the studio began to build sets in a wooded area along the studio's southeastern boundary. Thereafter known as "The Jungle," part of that area became, in 1958, the site for a second studio western town to be used primarily for TV productions. Constructed for the "Lawman" series with John Russell and known as Laramie Street after that series' Wyoming locale, that set was dismantled several years ago. It stood for years, though, with its general outline, if not its specific facades, remaining largely as it had in WB's heyday as a TV production factory. Laramie Street played host not only to "Lawman" (1958-62)

The north end of main street on the Laramie set, with its bank backdrop.

but also to "Cheyenne" (1955-63), "Maverick" (1957-62), "Sugarfoot" (1957-61), "Colt .45" (1957-60), "Bronco" (1958-62) and "The Dakotas" (1963) in the old days, as well as "The Adventures of Brisco County, Jr." (1993-94) of more recent times.

The lot provided the setting, of course, for non-western series as well. The farmhouse and general store sets for "The Waltons" (1972-81) were situated in woods north of the Laramie set and scenes for that series also occasionally used the Laramie street as well as Warner Bros.'s Midwestern and New York streets. Later, "The Waltons" farmhouse was moved to the old Columbia Ranch, about a mile north on Hollywood Way from the studio front gate, which Warner Bros. purchased in the 1980s.

The wide main street on the Laramie Street set ran north-south, but with slight changes in direction at various points along the way to maximize filming angles. The north end of the main street featured a courthouse/bank-type structure that was altered in appearance at various times over the years. In fact, when I visited that set, its current facade was superimposed over what appeared to be the original one, a portion of which could be seen protruding camera left from the rear of the current structure.

A north entrance road to the Laramie set ran camera right by the courthouse/bank set onto main street. Another entrance road ran east onto the main street at its south end. Storefront facades on the west side of the main street then included a bank; the east side of the street hosted a saloon and a hotel-saloon with balcony. Interior scaffolding behind the storefronts permitted camera shooting from second floors to the street below. During the TV era, the Laramie main street may have included only one side street. But by the 1990s, one of the saloons on the east side of main street cornered on a side street running east from the main street near its north end, while the other saloon, situated nearer the south end of main street, corned on a second side street that ran parallel to the first side street. Those two side streets ran east into a second north-south street. That north-south street hosted various storefronts as well as a white church building with steeple. At its north end, the street curved slightly westward and merged with the town's north entrance road.

A side street on the Laramie set.

With such an arrangement of its streets, the Laramie set could pose as two or more towns in a single episode and could also be used for shooting as many as four or five TV episodes at once–albeit creating, at times, extremely cramped filming quarters. While filming a "Sugarfoot" episode, Will Hutchins recalls, he once drove several cattle onto a "Maverick" set!

Location shooting, however, was extremely rare. "Sugarfoot," for example, was filmed entirely on the Warner Bros. lot. Even the exciting horse race in the first episode ("Brannigan's Boots") was entirely stock footage from *Boy from Oklahoma* (1954), with Will Rogers, Jr., filmed on the studio's Calabasas ranch.

In an area about a hundred feet north of the Laramie set, and later occupied by "The Waltons" farmhouse and general store, Warner Bros. maintained a ranch set for its TV oaters and features. The ranch and its outbuildings can be seen in the "Colt .45" episodes "Saga of Sam Bass" and "Devil's Godson," as well as "Bronco: Bodyguard," among many others.

Other sets included a small lake with a waterfall, a mine/cave entrance and various fake boulders and trees. A railroad station set, in which the health-conscious Clint "Cheyenne" Walker maintained a small gym, sometimes appeared in Warner Bros. westerns, too. Western Tvers and features also used the studio's Midwestern street. John Wayne's last feature *The Shootist* (1976), for example, gave prominent display to a house on that set, as did two "Sugarfoot" episodes ("Highbinder" and "Fernando") set in San Francisco.

With the demise of the TV western in the 1960s and early 1970s, Laramie Street was used less frequently but still made an occasional appearance in TV shows, commercials and even features, including Clint Walker's *The Great Bank Robbery* (1969) and *Sam Whiskey* (1969), as well as the more recent *Wild Bill*(1995), portions of which also lensed at the rebuilt Melody Ranch in Newhall.

By popular demand, Laramie Street was also eventually made part of Warner Bros.' excellent schedule of small-group walking tours of the studio and its fine museum. Ultimately, though, the incessant demand for more studio space for construction took its inevitable toll and Laramie Street, like so many other remnants of the golden age, succumbed to a demolition crew.

Directions: To reach the studio, take Vineland Avenue in North Hollywood to Riverside Drive, Riverside east to Hollywood Way and Hollywood Way south to the Warner Bros. gate. Please telephone the studio for tour reservations.

The Columbia Ranch

Columbia Pictures maintained studio facilities on Gower Street in Hollywood from its founding in 1924 until 1971, then shared facilities with Warner Bros. in Burbank until 1991, when it relocated to MGM's Culver City lot. But in 1935, Columbia also established ranch facilities for use in westerns and serials as well as studio exteriors for other productions.

The Columbia Ranch, now called the Warner Bros. Ranch after its current owner, is situated along Hollywood Way in Burbank, about a mile north of WB's main lot. In the golden era, its impressive western streets played host to Charles Starrett, Bill Elliott, Gene Autry, Russell Hayden, Randolph Scott and other Columbia stars.

The ranch also included a large park seen in *Batman and Robin* and other serials and features, as well as an impressive public building, which often played a library or scientific institute, and English/colonial and Mexican villages. Suburban homes abutting the park on two sides were featured in serials, as well as the *Blonde* movie series, other theatrical releases and such TV sit-coms as "Hazel." The "Hazel" house also appeared as the abode of *Batman and Robin* in that 1949 cliffhanger and even served as Danny Glover's home in the *Lethal Weapon* features, with its large evergreen tree seen in so many titles filmed there still standing in the front yard. (Ranch personnel did not know what to think of my friends and me when we declined an offer to watch Glover and Mel Gibson in late-night filming at the house for the first *Lethal Weapon* entry–explaining that we were leaving North Hollywood early the next morning for a trip to Victorville and visit to the Roy Rogers Museum!) Located north of the park were brownstones and an office building, what was left of the lot's "New York" street and a fake cliff sometimes seen in later Durango Kid and Autry entries.

Since Columbia's western street was not constructed until the mid-1930s, street scenes for the studio's early sound entries with Ken Maynard, Buck Jones, Charles Starrett and Tim McCoy were shot at the Monogram (later Melody) Ranch at Newhall and on the Paramount Ranch in Agoura. Later titles released through Columbia, but produced by independent outfits, such as Bill Elliott's first Larry Darmour-produced series, also used the Monogram facility. A number of post-war Gene Autry productions utilized Pioneertown, Monogram, Corriganville and the Iverson Ranch's "El Paso" street.

But beginning in 1936, with such features as Starrett's *The Cowboy Star*, Columbia relied mainly on

The north end of the Columbia Ranch's main street in the 1990s, with its courthouse backdrop.

Main street made its most impressive appearance in Gary Cooper's High Noon *(1952).*

But for most "front row kids," the street was mainly the domain of the Durango Kid.

its own western streets, among the most elaborate in the business, for in-house productions. The western set covered nearly the entire west end of the lot. Its main street ran south to north, with the familiar courthouse building seen in countless Columbia oaters located at the north end of the street. (Camera left of the courthouse was another structure that often served as a public building, while the rear of that building sometimes played the loading area of a feed store. Camera right of the courthouse set was a private home set that sometimes impersonated a distant ranch, when budget restrictions were particularly tight.)

Intersecting the main street near its south end was a side street running west into a second south-north street that featured a large hotel structure with tall columns on its front veranda. One of the town's two livery stables was located at the north end of that street with the other situated near the end of the principal street.

Yet another street, running southeast to northwest across the south end of the western set was rarely the focus of scenes, and was probably placed there to keep adjacent residential and commercial development out of camera range. It appeared, for example, in "Wild Bill" Elliott's *The Devil's Trail* (1942).

Rounding out the western set were a railroad track, train and depot located near the south end of the lot and a Mexican plaza seen in some later Durango Kid titles (e.g., *Bandits of El Dorado*, 1949).

Over the years, the lot underwent much change. A Mexican cantina at the north end of the main street soon became a western-style saloon with balcony. During rebuilding of the western set following a fire in the 1950s, a grain silo at the south end of the principal street, seen in countless films, was replaced with another facade.

The intersection of main street with a side street leading up to another north-south street and the ranch's hotel backdrop was the setting for this scene in Gene Autry's Cow Town *(1950).*

The impressive hotel set appears in the background of this scene from a Charles Starrett/Russell Hayden starrer.

In this scene with "Wild Bill" Elliott, the camera looks south on main street toward a feed store with silo familiar to all fans of Columbia westerns. Note also the backdrop of buildings at the south end of town, which also served as a street.

And here we see the barn at the north end of town near the courthouse set, as well as an inset shot of the rebuilt barn in the 1990s.

In 1960 the studio sold nearly 35 acres of the lot to real estate developers. From 1972 to 1991, Columbia shared the facilities (briefly called the Burbank Studio) with Warner Bros. Then WB assumed full ownership.

The street at the south end of the western set was demolished before my initial 1986 visit. And although the main street was still there, impressive as ever, its days were numbered. In later years, it appeared in several commercials. *The Wild Westerners* (1965) with James Philbrick and Don Meredith's *Banjo Hackett* (1976) were among later titles using the street set, which apparently made its last appearance, playing a movie set, in Robert DeNiro's *Guilty By Suspicion* (1991). In June of 1993, Warner Bros. razed the entire western set–another sad end for a wonderful celluloid landmark.

Twentieth Century-Fox

Twentieth Century-Fox was formed from two studios. In 1915, Hungarian immigrant William Fox, who had built a successful chain of nickelodeons in New York, formed the Fox Film Corporation in Los Angeles. Originally operating from facilities near the intersection of Sunset Blvd. and Western Avenue, Fox in 1925 purchased from studio star Tom Mix 176 acres between what would become Pico and Santa Monica boulevards, establishing there a much larger studio with a huge back lot.

Facing increasing financial legal pressures, however, Fox was obliged in 1935 to agree to a merger of his studio with Twentieth Century Films, headed by Darryl Zanuck and Joseph Schenck. Zanuck became boss of the new Twentieth Century-Fox studio and Schenck became its board chairman. In 1940, the new studio acquired a neighboring golf course, enlarging its size to 260 acres.

The Fox back lot was one of the finest in Hollywood. Its western set, Tombstone Street, situated on a sloping hill and bordered by a side street on its lower end, was constructed for *The Cisco Kid and the Lady* (1939), and later appeared in *Belle Starr* (1941), *The Ox-Bow Incident* (1943), *Yellow Sky* (1948), *Broken Lance* (1954) and *North to Alaska* (1960), among other titles. Its Omaha Street, originally built for *Brigham Young* (1940), also appeared in westerns, including *Belle Starr*, as did an impressive plantation set first built for Shirley Temple's *The Little Colonel* (1934) and later used in such westerns as Robert Wagner's 1957 etelling of the Jesse James saga.

In 1946, Fox also purchased ranch property in the Santa Monica Mountains. The Brent's Crag area of Agoura, along the Las Virgenes Road, apparently had first been used in films when MGM built a tree house there for *Tarzan Escapes* (1935). Fox had also filmed in the area, most notably when it constructed a Welsh village on eighty acres there for *How Green Was My Valley* (1941). Apparently, the studio purchased the property with the intention of moving its entire studio to Agoura. Those plans never materialized. But the area–known as the Fox Ranch or Century Ranch–was ideal for filming. Malibu Creek, a portion of which had been dammed up by the previous owners to form a small, scenic lake, ran through the property. A cliff overlooking a pool furnished the setting in *Butch Cassidy and the Sundance Kid* (1969) for the end of the famous cliff jump scene in that film that had begun in Durango, Colorado.

Over the years, the ranch continued to grow in size. In fact, with purchases of acreage from Ronald Reagan and Bob Hope, among others, it grew to around 6,000 acres. Westerns partially filmed there included Elvis Presley's *Love Me Tender* (1956). RKO constructed "Mr. Blandings['] . . . Dream House" there for its 1948 Cary Grant picture. Fox built a water tank on the property to film battle ship miniatures for its *Tora,*

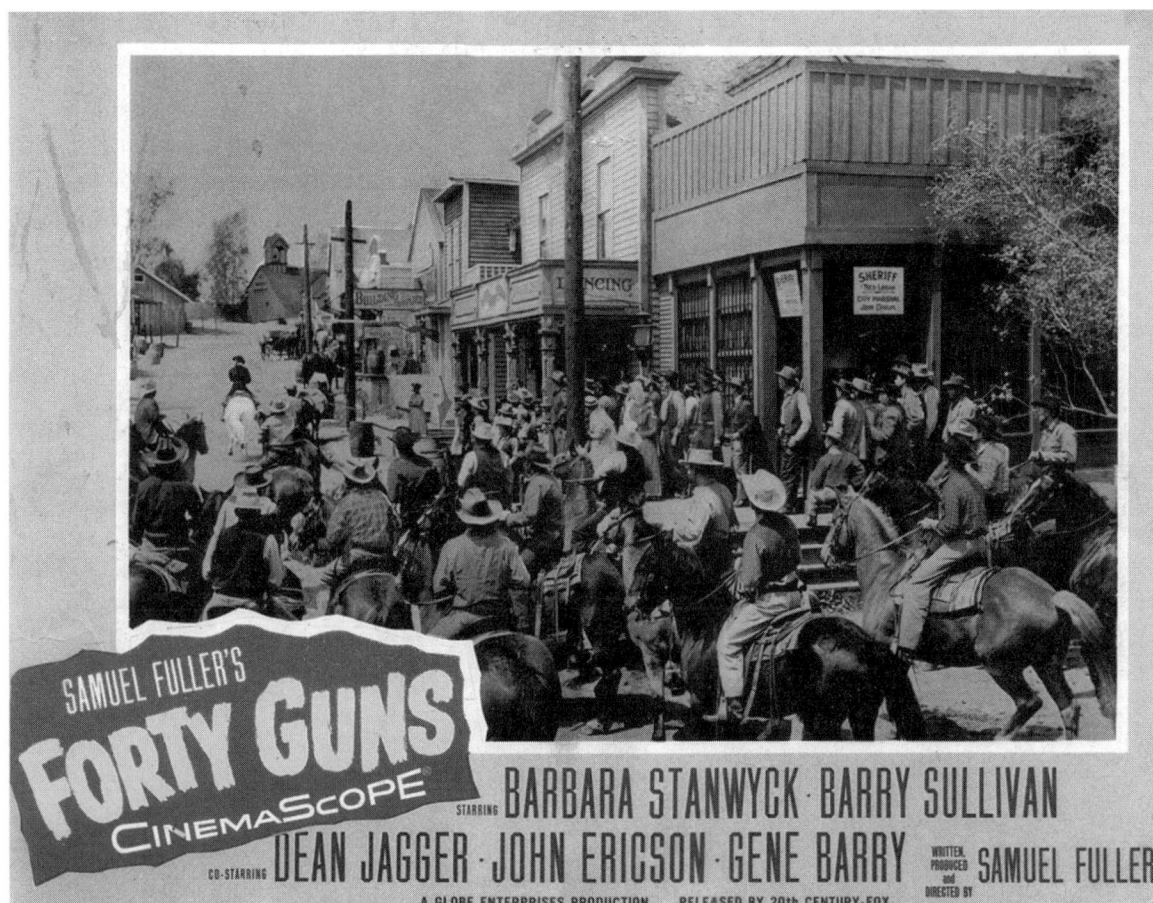

Tombstone Street on the 20th Century-Fox lot.

Tora, Tora (1970); parts of the office building burned in *The Towering Inferno* (1974) were also constructed there. The ranch was the setting, too, for the TV "M*A*S*H" hospital camp, as well as the location for many other TV series.

Confronted with impending financial difficulties, in 1960 Fox sold its studio property to Alcoa for development of Century City, then leased back 75 acres (the studio portion of the property) for its further operations. The next year, the studio began dismantling its back lot. And in 1974, it sold the state of California its ranch property, which became the Malibu Creek State Park. A visit to the park will bring back memories of its film history.

The Fox Ranch pool.

RKO Encino Ranch

RKO's "Forty Acres" back lot in Culver City sported a number of exterior sets, including the small town that served as "Mayberry" in the Andy Griffith Show and had earlier appeared as "Metropolis" in "Superman" episodes. Next to that set was a back lot western street near Balonna Creek that appeared, for example, in a number of later "Bonanza" episodes. But most RKO western street scenes were shot at the studio's Encino ranch on one of the most impressive studio western streets of them all.

George O'Brien confronts heavies on the RKO Ranch street. Note the "Lodge Hall" at upper right. That building, with an assortment of names, appeared in most scenes filmed on the street.

That 500-acre facility, constructed in 1929, was home to the elaborate set made for the studio's 1939 version of *The Hunchback of Notre Dame*, starring Charles Laughton and Maureen O'Hara. "Bedford Falls" was also built there for Frank Capra's *It's a Wonderful Life* (1946). That set included 75 stores and buildings, a main street, factory district and a large residential and slum section. The main street alone was 300 yards long. According to various reports, some of the snow scenes for *The Thing* (1949) were also done on the ranch, when nature failed to furnish adequate precipitation at the Montana site originally selected for that fine thriller.

The ranch appeared primarily, however, in RKO's western features, including not only the B-series of Tom Keene, George O'Brien, Tim Holt and the brief Zane Gray series of Robert Mitchum and James Warren, but also such A-westerns as Randolph Scott's *Badman's Territory* (1946). Almost from its beginnings, the ranch's western street assumed the shape it was to have throughout its existence. Although it included two side streets, most scenes were done on the main street, with the camera directed toward a backdrop of buildings at one end, one of which usually bore a "Lodge (or Assembly) Hall" sign. In fact, given the set's great look, it was disappointing that scenes on the street varied little from title to title.

The RKO Ranch boasted another set that appeared most often in westerns as well. As noted elsewhere in this book, the Southern Pacific's Chatsworth branch ran through the ranch until the mid-1940s. When it was relocated, 2000 feet of old track left on the ranch formed a dead-end spur, giving RKO its own ready-made "railroad," which first appeared in *Badman's Territory*.

When RKO began to collapse in the 1950s, the ranch unfortunately was one of the first studio properties to go. In 1953, the ranch was sold to a real estate company to help defray the huge deficits the studio amassed under the eccentric Howard Hughes'

Tim Holt and sidekick Richard "Chito" Martin on the depot set.

leadership. Two RKO releases, John Payne's *Silver Lode* (1954) and Jane Russell's *Montana Belle* (1952), were shot on the Republic lot. But in 1955, Hughes sold RKO to General Teleradio, Inc., and in 1957 the studio ceased making films altogether.

The once grand western set probably made its last appearance in "The Big Producer," a 1954 Dragnet episode about a has-been film producer reduced to selling teenagers obscene books and pictures. Another sad ending for a western film landmark.

Monogram Sunset Studio

Efforts to locate a tiny western street set often seen in independent cheapies of the 1930s led ultimately to KCET-TV, the L.A. PBS station at 4401 W. Sunset Blvd., which once housed Monogram-Allied Artists and a host of other studios. Initially part of the Colegrove community, annexed by L.A. in 1909, the facility's original address was 1425 Fleming Street (now Hoover Street). It first became the setting for film makers in 1912, when one of the Lubin Co. units opened a small studio there for filming instructional titles featuring local tourist attractions.

Bob Steele on the tiny Monogram Sunset Studio western street, which was built along the wall to its equally small sound stage building.

The Lubin venture quickly folded to be replaced the next year by the Essanay (S & A) Film Company, founded by George K. Spoor and "Broncho Billy" Anderson for production of one-reel westerns (*The Sheriff's Story*, 1913). After making around 20 titles, Essanay vacated the property in April 1913. The following October the Kalem Company moved onto the lot with a company that included director, and later western heavy, J. P. McGowan in its ranks.

Following Kalem's departure in 1917, Willis and Inglis, a theatrical agency and story brokerage firm, acquired the property as a rental studio. By the beginning of 1918, its facilities included an enlarged outdoor stage and an indoor stage, as well as offices, scene docks, property shop, dressing rooms and a carpentry shop.

For the next two years, several companies leased the facilities. But in 1920, silent star turned producer

Charles Ray purchased the property and established a company on the lot for the production of films to be released through First National (*The Courtship of Miles Standish*, 1923). By July, Ray had completed construction of a new stage (with pool beneath the floor), still in use today as Stage A. By October 1922 the lot boasted a Spanish-style administration building, which is also still standing, as well as backlot sets, including the very small, narrow western street with a backdrop of buildings and a side street at its one enclosed end, the location of which had long intrigued me.

Ray's company went bankrupt in 1923 and for several years the studio went largely unused. By 1927 it was again active as a rental studio operated by Jean Navelle, with Tiffany and other small companies leasing its western street and other facilities. In 1931, recording engineer Ralph Like purchased the lot for leasing, revamped Stage A for sound and the next year erected what is now Stage B on the current property. For the next several years, a number of independents produced cheapie features on the western street and also utilized a tiny saloon set with balcony seen in many titles.

Although headquartered at a lot nearby, Trem Carr's Monogram studio also used the Like lot frequently. In 1942, Carr purchased the studio as well as adjoining property to be used for additional scene docks, a New York street and offices. The next year, a building on Sunset Blvd., which bordered the studio on the south, was acquired to house the studio's costume department and, by 1946, Monogram had purchased bungalows on Commonwealth Street for use as offices.

During the 1940s and early 1950s, the little studio was kept busy with a seemingly endless outpouring of western titles as well as its Charlie Chans, Bowery Boys, Bomba the Jungle Boy, Jiggs and Maggie, Latham Family, Kirby Grant/Chinook and Bill Elliott detective series, along with a few B+/A Monogram features, including *Dillinger* (1945) and, beginning in 1946, the studio's bigger budget Allied Artists releases (*Black Gold*, 1947, *The Babe Ruth Story*, 1948).

Stage A hosted a tiny jungle set for the Bomba entries but the studio's limited back lot facilities obliged much location shooting on L.A. streets, at the county arboretum across from the Santa Anita racetrack in Arcadia, at Corriganville, at other locations for its non-western titles and at Big Bear/Cedar Lake for the Kirby Grant Mountie series. Gary Gray, who played Raymond Walburn's son in the Latham Family entries (*Father's Wild Game*, 1950, *Henry, the Rainmaker*, 1949) recalled, for example, that a North Hollywood residence, still standing when this book was written, served as the exterior to the family home in that series.

The studio's long-term lease in 1937 of Ernie Hickson's Newhall Ranch, thereafter called the Monogram Ranch until Gene Autry's purchase of the property as his "Melody Ranch" in 1952, began a long period in which the studio western street fell into disuse. With rare exceptions, such as Tex Ritter's *Rollin' Plains* (1938), the studio preferred the spacious Newhall streets to the cramped quarters of its studio set through the late 1930s, 1940s and early 1950s. In fact, after Monogram lost its Newhall lease, it used the Iverson, Corriganville and Ingram Ranch streets rather than its home set for the balance of the B-western era.

The company did enlarge its studio western street for occasional use in later Allied Artists titles (George Montgomery's *King of the Wild Stallions*, 1959), as well as rental to TV shows, including "Have Gun, Will Travel." In fact, it even prepared an elaborate advertisement in efforts to attract TV productions to its western street, which it erroneously termed the "best" in Hollywood. But some of the best Allied Artists titles of later years (e.g., *Gunfight at Dodge City*, 1959) returned to the Newhall western street for at least part of their town scenes.

In later years, Allied Artists released a number of excellent features, including the superb *Invasion of the Body Snatchers* (1956), Phil Karlson's gritty *The Phenix City Story* (1955), Gary Cooper's *Friendly Persuasion* (1956), *Al Capone* (1959), a number of solid westerns (*At Gunpoint*, 1955, *Wichita*, 1955) and several big-budget epics (e.g., *El Cid*,1961), as well as a number of exploitation features (*I Passed for White*, 1960, *Sex Kittens Go to College,* 1960).

By the early 1960s, however, the company, facing $4 million in losses, had largely abandoned its production activities to concentrate almost exclusively on film distribution. In 1964, it moved its operations to New York, began leasing the Sunset lot as a rental studio, then, in 1967, sold the property to Colorvision, which continued use of the lot as a rental studio. In 1970, KCET's parent company purchased the studio. The studio western street, of course, is long gone. But a tour of the facility was well worth the time. Its original brick sound stages and other buildings, which were still there, often appeared in the background of Monogram non-western titles, such as Bill Elliott's detective entries. Visiting them brought back many fond memories of Hollywood's old days.

Directions: To reach KCET, go east on Sunset after exiting the Hollywood Freeway. The studio is on the left.

Providencia Ranch

Some of our western favorites not only rode the Hollywood range; they are buried there, too. Burbank's Hollywood Hills Forest Lawn cemetery, situated west of Griffith Park, is the final resting place not only for Gene Autry, but "Gabby" Hayes, "Smiley" Burnette and such celluloid heavies as Bud Osborne, among many other stars and character players.

From 1916 to 1948, however, the area also regularly played host to movie crews. In fact, when I asked stuntman/actor Jock Mahoney years ago about a filming site with no rock formations that appeared in a lot of the post-war Durango Kid titles, he said that much filming for that series was done at the old Providencia ranch, which later became Hollywood Hills Forest Lawn.

Burbank's southern portion was once part of a Spanish land grant, Rancho La Providencia. For about twenty years in the late 19th century, Dr. David Burbank, the Los Angeles dentist for whom the L.A. suburb is named, operated a large sheep ranch there.

Burbank sold his holdings in 1887 to the Providencia Land, Water and Development Co. and in 1915 Carl Laemmle built his Universal lot southwest of the Providencia Ranch. The next year, Laemmle and Jesse Lasky of the Famous Players-Lasky Corporation co-leased about a thousand acres of the ranch for film-making. Not surprisingly, given its close proximity to Laemmle's studio, the property was originally called the Universal Ranch. But largely as a result of Lasky's investment of $1.5 million on the spread, it soon became better known as the Lasky Ranch. For about ten years, Lasky and others used the ranch for silent productions, including Wallace Reid comedies and the William Desmond Taylor version of *Huck and Tom* (1918).

In 1927, the Lasky company, which had been renamed the Paramount Famous Players-Lasky Corporation, bought a ranch along the Ventura highway west of Calabasas. The new Paramount Ranch and its western street, examined elsewhere in this volume, would become a favorite filming site for Paramount, other studios and independents.

But the Providencia Ranch's filming days were not over. In the early 1920s, Ace Hudkins, a prizefighter, moved to L.A. with his six brothers from Valpariso, near Lincoln, Neb., where he had fought as "The

The western street set on the Providencia Ranch during production of Famous Players-Lasky's
The Pony Express (1925). Photo Bison Archives

Nebraska Wildcat." Ace won a $500 purse in his first match at the Hollywood Legion Stadium, then went on to win all but two of 104 additional contests.

But the family's fortunes did not depend solely on Ace's pugilistic prowess. His brother Ode had moved onto the Providencia Ranch when he came out to L.A. from Nebraska. In the mid-1930s, the family leased 989 acres of the ranch for $500 a month from its owner, the W.I. Hollingsworth Co., and established a ranch there off Barham Blvd. Ace and his brothers primarily supplied livestock, wagons, coaches and other equipment to the movie companies, especially Warner Bros., Universal, Republic and the Columbia Ranch. In fact, Universal and Warner Bros. were so close that Hudkins' wranglers would simply herd livestock on horseback over the short distance to those studios.

The Hudkins also rented the property, however, to the movie companies for filming. Stuntman Roydon Clark began working for the Hudkins brothers in the early forties while still a young boy, eventually living in a bunkhouse on the property and becoming essentially part of the family.

According to Clark and others, a dirt road leading into the ranch began about where the entrance to the Forest Lawn cemetery now stands. "What you would see as you pulled into the ranch road, which was dirt, was a barbed-wire fence. On the left was a racehorse barn and a fenced, dirt racetrack about a half-mile around, with a starting gate. As you kept going up the road, you would see on the right Ode's home. . . . [The boxer] Max Baer trained in the back yard–big arena there. To the right of Ode's home on a hillside was a rather large structure, the caretaker's house. Across from Ode's house were two very, very large corrals and a very large barn that had probably fifteen to twenty box stalls and about fifty tie stalls. Farther up the road was an office and, across from it, another barn, which held approximately sixty head of horses in tie stalls, and two additional corrals. To the left of the office was a blacksmith barn and tie rack where the horses were washed."

Beyond there on the road was the home of Art, another of the Hudkins brothers, who lived on the ranch until about 1946, when he moved across the L.A. river to another residence. (Ace and the other brothers had homes off the property.) "On Saturdays and Sundays," Clark remembers, "a Who's Who of Hollywood–the Cagneys, the Waynes, everybody–was there." In the thirties, according to veteran stuntman Jack Williams, the inside of the racetrack also sometimes served as a polo field for local celebrities.

Near the entrance to the compound, about 400-500 feet east toward Griffith Park, was an area known as Gopher Flats or Lasky Mesa (not to be confused with the huge Lasky Mesa out from Calabasas, used for filming of cavalry charges and other large-scale action scenes). The Hudkins maintained a graded insert road on Gopher Flats, which saw service in *Hoppy's Holiday* (1947) as well as for frequent stagecoach and wagon chase scenes for Durango Kid entries, with stunt great Jock Mahoney transferring effortlessly from Durango's white steed Raider to the stage or wagon horses in some of those titles. The Hudkins also maintained a few false fronts for use by the moviemakers, although not a full-fledged western street, and the studios occasionally constructed elaborate sets there.

The Durango Kid (or his stunt double) on the Gopher Flats insert road.

Richard Dixon, who was raised on the Mack Sennett ranch at the foot of Mount Lee, south of the Hudkins ranch, recalled that a giant New York set was built on Gopher Flats for Don DeFoe's *It Happened on 5th Avenue* (1947), with cars and double-decker buses passing before the camera, circling around and passing by again. Films Dixon watched being filmed there included *The Boy with Green Hair* (1948), *A Boy and his Dog* (1946), *Hoppy's Holiday* and *Stallion Road*, some of which was shot on the Kentucky Park thoroughbred farm (now Ventura Farms) in Hidden Valley near Thousand Oaks, where *My Pal Trigger* (1946) and other Roy Rogers titles were filmed. Stuntman Jack Williams recalled going over to the ranch after WW II to watch filming of some riding scenes for *Stallion Road*.

Providencia's rolling hills and woodland also served as the English countryside for the Columbia chapterplay *Son of the Guardsman* (1946), as well as the locale for several Hoosier Hotshots titles and other Columbia musical westerns. But the ranch was used most during the Hudkins years for Columbia's Durango Kid series, including *Roaring Rangers* (1946), *Galloping Thunder* (1946), *Blazing the Western Trail* (1947), *The Stranger from Ponca City* (1947), *Riders of the Lone Star* (1947), *Buckaroo from Powder River* (1947) and *Phantom Valley* (1948).

In fact, viewers can be reasonably confident that scenes without rocks in Pre-Durango Charles Starrett titles were shot either at Agoura or on the Walker, Monogram and Jauregui ranches near Newhall, while such scenes in the 1946-48 Durangos were nearly always filmed at Providencia.

Two houses used for one Durango each–*Texas Panhandle* (1945) and *Last Days of Boot Hill* (1947), scenes for both of which were shot at Providencia–and never, to my knowledge, ever seen in another title may also have been situated on the ranch. Neither veteran movie-maker Earl Bellamy, who served as an assistant director on many Columbia Durangos, nor Roydon Clark could remember either structure. Clark recalled the caretaker's house at Providencia, for example, as being smaller than the ranch used in *Last Days of Boot Hill*. But Clark did remember, as noted above, a stable with tie stalls and a racetrack. And such a stable and a track were across from the ranch house used in *Last Days of Boot Hill*.

Sometimes Providencia served as the main exterior location, at other times only for pickup shots, filling gaps in principal photography done at Iverson's, Corriganville and other more familiar sites.

But all good things must come to an end. One day in 1948, Earl Bellamy and other crew members shot portions of a Durango at Providencia. When they returned the next day, they discovered that the Forest Lawn folks had opened several graves (the number varies–from three to twelve–depending on the source relating this story) the previous evening and were beginning to enclose their new cemetery in fences.

The beginnings of the ranch's conversion into a cemetery.
Photo Bison Archives.

The stepson of Clyde Hudkins, another of the brothers, shared with me his recollections of the events leading to Forest Lawn's acquisition of the property. Also known as Ace Hudkins after his uncle (who died in 1973), the stepson recalled that Providencia's owner died in the late forties and his son, heavily in hock to Las Vegas gamblers, was forced to sell the property to Forest Lawn. The Hudkins brothers were given time to move their operations and by 1950 had relocated to Coldwater Canyon and Sherman Way in North Hollywood, where they would remain until the 1960s, when rezoning ended that area's use for horse stables, too.

The Hudkins, according to Clyde's stepson, eventually sold everything "on top of the ground"–horses and equipment–to Trigger's trainer Glenn Randall, another stable operator, for $125,000. When Randall, who had moved his stable from North Hollywood to Newhall, got into financial difficulty, he sold everything to an auctioneer for little more than he had paid the Hudkins. The auctioneer then got $800,000 for the business. "So he screwed Glenn pretty good."

Raleigh/California Studios

When Harry Sherman was producing his Hopalong Cassidy features for Paramount release, he relied mainly on the western streets at the Paramount Ranch and at the Monogram Ranch in Newhall. But in 1941, he contracted with United Artists for release of further Hoppys and moved his production facilities to a rental studio that he dubbed the California Studios and which was located at the intersection of Melrose and Bronson in Hollywood. The studio's western street, which Sherman may well have built, first appeared in Hoppy's *Undercover Man* (1942), probably had its most extensive role in *False Colors* (1943) and also appeared in nine other Hoppys, the last of which was *Devil's Playground* (1946), the first

The California Studios western street in False Colors (1943).

of the twelve final titles in the series that William Boyd personally produced.

Over the years, the California Studios–now the oldest continuously operating studio in Hollywood–sported a variety of names. Filming first began there in 1915, when the property was undeveloped. The next year, theater owner William H. Clune, bought forty acres there and built a sound stage, creating his Clune Studio. Largely a rental facility, it would go on to host several of Douglas Fairbanks, Sr.'s productions, Walt Disney's Mickey Mouse shorts, and many small independents, among many other titles. In 1934, it became the home of Prudential Studios and bore that name until Harry Sherman began his tenure there. Beginning in 1946, it was briefly known as Enterprise Studios, then once again became California Studios. In the 1960s, it acquired the name Producer's Studio, which it retained until 1980, when it got its current name, Raleigh Studios.

Reportedly, Producers Releasing Corporation (PRC) used the studio for some of its interior filming. Scenes for such TV series as "Gunsmoke," "Death Valley Days" and "Have Gun Will Travel" were also filmed there, as were many major productions, including the Fredric March version of *A Star Is Born* (1937), *The Best Years of Our Lives* (1946) and *In the Heat of the Night* (1967). But western fans will remember it best for its little used western street.

The California Studios western street in 1958. Photo Bison Archives.

Samuel Goldwyn Studio

Although it also rarely appeared on screen, yet another western street set was located at the Samuel Goldwyn Studio, an 18-acre lot on the corner of Santa Monica Boulevard and Formosa Avenue in West Hollywood. Originally the Pickford-Fairbanks Studio, its name was changed to the United Artists Studio in the 1920s when Mary Pickford and Douglas Fairbanks, Sr., formed UA with Charles Chaplin and D. W. Griffith. In 1925, producers Samuel Goldwyn and Joseph Schenck rented offices and sound stages on the lot and began releasing their films through the studio. They also financed the studio's expansion, creating an awkward arrangment whereby Pickford and Fairbanks owned the land, while Goldwyn and Schenck controlled production facilities. Ultimately, Schenck left UA and Fairbanks died, leaving Goldwyn and Pickford joint, and often bitter, owners. By 1940, Goldwyn had acquired sufficient clout to force giving the lot his name and in 1955, he became sole owner of the property. In 1980, Warner Bros. purchased the lot as an auxiliary to its Burbank headquarters, renaming it the Warner Hollywood Studio. In 1999, WB sold it to another company, which renamed it simply The Lot.

Over the years, a number of major films were produced there, including *Wurthering Heights* (1939), Bette Davis' *The Little Foxes* (1941)*, Some Like It Hot* (1959) and *West Side Story* (1959). Interiors for *Stagecoach* (1939) were also filmed there. The studio's western street may have been used for the exciting final scenes of *Stagecoach* and also served as "Mineral City" in various episodes of the Roy Rogers television

The Goldwyn western street in 1953. Photo Bison Archives.

show, although the Iverson, Jack Ingram and Corriganville ranch town sets played that role as well.

Metro-Goldwyn-Mayer

For a quarter century beginning in the 1920s, MGM boasted the largest, most elaborate studio in Hollywood. Permanent exterior sets, located mainly on Lot 3 of its five Culver City lots, abounded. They included, of course, western sets. But MGM produced relatively few westerns, those often involved little or no filming on its western sets and they thus were not nearly so familiar to moviegoers as the streets and other western sets of such studios as Republic, Columbia and Universal. In fact, the most sustained glimpses of MGM's western streets appear to have been those in the "Hondo" TV series, which ran briefly on ABC in 1967 and later in syndication. Features in which the western set can be seen include *The Harvey Girls* (1946), *Stars in My Crown* (1950) and *The Hired Gun* (1957).

The MGM western street in Ride Vaquero (1953). Photo Bison Archives

The MGM street in 1963. Photo Bison Archives

Bronson Canyon

Originally a quarry for construction of L.A.'s first street-car system, Bronson Canyon has been a favorite filming site for low and high budget titles at least since 1919, when the Jack Hoxie silent serial *Lightning Bryce* used the canyon when some of the quarry equipment was still in place. Bronson is part of the 4,000-acre Griffith Park, largest municipal park in the nation. The horseshoe-shaped canyon hosts four tunnel entrances–two large entrances, one at each end of a main tunnel, as well as an entrance to a medium-size tunnel branching off from the main tunnel near its east end and a small cave entrance that also merges with the main tunnel on its east end. The walls of the canyon are steep but were accessible to production crews for rare shots near or at the top of the canyon.

The large entrance at the west end of the main tunnel played a mine in Gene Autry's *Under Fiesta Stars* (1941), cattle were herded into the its main east entrance in an exciting scene for Autry's *Call of the Canyon* (1942) and the strangely shaped mid-sized tunnel served as the entrance to the underground city of Murania for his futuristic serial, *The Phantom Empire* (1935).

Nor was that Autry serial the only cliffhanger to feature Bronson Canyon. Ken Maynard's *Mystery*

Bronson Canyon's west tunnel entrance.

Two of the east tunnel entrances, with the "Murania" entrance at right.

Mountain (1934), in which Autry also appeared, used the canyon, as did other Mascot chapter plays, including *Lightning Warrior* (1931), several Republic serials, among them *Robinson Crusoe of Clipper Island* (1936), *S.O.S. Coast Guard* (1937) and *The Adventures of Captain Marvel* (1941), in which the diabolical Scorpion sealed a seemingly doomed Captain Marvel in the walls of a melting canyon.

Bronson's smallest cave opening made a rare appearance in a scene with that great character player Tom London for Columbia's *Superman* (1948). In another scene for that same title, heavies drove into

The Thunder Riders exit the "Murania" entrance in The Phantom Empire *(1935).*

Buck Jones at the largest east entrance for Hello Trouble *(1932).*

the west tunnel after first driving up the tree-lined road leading to the canyon entrance (perhaps the only film use ever made of that road) and stopping at what appeared to have been the actual chained entrance to the canyon.

Western stars, however, were the most frequent Bronson visitors. Buck Jones made impressive use of the east entrance to the main tunnel in *Hello Trouble* (1932). Wagons raced through the tunnel in an exciting scene for Wayne's *Sagebrush Trail* (1933). Hoppy put it to use in *Leather Burners* (1943). In a beautifully photographed sequence, Durango fought off bandits in the Bronson caves below villainess Mary Newton's ranch house (actually the Middle Iverson ranch set at Chatsworth) in the climax to *Desert Vigilante* (1949).

A-westerns and TV episodes were hardly strangers to the area either. While most of Wayne's *The Searchers* (1956) was filmed at Monument Valley near the Utah-Arizona border, the crew returned to Bronson for that great film's exciting and moving climax. Randolph Scott and Joel McCrea shot part of *Ride the High Country* (1962) there. The ambush scene for the Lone Ranger TV series ("Enter the Lone Ranger") lensed at Bronson, as did many other video series, including "Rebel" and "The Iron Horse."

The Durango Kid after his man in Bronson cave.

The canyon was also a familiar locale for science fiction-horror film fans. Not only did such classics as *Invasion of the Body Snatchers* (1956) use Bronson but also such Grade-Z clunkers as *Robot Monster* (1953), featuring the space-helmeted gorilla Ro-man, and *It Conquered the World* (1956) ("*That* conquered the world?" asked "It" star Beverly Garland on being introduced to the silly-looking monster created for Roger Corman's campy cheapie), as well as *King Dinosaur* (1955) and *Teenage Caveman* (1958), among other titles.

Bronson Canyon is very close to Hollywood & Vine, so close, in fact, that a slight upward shift of a moviemaker's camera would bring Tinseltown's famed "HOLLYWOOD" sign into view.

Directions: To reach the canyon, take Hollywood Blvd. to Bronson Avenue, Bronson north until it becomes Canyon Blvd. and Canyon north to the Bronson parking lot. Walk up the gravel entrance road and enter one of the few sites that still looks almost exactly as it did in the golden era.

Chapter 2

Chatsworth and
the Simi Valley

Today, Chatsworth, in the northwest corner of the San Fernando Valley, about twenty miles from North Hollywood, is reputedly the center for the pornography industry. For many years, however, Chatsworth and its neighbors Canoga Park and the Simi Valley were home to two of the most active movie location ranches, plus other sites that regularly appeared in western films.

The Iverson Ranch

Few film makers have fond memories of working on Chatsworth's Iverson Ranch. Ace Republic director Bill Witney called it the, uh, "armpit" of filming locations. Actors and crew members complained of the sweltering Iverson summers, the bitter cold winters and the gale-force Santa Ana winds that regularly challenged the most securely attached hairpieces of our stalwart western heroes.

But for movie location fans, Iverson–with its cliffs, chase roads, enormous rock formations and elaborate sets–was the premier filming site of the western and serial era. When we hear the word "West," we think first not of the real west but of the "reel west" that Iverson's landmarks conjure up in our minds.

In 1880, Augusta Wagman, a native of Sweden, established a 160-acre homestead on the property that would one day become the Iverson Movie Ranch. In 1888 she married Karl Iverson, a native of Norway who had obtained an adjacent 160-acre homestead. Their ranch, eventually to comprise about 500 acres, apparently first played host to a movie company for a 1912 silent *Man, Woman and Marriage*, shot on the ranch for a fee (set by Mrs. Iverson) of $5 per day. Later, other silent titles were filmed on the Iverson, including *The Amazonians* (1920), Tom Mix's *Wagon Train* (1914), the original *Ben Hur* (1925), *Noah's Ark* (1928) and Buster Keaton's first starring feature *The Three Ages of Man* (1923).

But Iverson would reach its prime in the sound era, ultimately serving as a filming site for more than 2,000 features and TV episodes and at times hosting as many as eight movie crews at once, with fees of $100

The Iverson Ranch's famous "Garden of the Gods" formations in the 1970s.

per day and up by the mid-1940s. Many major features were filmed there, including not only westerns and a variety of Tarzan and other jungle features, but also such non-western comedies as Laurel and Hardy's *Flying Deuces* (1939), as well as western comedies, including Abbott and Costello's *Ride 'Em Cowboy* (1942), Bob Hope's *Son of Paleface* (1952) and Martin and Lewis' *Pardners* (1956). But we perhaps have fondest memories of the countless B-westerns and serials filmed at Iverson's during the golden age.

Of the Iversons' five children, sons Aaron and Joe would devote most of their lives to managing the ranch's film operations. In the 1930s, when the ranch became a major filming site, a three-way split was arranged, with Aaron, Joe and their parents each receiving a third of the profits from location rentals. In the same period, the elder Iversons built a home on the south end of the property. Later called the "Old Folks' Home," it overlooks the San Fernando Valley. Joe built a home that is still on the property and Aaron built a three-story house (no longer standing) near where the Ronald Reagan Freeway (Highway 118) now passes through the ranch.

Augusta and Karl Iverson died in the late 1940s and in 1947 the brothers worked out another split, with Joe taking over the portion of the ranch known as the Lower Iverson (the area south of the freeway) while Aaron assumed control of the Upper Iverson (north of the freeway), each parcel totaling about 250 acres. In 1958, Aaron had a stroke and his son Edwin took over management of upper Iverson filming sites. As filming dwindled on the ranch in the early 1960s, Joe Iverson sold 16 acres of the Lower Iverson in 1963 for construction of what became the Indian Hills trailer park on the site where the ranch's only western street previously stood. Construction of the Simi Valley (now Ronald Reagan) freeway through the property in 1965-67 further diminished the site's value as a filming location and, in 1965, Aaron Iverson sold approximately 90 acres of the Upper Iverson.

On September 25, 1970, a huge fire swept through the ranch, destroying most of the movie sets, as well as those at the nearby Corriganville movie ranch. Later, Joe Iverson sold an additional 200 acres of the Lower Iverson, leaving around 22 acres in his hands. In the 1980s, Joe sold that parcel to Bob Sherman, a relative of his second wife, whom Joe had married in the late 1940s, following his first wife's death in an automobile accident.

With Sherman living in Joe's house and the elder Iverson occupying the "Old Folks Home" overlooking the San Fernando Valley, Sherman attempted to revive the spread as a motion picture location, but with limited success. A few commercials and TV shows lensed there and at least one low budget thriller (*Out of the Dark*, 1988) included a brief scene shot on one of the chase roads and in front of the "Old Folks Home" But the lower ranch's heyday as a filming Mecca had long past.

By the early 1990s, a condo complex covered much of the Lower Iverson, huge mansions were desecrating the upper spread and an apartment complex occupied much of the valley east of the Upper Iverson–the so-called Middle Iverson area where the main Iverson ranch set had once stood. In fact, when a film crew came to the Iverson to shoot scenes for Darryl Hannah's 1993 cable movie, *Attack of the 50 Foot Woman*, they used one of the upper spread mansions rather than the ranch's famed rocks. *The Hollywood Mom's Mystery* (2004), a cable movie with Justine Bateman, was also filmed in part at an Upper Iverson mansion, with one of that area's most distinctive rock formations sometimes visible in the background of scenes.

Finally in 1997, Bob Sherman, faced with growing financial difficulties, produced a cheapie entitled *Motorcycle Cheerleading Mamas* on the ranch (which must have sent Karl and Augusta spinning in their graves), announced plans to move his film operations to Costa Rica and sold the six Iverson acres still in his possession to Van Swearingen of North Hills, California, a classic car collector who planned to construct a western set, a 1950s-era set for display of his automobiles and a number of children's attractions on the property. Swearingen also hoped eventually to obtain the remaining 16 undeveloped acres (including the famed Nyoka Cliff) of the Lower Iverson, which a Chatsworth resident had recently purchased from an investor group.

Swearingen's plans were never realized. Fortunately, however, the most famous rock formations on the ranch, the Lower Iverson's Garden of the Gods area–so named because of its resemblance to Colorado formations of that name–were donated in the 1980s to the Santa Susanna Conservancy for preservation as a nature area. Several years ago, Edwin Iverson still owned 140 undeveloped acres of the Upper Iverson but in the 1980s had sold 12 acres of a large hill separating the lower and upper spread. Much of the most famous filming location of them all has thus become a developer's paradise–and movie fan's nightmare!

Lower Iverson

But we still have our memories. Although Iverson is now largely finished as a filming site, in its heyday it boasted, by far, the most extensive facilities, sets and landscape of all the location ranches, including more than 25 miles of chase roads.

The Lower Iverson is now bordered on the north by the Ronald Reagan Freeway, on the south by the Santa Susanna Pass Road, on the east by Topanga Canyon Blvd. and on the west by Iverson Road–an entry road to the gated community that now occupies much of the upper spread and the neighboring Brandeis Ranch, examined later in this chapter.

The lower spread included numerous filming sites. An unidentified ranch entrance road off the Susanna Pass Road took crews first by side roads leading up to the Garden of the Gods–perhaps the most recognizable location in all filmdom. The Garden of the Gods featured two huge rocks separated by a chase road. The larger and more prominent of those two rocks was usually referred to as the Sphinx Rock. But

The Garden of the Gods in George O'Brien's Silver Treasures *(1925).*

it had the shape of an Indian head. And it was even so designated in the script to Johnny Mack Brown's *Overland Trails* (1948), about a search for a lost gold mine. TV's Lone Ranger rode between the Garden of the Gods rocks at the conclusion of each episode and they are prominent in countless other westerns, TV series and serials, including *Zorro's Fighting Legion* (1939) and *Zorro's Black Whip* (1944).

West of the Garden of the Gods was a field rarely used for filming, which now hosts a church complex. At the end of that church parking lot, however, you can find one of several ambush rocks (*Out California Way*, 1946) on the ranch.

A bit north of the roads leading up to the Garden of the Gods area, a two-story relay station set, which sometimes doubled as a small ranch, once stood. Its proximity to the Garden of the Gods can be seen in Don "Red" Barry's *Stagecoach Express* (1942). It was also used in the treasure hunt scenes for Roy Rogers'

Ambush Rock.

Relay station set near the Garden of the Gods.

Heldorado (1946), the 1940 Columbia serial *Deadwood Dick* and Republic's *Haunted Harbor* (1944) chapter play.

Farther north on the ranch entrance road, which itself often served as a chase road in serials and features, one side road to the east took riders into a Lower Iverson gorge that separated the Garden of the Gods area of the lower spread from the rest of that section of the ranch.

Yet another side road led to another of the Lower Iverson's most familiar formations–a "Devil's Doorway" arch rock through which Gene Autry rode in *Oh, Susanna* (1936) and "Wild Billl" Elliott, as Red Ryder, got the drop on heavies raiding a wagon train in *Wagon Wheels Westward* (1945). (As noted below, another arch rock was situated next to a cabin/mine set in the gorge. The third arch rock, seen in Lash LaRue's *King of the Bull Whip* [1950] and in the second chapter of the Buck Jones serial *White Eagle* [1941], still stands near the Indian Hills trailer park's swimming pool.

Next, the entrance road went past the Iverson family homestead, which apparently never appeared in films, then wound on up to the Upper Iverson and to the neighboring Brandeis Ranch, which was also used

The "Devil's Doorway" Arch Rock.

for filming. In a chapter of Columbia's *Blackhawk* serial (1952), heavies can be seen in a rare shot driving up that road, with the relay station set in the Garden of the Gods area visible in the distant background.

In an area east of the arch rock was an adobe village that was apparently first built as Cesar Romero's mountain fortress in Shirley Temple's *Wee Willie Winkie* (1937). The village was later seen in such titles as Eddie Dean's *Romance of the West* of the West (1946) and Lash LaRue's *Outlaw Country* (1949), as well as Burt Lancaster's foreign legion title *Ten Tall Men* (1951). It overlooked the Lower Iverson gorge, which was bordered on the west by a rarely used road (site of the wagon train attack in *Wagon Wheels Westward*) that ran south toward the Santa Susanna Pass Road, then split into two roads, one running up to the Garden of the Gods area, the other running beneath a cliff situated east of the

The adobe village in Ten Tall Men. *The Nyoka Cliff can be seen in the distance.*

Garden of the Gods. That cliff served as the site for the thrilling cliff-fight climax of two chapters in *Zorro's Black Whip*, as well as many other titles.

Running along the east boundary of the Lower Iverson gorge was a winding stagecoach road featured in many titles and the scene of a terrific wagon explosion first filmed for the Red Ryder entry *Vigilantes of Dodge City* (1944), then utilized as stock footage in countless later Republic titles. Overlooking the stagecoach road and the Santa Susanna Pass Road was another prominent Lower Iverson landmark, the Nyoka Cliff, which not only appeared in that great 1942 Bill Witney serial but was also utilized for exciting

The stagecoach road and, above it, the Nyoka Cliff, in the 1970s.

The Nyoka Cliff.

*Kay (Nyoka) Aldridge and Clayton Moore,
menaced by the ape Satan on the Nyoka Cliff.*

cliff fights in *The Crimson Ghost* (1946), *Valley of Vanishing Men* (1942), *Haunted Harbor* and "Wild Bill"
Elliott's *Taming of the West* (1939), among many other titles.

*The cliff east of the Garden of the Gods and across the gorge from
the Nyoka Cliff, seen at left in this shot from*
The James Brothers of Missouri (1950).

Incidentally, both *Valley of Vanishing Men* and *Haunted Harbor* featured chapter endings in which tall ladders our heroes were attempting to climb from the stagecoach road to the top of Nyoka Cliff were pushed away from the cliff by dastardly villains, hurling our stalwarts to (almost) certain death. Interestingly, shots of the top of the cliff in both those chapter endings actually used the cliff east of the Garden of the Gods rather than the much more hazardous Nyoka precipice. But the exciting *Crimson Ghost* cliff fight, among others, was shot on the Nyoka Cliff itself.

Beyond the south end of the Lower Iverson gorge, across the Santa Susanna Pass Road, was a railroad cut and stretch of track that appeared in numerous films, especially Mascot and other early serials.

On a side road running off to the left from the stagecoach road and near the upper (north) end of the gorge was another landmark–the famous Lone Ranger rock, before which the Ranger reared his trusty steed

Railroad cut.

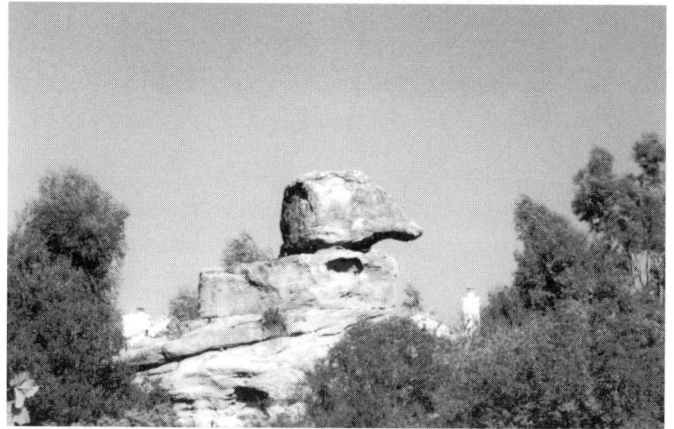

The Lone Ranger Rock.

Silver at the beginning of each episode.

Nestled in large rocks farther up the gorge to the north was a mine entrance, another rock doorway and a stone cabin that appeared in Bob Livingston's *Pride of the Plains* (1944) and *Death Rides the Plains* (1943), as well as *The Adventures of Red Ryder* (1940), among other titles. That cabin, incidentally, was moved to the upper Iverson in later years, where it appeared in several of Lash LaRue's titles, among others.

At the northeast end of the gorge, near the beginning of the stagecoach road, was a favorite spot for scenes depicting our heroes bulldogging baddies from their horses. In *Bandits of Dark Canyon* (1947), for example, "Rocky" Lane

Gorge cabin/mine set. The cabin was later moved to the Upper Iverson.

(compliments of stock footage from a Red Ryder entry) bulldogs a heavy at that spot, then dispatches another baddie (Art Dillard) with some fancy gunplay.

Near the bulldogging site, the stagecoach road merged with a road running west to east across the north end of the gorge and continued east past the two most famous Iverson cave entrances (*Zorro's Fighting Legion*, *The Adventures of Red Ryder*, *Perils of Nyoka*, *Vigilantes of Dodge City*)–actually the two ends of an extended arch rock, with each "entrance" appearing in movies. In *Perils*, Vultura's ape "Satan" chased Nyoka from the west

Nyoka flees the west "cave" entrance.

entrance, essentially A-shaped in form. The east entrance was put to good use in *Red Ryder* and *Vigilantes*.

Iverson east "cave" entrance in the 1990s.

Several other chase roads were also situated in the Lower Iverson hills. At the south end of one road that ran up toward the Nyoka Cliff area, a distinctive rock protruded from the ground. The exciting stagecoach chase in the climax of *Vigilantes of Dodge City* used that road. East of it was another north-south

68

chase road that ran south up a hill to the "Old Folks Home." On the left up that hill, the remains of one of the few Iverson cabins to survive the 1970 fire could still be seen on my last visit to the ranch in the mid-1990s. Best used for an exciting shootout scene between Red and crooked sheriff Tom Chatterton near the beginning of the Red Ryder entry *Lone Texas Ranger (*1945), that cabin also appeared in *Batman and Robin* (1949) and other later Columbia serials as well as numerous features. In several western titles, it served as a false front to a cave hideout for stolen cattle.

Cabin remains near the "Old Folks Home."

 Rocks from a third chase road, including a mushroom-shaped rock, can still be seen in the Indian Hills trailer park. Construction of the trailer park makes it impossible to pinpoint that road's precise location in

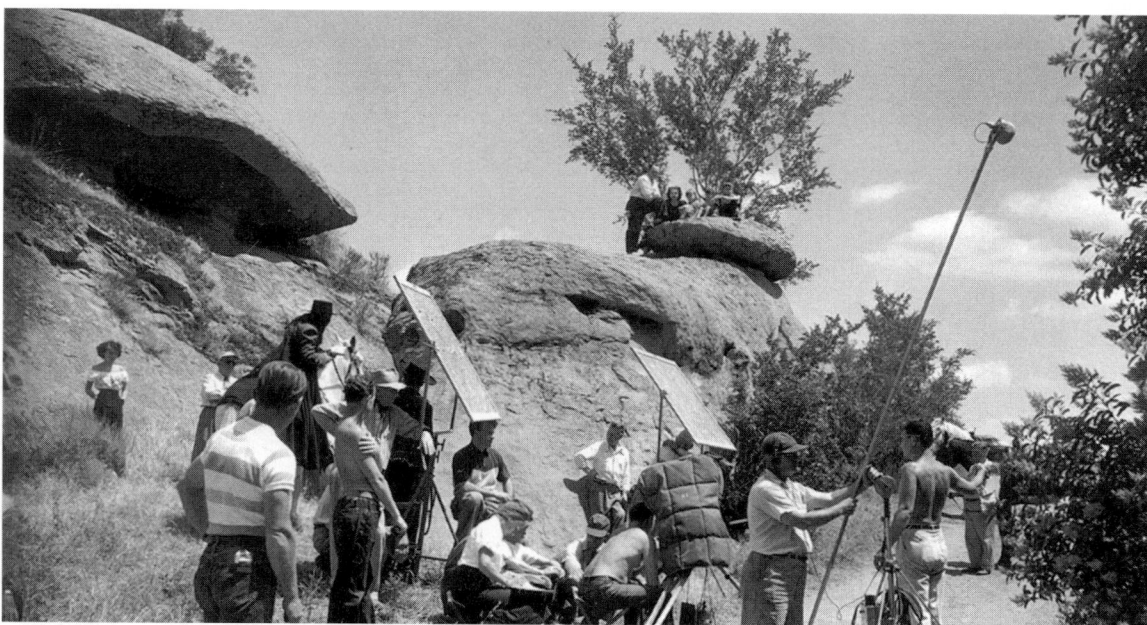

The Mushroom Rock can be seen in this production shot from Lash LaRue's King of the Bullwhip (1950).

relation to the rest of the Lower Iverson. But a cliff-lined clearing near that road hosted a mine/cave entrance often seen in films. It served, for example, as Jennifer Holt's hideout in Eddie Dean's *Hawk of Powder River* (1948) and in many later serials, but was perhaps first seen in *Zorro's Fighting Legion*. Those rocks now provide a backdrop, incidentally, to the trailer park's swimming pool.

In a grove of eucalyptus trees near where the trailer park now stands were other distinctive rock formations and two hideout cabins. That area hosted a two-story relay station set seen in the climax of *Stagecoach to Denver* (1946), blown up in miniature in *The Tiger Woman* (1944) and crushed beneath a dynamite avalanche in *Zorro's Black Whip*. A utility pole could sometimes be seen in sequences shot on the relay station set (for example, in *Stagecoach to Denver*). The area was also home to a nearby second cabin seen in *Prairie Gunsmoke* (1942) with Bill Elliott and Tex Ritter, as well as *King of the Texas Rangers* (1941) and *Bells of Rosarita* (1945), among many other titles.

The Mushroom Rock, concealed by foliage, is situated on the hill to the left, just beyond the fence, in this 2007 photograph.

The cabin in the eucalyptus grove, in King of the Texas Rangers (1941).

Relay station set, in Zorro's Black Whip (1944).

That area was very close to the Iverson Ranch western street set. In fact, the tree-lined entrance road to the town was sometimes visible in the background of scenes shot at the relay station set.

The town set itself was first constructed by Gary Cooper's production company for *Along Came Jones* (1945). Several years later, it appeared in John Payne's *El Paso* (1949) and thereafter was often referred to as the "El Paso Street." Earlier, that portion of the Lower Iverson, known as the Sheep Flats, had hosted the colonial Indian outpost built for *Wee Willie Winkie* and later used in Republic and Columbia serials (*Drums*

This production shot on the edge of Iverson's "El Paso" street underscores the town set's close proximity of the eucalyptus grove.

In this picture, the eucalyptus grove is behind the camera.

This scene from a Whip Wilson title captures the backdrop of buildings at the lower end of "El Paso" Street.

And this shot features a portion of the middle of the street.

of Fu Manchu, 1940, *Adventures of Captain Marvel*, 1941, *Valley of Vanishing Men*, 1942). Later, portions of the outpost formed part of Iverson's western street set.

The Iverson town was a regular fixture in later westerns, including PRC's Eddie Deans, a number of Lash's PRC titles and the films he did for Ron Ormond, and later Monogram/Allied Artists entries in the Johnny Mack Brown, Whip Wilson, Bill Elliott and Wayne Morris series. Gene rode the street in *Hills of Utah* (1951), as did Roy, albeit in Bob Hope's *Son of Paleface* and Roy's TV series rather than his Republic features.

Middle Iverson

A valley east of the large hill separating the lower and upper spreads, sometimes referred to as the Middle Iverson, hosted the Iverson Ranch's main ranch set. Termed "Halfway House" by the Iverson family and the actual residence of the Iverson caretaker, the ranch set was constructed in the early 1940s and made one of its first appearances in "Wild Bill" Elliott's *Prairie Gunsmoke* (1942).

Heavy John Hart is no match for Jim Bannon in this scene filmed on the Middle Iverson ranch set in later years. The bunkhouse at upper left replaced a large barn that originally stood on that spot.

The ranch originally featured a main house with three front entrances, two of which were frequently used in filming, a large barn (through which a driverless car with Gabby Hayes in the trunk raced in *Bells of Rosarita*) and one or two small outbuildings. One of the two most used entrances to the main house can be seen in late-forties PRC/Eagle-Lion films (for example, *Hawk of Powder River*, *Cheyenne Takes Over*, 1947), as well as Columbia's later Durango Kid entries. The other was used not only in Durangos but in Sunset Carson's *Rough Riders of Cheyenne* (1945), one of the relatively few Republic titles to use the ranch set.

The original barn burned in the mid-1940s (torched, locals joked, by "Crash" Corrigan, who was jealous of the competition Iverson gave his location ranch) and was replaced with a long, low bunkhouse-style building. In the mid-fifties, the barn seemed to reappear in TV series and B-plus features. Actually, however, the "Fury" TV series company had simply built a very similar ranch set, complete with large barn, about a half mile north of the original ranch. The 1970 fire destroyed both sets.

Another, less frequently used "front" to the Middle Iverson ranch set.

Upper Iverson

Although the Lower Iverson boasted the most recognizable filming sites, the upper spread was probably used more for filming, especially in the later western and serial era. A large hill, it will be recalled, separated the upper and lower filming areas. A field at the north base of that hill was the principal filming area on the Upper Iverson. It featured a large rock formation that could be seen in numerous titles jutting through trees at the base of the hill (for example, in *Tiger Woman*) and was also sometimes used for cliff fights, as in the climax to Allan Lane's *Silver City Kid* (1944). A road running west up into the hill from the base of that centerpiece rock formation could also be seen in Lane's *Leadville Gunslinger* (1952), as well as many other titles, and a chase road running west to east and northeast along the base of the hill was a frequent site for stagecoach and buckboard chases. Another road ran east-west through the middle of the field. Both field roads hosted an early chase in Sunset Carson's *Rough Riders of Cheyenne*.

Most prominent rock formation on the Upper Iverson.

That rock appears in the background of this Upper Iverson scene.

Just below a prominent and frequently seen eagle-beak rock overlooking the east end of the field was a favorite lookout site for bandit gangs, who would then swoop down onto the Upper Iverson's long, wide, east-west insert road (actually several parallel roads) for yet another thrilling chase. That insert road was prominent in countless titles, from such cheapies as Buster Crabbe's *Devil Riders* (1943) to Roy Rogers' *Twilight in the Sierras* (1950) and *Spoilers of the Plains* (1951). Its position in relation to the main field chase area can perhaps best be seen in the climax to Gene's *Hills of Utah*. The lookout spot also served as the site for some exciting cliff fights, as in the Red Ryder entry *California Gold Rush* (1946).

This eagle-beak rock appeared in the background of countless Upper Iverson scenes.

The eagle-beak rock can be seen in the background of this scene from Spy Smasher (1942) *on the Upper Iverson's insert road.*

At its east end, at a point below that cliff (which is actually quite shallow despite its appearance on cameras shooting up to the top of the cliff), the Upper Iverson's insert road split into several narrow roads. One turned north over a small bridge (see the road gang scene in Roy's *Golden Stallion* (1949) and into a large field area used extensively in later Monogram/Allied Artists titles. A second road curved southward by a section of very unusually shaped rocks, including one resembling an Indian head (*Valley of Hunted Men*, 1942, with the Three Mesquiteers) and led into a "Hidden Valley" section of the upper spread where a cabin originally situated in the Lower Iverson gorge was relocated for later B-western entries.

The Indian Head Rock in a production shot and (inset) in the 1990s.

The cabin that was moved from the Lower Iverson gorge to the Upper Iverson in later years appeared in "Wild Bill" Elliott's Bitter Creek *(1954).*

A third road wound southward up the east side of the hill separating the upper and lower spreads, by a huge rock formation resembling a turtle's head and beak, and past an often-used hillside hideout shack with stone steps and two fake mine entrances, embedded side-by-side in the rock just south of the shack. Among countless titles featuring that shack, see the exciting climax to Durango's *Snake River Desperadoes* (1951).

Turtle Rock.

The Upper Iverson main cabin, which included two mine entrance facades in the rocks next to the cabin.

Farther up the hill, that road forked. One fork led south, ultimately down into the Middle Iverson valley and the ranch site. The other ran west in switchback fashion to the top and across the hill separating the lower and upper spreads. Russell Hayden's *Lone Prairie* (1942) features a musical opening filmed along the rarely used hilltop road, which also included a cactus garden the elder Iversons carefully tended but was rarely seen in films. The hilltop road eventually led down the west end of the hill, connecting at one point with the previously mentioned road that ran up the hill from the Upper Iverson's main field chase area and centerpiece rock formation.

Some chases and other action scenes took place on a "figure eight" set of roads in the valley east of the main Upper Iverson filming area. Northwest of the main insert road was a tree-lined chase road running northeast across the Upper Iverson. It also sometimes appeared in films. But the field chase area and main insert road were by far the most used Upper Iverson filming sites.

The Brandeis (Lazy A) Ranch

For years I struggled to pinpoint the location of a western street that often played the role of a ghost town in cowboy films, as well as the small ranch house and bunkhouse that frequently appeared in titles featuring the town. The street appeared often in films through the late 1930s and early 1940s, then vanished. It was the ghost town in the Three Mesquiteers' *Ghost Town Gold* (1936), Wayne's *Winds of the Wasteland* (1936), Charles Starrett's *Cowboy Star* (1937), Bob Baker's *Ghost Town Riders* (1938) and *The Lone Rider in Ghost Town* (1941), among many other titles. The rocks and distant peaks closely resembled those at Chatsworth's Iverson Ranch. Character player Marc Lawrence was uncertain but thought that the ghost town scenes for *Cowboy Star*, in which he appeared, were shot "up at Iverson." Some location buffs were even erroneously convinced that it was the original Iverson town set, in use before construction of the town seen in Cooper's *Along Came Jones* (1945). But the street built for the Cooper title, also seen in John Payne's *El Paso* (1945) and many later films, was the first and only Iverson western street.

Finally, I sent clips of my "lost" town to Edwin Iverson, whose father Aaron was one of the Iverson Ranch owners. Edwin Iverson and Sigurd Furubotten, an Iverson worker 1933-37, readily identified my ghost town as part of the small Brandeis Ranch, situated on the western edge of the Upper Iverson. Edwin also recalled that film crews using the Brandeis Ranch entered it via the entrance road to the Upper Iverson, which tended to explain Marc Lawrence's recollection that *Cowboy Star* was shot "up at Iverson."

The Brandeis Ranch was first homesteaded in the 1870s by early Chatsworth settlers Niles and Ann Johnson and known as the Johnson Ranch, as well as the "Lazy A," the name by which movie makers generally knew it in the filming days. The property was later purchased by John Brandeis, scion of the wealthy Omaha, Nebraska, family, whose patriarch Jonas L. Brandeis founded one of the nation's largest department stores.

The origin of the Brandeis town set (called "Hickyville" by locals, perhaps because of its ramshackle appearance) is unknown. It was the most prominent set on the ranch but studios also staged chases and fights in the small stretch of surrounding countryside, which included many eucalyptus trees and evergreens, as well as rock formations of the Iverson variety.

At least two houses on the Brandeis Ranch were also used for filming. One resembled Joe Iverson's own home; and Edwin Iverson erroneously identified it as his Uncle Joe's house when first shown clips of films shot there. But

The Brandeis ghost town set, looking toward Rocky Peak.

this single-story, white house with a slightly pitched roof, standing before a huge boulder, was actually the Brandeis Ranch caretaker's house, often used in films. (According to locals, the remains of the wine cellar to the main house could still be seen before the area was covered with development. But the main house, to my knowledge, was never used in films.)

The Brandeis caretaker's house, playing a ranch once again, in
Charles Starrett's Cattle Raiders *(1938).*

The caretaker house can be seen in the Three Mesquiteers' *Heroes of the Hills* (1938) and *Santa Fe Stampede* (1939), as well as Gene Autry's *Prairie Moon* (1938) and Starrett's *Cowboy Star*, among other titles. In a great shot from *West of Tombstone* (1942), connecting the ranch with the Iverson Ranch and Chatsworth, Charles Starrett and Cliff ("Ukelele Ike") Edwards ride toward the Brandeis caretaker's house. In the distant background behind them can be seen Stony Point, a huge rock formation with a chimney rock at one end, which stands on the outskirts of Chatsworth and was visible in the background of so many scenes shot at the Iverson Ranch. In the far distance from the front of the Brandeis house could also be seen the main chase area of the Upper Iverson and the hill separating the upper and lower portions of the Iverson Ranch.

The caretaker's house burned in the 1970 fire that also destroyed most of the Iverson sets. It was later rebuilt. In fact, I videotaped it and the adjacent area in 1986, on my second visit to the Iverson Ranch, without realizing its significance, or that it was not part of the Iverson spread.

Near the caretaker's house, against a backdrop of rocks, was a small bunkhouse with an unusual ramp-like structure with crude railing on the right side of the stoop to the cabin. In Tim McCoy's *Ghost Patrol* (1936), Claudia Dell can be seen walking up to the bunkhouse, with Stony Point again clearly visible in the background of the scene. Rex Bell's *Stormy Trails* (1936) also used the bunkhouse, as well as the town set and caretaker's house, as did Tim McCoy's *Two-Gun Justice* (1938).

The Brandeis bunkhouse with the unusual ramp entrance probably made its last appearance in Bill Elliott's The Last Bandit *(1949).*

The caretaker's home, bunkhouse and several other outbuildings were about a quarter mile west of the Upper Iverson Ranch. and near the base of Rocky Peak, another distinctive area rock formation. The ghost town was located at Hialeah Springs, near the base of Rocky Peak and about a half mile from the caretaker's house. A stream from the spring ran beneath a bridge located at one end of the ghost town's only street.

At some point in the early 1940s, John Brandeis largely ended filming at his ranch. *West of Tombstone,*

Trail of the Silver Spurs (1941) in the Range Busters series and *Wells Fargo Days*, a color short filmed in 1940 and released theatrically in 1944, were among the last titles to feature the ghost town. But the caretaker's house, which succumbed to suburban development in the 1990s, did appear in an important early scene for Bill Elliott's *The Last Bandit* (1949).

Chatsworth

As if these familiar and wonderful locations were not enough, film crews often shot at other Chatsworth sites as well. The winding Santa Susanna Pass Rd. hosted serial chases in several later Republic and Columbia chapterplays, including *Invisible Monster* (1950) and the 1948 *Superman* serial. A railroad tunnel running beneath the Santa Susanna road and used in many titles, including the opening of James Cagney's *White Heat* (1949), provided the climax (via back projection) to a chapter of *Batman and Robin* (1949).

Chatsworth's Stony Point, with its distinctive chimney rock, could be seen in the background of many scenes filmed here on the Lower Iverson cliff east of the Garden of the Gods. Note the track to a camera dolly embedded in the ground on the cliff.

Stony Point, a huge rock formation with a chimney rock on top, was situated on the outskirts of Chatsworth along Topanga Canyon Blvd., southeast of Iverson. It can be seen in the background of many scenes filmed at Iverson and on Chatsworth streets. Devonshire Blvd. and other Chatsworth streets were often used for car chases. A building at the corner of Devonshire and Topanga (Topanga ended at Devonshire in the filming days) once housed Chatsworth Hardware, the post office and a drug store, which can be seen in several later Republic serials. A local gasoline station was also a frequent filming site as well as a parking lot for actors and crew obliged by insurance/union regulations to take a bus onto the ranch.

Chatsworth Lake west of town may now only be a small pond feeding into a reservoir. But it once hosted Roy's *Susanna Pass* (1949) and Monte Hale's *Home on the Range* (1946), among other titles. The man who drove the sandwich wagon for film crews lived in Chatsworth. The Chatsworth railroad depot, with its several palmetto trees at one end, was featured in countless titles, including *Mysterious Dr. Satan* (1940), *Heldorado* (1946) and *Superman* (1948), before being demolished in the 1970s.

Now Chatsworth, like that greatest of all location ranches nearby, has fallen victim to urban sprawl. Fortunately, though, we fans have our memories and our timeless films.

Directions: To get to Iverson and Brandeis, take Freeway 170 north to I-5, I-5 north to Freeway 118 (Ronald Reagan Freeway), 118 west to the Topanga Canyon Blvd. exit, south on Topanga to Santa Susanna Pass Road and Santa Susanna Pass Road west to Red Mesa Drive, in what was once the Lower Iverson gorge, and Iverson Road, the current entrances to the upper and lower spreads. (Alternatively, take the Ventura Freeway northwest from North Hollywood to Topanga Canyon Blvd. and Topanga north to Santa Susanna Pass Road.) Unfortunately, the upper and middle portions of the ranch, as well as the adjacent Brandeis Ranch, are now closed to the public. But the Garden of the Gods is open. Along Red Mesa Drive, one can also see the Lone Ranger Rock, Nyoka Cliff and the faint outlines of the stagecoach road. Resourceful persons, of course, may be able to access other parts of the ranch.

Marwyck Farm

Another Chatsworth ranch made an impressive appearance in *South of Caliente* (1951), one of Roy Rogers' last starring features. That story of thoroughbred racehorse rustlers included scenes made at an obviously upscale ranch, complete with an exercise-race track. When I asked director Bill Witney, he readily recalled using Marwyck Farm in the Chatsworth area for those scenes.

Following her divorce from Frank Fay in 1935, actress Barbara Stanwyck had briefly gone into the thoroughbred business with Zeppo Marx. Their Marwyck Farm consisted of 140 acres situated along north Reseda Blvd. in Northridge, near where Reseda's pavement ended at Devonshire. In 1940,

Roy Rogers at Marwyck Farm in South of Caliente *(1951).*

Stanwyck sold her share of the business to Marx and her house at 18650 Devonshire to actor Jack Oakie. At some point, the name of the ranch was changed to Northridge Farms. Its site is now part of California State University at Northridge.

The swimming pool at the Oakie house was on a hill and may have been the pool that appears briefly in Roy Rogers' *Rainbow over Texas* (1946). The ranch's track not only appeared in *South of Caliente* but also in Shirley Temple's *The Story of Seabiscuit* (1949). Although set, of course, in Kentucky (courtesy of stock footage), the title's thoroughbred farm scenes appear against a backdrop of rocky ridges one would hardly expect to see in the Bluegrass State!

Rowland Lee Ranch

A Canoga Park ranch owned by director Rowland Lee also appeared in a few features. Lee purchased his 214-acre spread in 1935, naming it Farm Lake Ranch. But it was always known as the Lee Ranch and for years one of its two lakes appeared on San Fernando Valley maps as "Lee's Lake."

For its big-budget musical *I've Always Loved You* (1946), Republic constructed an elaborate farm set, complete with a stone and wood bridge, on the ranch. That set later appeared also as a period French farmhouse in RKO's *At Sword's Point* (1952). For *The Big Fisherman* (1959), which Lee produced, one of the lakes reportedly served as the Sea of Galilee, with filming periodically interrupted on that shoot by clouds of black smoke erupting from the testing of rockets at Rocketdyne's facility on Burro Flats, in the hills above Canoga Park.

A 1949 photograph of the set built for I've Always Loved You *(1946). Photo Bison Archives.*

The closest to a western feature filmed there was Gary Cooper's *Friendly Persuasion* (1956), in which the set served as an Indiana Quaker family's farm during the Civil War. To give the property an authentic look, director William Wyler had a cornfield planted, sycamore trees imported and huge areas covered with green grass. *Glory* (1956), a horse-racing title with Margaret O'Brien and Walter Brennan, used the farm set and lake, as did Ginger Rogers' *The First Traveling Saleslady*, released the same year.

The ranch also appeared in Robert Mitchum's *Night of the Hunter* (1955). But one of Lee's lakes had its most memorable role in Alfred Hitchcock's *Strangers on a Train* (1951), for which the great director had an amusement park constructed on the ranch. One of the most chilling—yet fascinating—scenes in that superb film depicts Robert Walker strangling Farley Granger's sluttish estranged wife (Laura Elliott) on an island in the amusement park, with the murder captured in the lens of the victim's eyeglasses. Years later, Elliott recalled Hitchcock's insistence on take after take in his effort to capture that scene perfectly on film. Obviously, he succeeded.

For observant location fans, *Strangers on a Train* also included an interesting bit of insider trivia. When Elliott and her two male companions boarded a bus for her fateful trip to the amusement park, the bus destination read, "Lee's Lake."

Much of Walt Disney's *The Light in the Forest* (1958), the 18th century story of a white boy (James MacArthur) raised by Indians, was filmed on location near Chattanooga, Tennessee. But an Indian village was constructed on the Lee ranch for those scenes. Reportedly, *Johnny Tremain* (1957), another Disney epic of early America, was also shot on the spread.

Lee died in 1975. Although one of the lakes is still there, the area is now occupied by a gated community, Hidden Lake Estates.

Corriganville

Corriganville in California's Simi Valley, about an hour's drive northwest from L.A., was second only to the Iverson Ranch as the busiest filming location of the golden era. It was generally home to the lowest of the low of western movies, Tvers and such non-western fare as several entries in the Jungle Jim feature series, but also boasted some fine features and serials.

The Scott Ranch since 1870, the property had once hosted a valley stagecoach stop and was an occasional site for filming in its pre-Corriganville days. B-movie star Ray "Crash" Corrigan purchased the 1,740-acre spread, later enlarged to 2,060 acres, in 1937 for a reported $11,354 and lost no time in developing the area for film use. According to a September 30, 1937, newspaper profile, work crews with bulldozers were already grading the property for three 50-foot-wide macadam insert roads at least a half mile each in length, constructing a lagoon to be fed by two springs on the property and clearing other areas of brush and rock. Lumber for construction of additional facilities had arrived and Warner Bros. location scouts, according to the article, were then inspecting the site for possible use in future productions. Although no footage for Warner's *Adventures of Robin Hood* (1938) was apparently shot at the ranch, the presence of Warner Bros. scouts there at the very time the studio was scouting sites close to L.A. for the Errol Flynn hit lends some credence to speculation that Corrigan constructed the 372-foot lagoon in an effort to lure that big-budget production to his new ranch, with plans that the lagoon become Robin Hood Lake, and the adjoining five-acre oak grove Sherwood Forest, at that time rather than in 1946 or 1950, when Columbia's *The Bandit of Sherwood Forest* and *Rogues of Sherwood Forest* filmed there. Some have suggested that the names originated with the Columbia titles. But that studio, contrary to various reports, was not involved in the lake's construction and the Robin Hood Lake is given very limited exposure in the Columbia titles.

While Corrigan did not land the Flynn title, our western and serial heroes were soon familiar sights at the ranch, with George O'Brien's *Gun Law* (1938) apparently the first film shot there under the Corrigan banner and the Three Mesquiteers' *Heroes of the Hills* (1938) and Tex Ritter's *Starlight over Texas* (1938) following close on O'Brien's heels. At least by the Trail Blazers' entry *Blazing Guns* (1943), our heroes were diving or falling off a fake cliff added to the lagoon, and the lagoon, albeit with a low water-level, can be seen in *Perils of Nyoka*. *Perils* and its predecessor *Jungle Girl* (1941) also featured the ranch's most prominent cave/mine entrance facade, and *Perils* put Corriganville's main insert road to thrilling use. The original ranch house, bunkhouse and barn were also put to regular use, as were several hideout shacks.

The Robin Hood Lake and cliff in the 1980s.

Gene Autry strums a serenade on the lake, with the cliff at upper left.

Corriganville's main cave/mine entrance.

Remains of the cave/mine facade in the 1970s.

Original buildings on the ranch.

*The original ranch entrance road appeared in the opening credits to early
"Trail Blazers" series titles. Note the ranch barn at upper right.*

In 1943, Ray Corrigan also began construction of a town set adjacent to the ranch buildings. Apparently first used, partially constructed, for Bob Livingston's Lone Rider entry *Law of the Saddle* (1943), the completed town appeared initially in Buster Crabbe's *Frontier Outlaws* (1944). It quickly became the "official" town set for PRC's Crabbe and Texas Ranger series as well as the site for several Lash LaRues and other cheapies and for entries in the Bill Elliott (*Vigilante Terror*, 1953) and Wayne Morris (*Texas Badman*, 1953, *Two Guns and a Badge*, 1954) Monogram/Allied Artists series at the end of the B-western era, with the ranch barn becoming the town's livery stable and the ranch house itself often posing as a residence on the edge of town rather than a ranch–a wise move since sharp-eyed Front Row kids had long noticed the distant ranch to which Buster Crabbe and other heroes often rode on leaving the Corriganville town was actually only a few yards away, at the end of the western street!

A shot of the western street in later years, with the camera looking toward the large rock formation that hovered over the end of town nearest to Robin Hood Lake.

And a picture with the camera looking toward the ranch house at the opposite end of town.

The street from another angle, with riders racing in the direction of the ranch house.

*Remains of the street in the 1970s, including the large livery stable
constructed for the ranch's amusement park days.*

1948 saw the appearance on a plateau above the town of John Wayne's "Fort Apache," later the setting for the "Rin Tin Tin" TV series and many features. Especially after Corrigan converted the site into a amusement park in 1949, other sets–most notably a huge stable at the end of town (called "Silvertown") and Mexican and Corsican villages–were added to the facility. Several hideout shacks/relay stations, including one constructed for *Fort Apache* and partially below ground, plus cave/mine entrances and a hideout rock the Durango Kid regularly rode behind for a quick change of costume, also dotted the landscape.

The Fort Apache set.

A slightly different perspective.

The Durango Kid at the dugout set adjacent to Fort Apache.

The hideout rock near the Robin Hood Lake.

The use of camera trucks for chases along the ranch's running insert roads added greatly to the excitement of our westerns and serials. Corriganville's three insert roads were the best in the business. One began up on the plateau where the Fort Apache set was eventually constructed and ran southeast down a hill, past a hideout shack (which could occasionally be seen in the background of films using the road) and by the edge of the town set, there separating into two roads at a point where a large, saddle horn-shaped rock protruded from the ground prior to the ranch's amusement park days. (For only one of many examples, see Wild Bill Elliott's *Man from Thunder River*, 1943.)

A photograph taken in the 1980s of the Corriganville chase road that ran by the town set (camera right), with the camera looking in the direction of Fort Apache. Note the large rock at upper left, which appears in the next photo. The large saddle-horn rock mentioned in the text does not appear in this picture. That rock was apparently removed when Corriganville became an amusement park.

Johnny Mack Brown on the first chase road. The large rock noted in the previous photo is at upper right in this picture.

"Wild Bill" Elliott and sidekicks "Gabby" Hayes and John James ride toward the site of the future Fort Apache on the first chase road.

The larger of these two photos shows the saddle-horn rock above the team horse's head, the insert a more distant shot of the saddle-horn rock.

A second insert road ran past the Robin Hood Lake, by the principal hideout rock and Corriganville's most prominent cave/mine facade, then split into two roads at the edge of town, with one road running into town and another running around the base of a hill with a prominent eagle-beak rock formation at the end of town to intersect with the first chase road. The third chase road began in Sherwood Forest, proceeded along a tree-lined and fence-row route toward the rear of the town set and ranch house. That road was separated by a gully from the second chase road and finally merged with Smith Road, the entrance road to the ranch in the pre-amusement park days. It and Smith Road itself were used in the opening credits to early Trail Blazers entries.

Chase scenes on the hilly second insert road, shot from a camera truck racing along the flat third road, with trees and rocks flashing between camera and riders, were truly exhilarating (see, for example, the Durango Kid entry *Pecos River*, 1951, and the Elliott/Ritter entry *Bullets for Bandits*, 1942), as were shots taken along the third road from a speeding camera truck positioned in front of riders, buckboards or stagecoaches (see especially Sunset Carson's *Firebrands of Arizona*, 1944).

Although Republic, Columbia and Universal (*Raiders of San Joaquin*, 1943) film crews probably put Corriganville's chase roads to best use, the cheapie companies also had their moments. Most notable perhaps

The larger photo is of the second chase road looking south toward the town set. The inset is a scene on this second chase road shot by a camera truck speeding along the third chase road. The hideout rock can be seen just above the stagecoach in the inset scene and lower mid-camera in the larger photo.

was the super relay race scene climaxing *Pinto Bandit* (1944), perhaps the only highlight of the lamentable James Newill/Dave O'Brien Texas Ranger series–even if Jack Ingram did fall off his steed at the end of the race–an unscripted goof only partially excised (in true zero-budget fashion) by the PRC film cutter!

Despite Corriganville's large overall size, the principal filming area was very compact; portions of the chase roads, for example, were only a few yards from the town set.

Virtually every western hero, along with not only both Nyokas but also other serial figures, such as "King of the Texas Rangers," "The Vigilante" and even "Sir Gallahad," saw duty at Corriganville. But it was home primarily to lowly PRC and Monogram, as

The tree-lined third chase road.

well as independents, including Ken Maynard's last hurrah *Harmony Trail* (1944) and nearly all the early western TV series. Republic used Corriganville's town only in Gene Autry's *Sioux City Sue* (1947), Roy

Corriganville was home mainly to such low budget B-westerns as PRC's "Texas Rangers" series. Here the first trio in the series is pictured before one of the ranch's distinctive slanted rock formations.

Rogers' *Down Dakota Way* (1949) and in a very quick clip for Elliott's *Overland Mail Robbery*. Columbia used it only in a few post-war Autrys and Durango Kid entries, and Universal and RKO never, to my knowledge, although those studios used other Corriganville sites extensively, especially before the post-war era.

Although star Rex Allen derided Corriganville as "a tourist trap," it reportedly drew as many as 20,000 fans on weekends and was rated at one point as one of the top ten U.S. amusement parks. But as the Simi Valley (now Ronald Reagan) Freeway was being constructed through the area in the mid-1960s, Corrigan sold his ranch in 1965 to comedian Bob Hope, presumably for real estate speculation. The next year, the facility, renamed Hopetown, was closed to the public. The same September 25, 1970 fire that destroyed much of the nearby Iverson Ranch also gutted most of the Corriganville sets and left only the chimney standing at the ranch house. *Land Raiders*, a 1969 Telly Savalas epic shot in Europe included an exciting Corriganville stagecoach chase. But alas, that scene was lifted from Columbia's 1946 B+ feature *The Renegades*. *Stage*

Ghost, a Z-grade horror spoof released in 2000, included scenes of the Corriganville countryside, by then heavily overgrown with weeds. But that epic was a sad end for the once-proud filming location–its producers could afford only two horses for their stagecoach!

In 1988 the city of Simi Valley purchased the property for use as a regional park. For several years, the Corriganville Preservation Committee, composed of people who had worked at the ranch or had fond memories of its years as an amusement attraction, attempted to establish a movie and natural history museum on the site, even beginning the process of rebuilding the town set. That effort failed and the amusement park entrance area is now covered with apartments. But we fans can still visit the now overgrown park our heroes once rode.

Directions: From L.A. take Freeway 170 north to I-5, I-5 north to Highway 118 (Ronald Reagan Freeway), 118 west to the Kuehner Road exit, Kuehner Road south to Smith Road and Smith Road east a hundred yards or so to the remains of the original ranch entrance on the left.

The Bell Ranch

In the mountains separating the famed Iverson movie ranch of Chatsworth and Corriganville in the Simi Valley, there was a third, less well-known western filming site–the Bell Ranch. Apparently, the area was a frequent location for silent flicks. In fact, a 1920s flyer carried real estate advertisements for the Bell Moving Picture Ranch area. A man named Berry eventually purchased the Bell holdings but later sold his 120 acres to Rosemary Couch and Jean Forsythe, who dubbed the area the Berry Ranch when leasing to movie companies.

In 1950, Couch and Forsythe sold five acres of the property to Tony Stimolo, a studio location manager, who resurrected the Bell Ranch name even though location listings for certain films shot there would continue

The Bell Ranch street. Note the Victorian home at the far end of the street. Photo Bison Archives.

to carry the Berry Ranch location. A native of Burbank, Stimolo had worked in his early years for the city, doing tree-trimming and landscaping, getting bit parts in a number of features and once serving as Rudolph Valentino's stand-in, but primarily arranging locations for Universal and other studios and producers, including the company producing the "Lassie" TV series.

In 1955 Stimolo built a western street on the Bell Ranch property from the remains of residences then being razed in L.A. Sets constructed for particular productions were also left behind for future use. A Victorian home built for Bing Crosby Productions, for example, was frequently recruited for other films and Tvers. Stimolo also formed Motion Picture Locations Unlimited, the first independent location service for film, television and commercial productions. Operating originally from offices at the ZIV studios on Melrose Avenue in Hollywood, he rented out his Bell Ranch property and also served as broker for owners of adjacent property and others interested in rental opportunities. Through

The "Zorro Cabin."

Stimolo's efforts, for example, an adobe cabin on property adjoining the Bell Ranch became a favorite filming site for Disney's "Zorro" TV series, as did the ranch's rocky terrain. Stimolo's western street and the ranch's chase roads and rock formations also played host to "Have Gun Will Travel," "The Big Valley," "How the West Was Won" and other Tvers, and the Bell countryside appeared in such A-features as Elvis Presley's *Love Me Tender* (1956), Laurence Harvey's *The Outrage* (1964) and, according to some sources, portions of Paul Newman's *Hombre* (1967). The ranch overlooked the San Fernando Valley, which was often visible in the background of chase scenes shot there.

A 1969 shot of the street. Photo Bison Archives.

The Bell Ranch's original western street, put to most extensive use perhaps in Audie Murphy's *Quick Gun* (1964), burned in the mid-1960s but was soon rebuilt. Lash LaRue's lamentable soft-porn turn *Hard On the Trail* (1971) used that street as well as the Spahn Ranch of Manson Family infamy. It as well as the surrounding countryside were also put to scenic use in "McCabe," a 1970 color "Gunsmoke" episode featuring Jim Davis and David Brian. The second street was last seen in *Sunset* (1988) with Jim Garner and Bruce Willis. In the early 1990s, the buildings were donated to the Wilderness Institute and moved. When Tony Stomolo died in 1994, only the adobe structure (which locals fittingly dubbed "Zorro's Cabin") still stood on the property.

Directions: Santa Susanna Pass Road west from Chatsworth a few miles. Turn left on Box Canyon Road, then left on Studio Road. But the area was developed several years ago and is no longer accessible.

Burro Flats

Rex Allen's *Phantom Stallion* (1954) was the last series B-western Republic Pictures released. At the film's end, Rex, not his stunt double Joe Yrigoyen on that occasion, rode off into the sunset at the site where most, if not all, the original non-studio exteriors for *Phantom Stallion* had been filmed.

But where was that site? The name and location of that little used but impressive filming locale eluded me for many years. It was the setting for the spectacular cliffhanger climaxing Chapter 7 of *Zorro's Fighting Legion* (1939), in which stunt ace Yakima Canutt suffered a seemingly near-fatal mishap executing his famous fall beneath a runaway stagecoach. The riveting stagecoach fight that concluded Chapter 1 of *The Adventures of Red Ryder* (1940) was filmed there also, as was the exciting stagecoach race ending Chapter 6 of the same serial. So, too, were a number of the Roy Rogers (*Robin Hood of the Pecos*, 1941), Don "Red" Barry (*Frontier Vengeance*, 1940, *Texas Terrors*, 1940) and Three Mesquiteers (*Kansas Terrors*, 1939, *Covered Wagon Days*, 1940) Republic titles of the late 1930s and early forties. Also, several other early fifties Rex Allen titles (*Utah Wagon Train*, 1951, *Iron Mountain Trail*, 1953, *Shadows of Tombstone*, 1953, *Red River Shore*, 1953), one of the last Allan "Rocky" Lane entries (Bandits of the West, 1953) and even early scenes for Columbia's fine Elliott-Ritter entry *Lone Star Vigilantes* (1942), as well as a number of A-westerns (e.g., *California*, 1948, with Barbara Stanwyck and Ray Milland, and Audie Murphy's *Ride Clear of Diablo* and *Drums Across the River*, both 1954) and at least one TV oater.

But *where* was that location? Scenes shot there were often combined with filming set at the Iverson Ranch outside Chatsworth and my mystery site's boulders did resemble those at Iverson's. But my "lost" site was not part of that famous movie spread. When asked, Rex Allen could not remember where his later titles were filmed, only that the site was in the mountains above Iverson's.

Finally, beloved movie baddie Pierce Lyden identified the beautiful grassy plateau surrounded by huge boulders featured in a Gene Autry TV episode, in which Lyden had appeared, as Burro Flats, or as most of the old cowboy actors called it, "Jackass Flats."

I had seen reference to Burro Flats as a filming site over the years but was told it had been developed long ago as a rocket testing facility. With the help of the Chatsworth post office, my friend John Leonard and I located Burro Flats on our next trip to California. The area was indeed now home to a rocket installation–the Santa Susanna Field Laboratory, owned by Rocketdyne Propulsion and Power of Canoga Park, formerly a

California (1946).

division of North American Rockwell and at that time part of the Boeing Corp.

The Santa Susanna field lab was normally off-limits to visitors. But we western location fans are a persistent lot. Within a few days, John and I were being given an extended guided tour of the area. Originally part of the Sage Ranch in the Santa Susanna Mountains overlooking the San Fernando and Simi valleys, 2,100 acres had been set aside there in 1948 to become part of the nation's then infant rocketry industry. Over the years, Rocketdyne's facilities became the test site for many household names of the space industry. A recent Rocketdyne brochure indicated that the company was familiar with the property's film history, but only vaguely so. The one photograph in the brochure supposedly representative of filming there was a still from a Trail Blazers entry shot at Corriganville! The elaborate rocket facilities scattered over the area gave the site an appearance more suited for sci-fi flicks than our favorite oaters. But much of the area was still readily recognizable to western fans. Several relatively distinct sections had been used for western filming on the flats. The most familiar was a gently sloping grassy plateau with large, unusually shaped boulders scattered mainly along the edge of the plateau. Running inserts of riders, coaches and wagons racing past those boulders at seemingly breakneck speed provided front-row kids with truly exhilarating visual delights. Other scenes utilizing that area would be shot from a distant, static camera. *California* included such shots as well as similar segments filmed for that title in the Rocky Oaks area of the Conejo Valley near Thousand Oaks. On one occasion, moreover, a camera fortuitously caught an unusual Burro Flats scene in that area of a stagecoach riding past a small herd of deer–a scene repeated in stock footage countless times.   A second, relatively flat plateau bordered on one edge by a sloping hill of solid rock, vaguely reminiscent of the Vasquez Rock s north of Newhall, provided another setting for chase scenes. Yak's fall beneath the coach for *Zorro's Fighting Legion* was shot on that part of the flats, as were portions of a race between two stagecoaches in Don "Red" Barry's *Frontier Vengeance.*

A third filming area featured a road bordered by scattered trees and rocks, while yet another consisted of large boulders overlooking the Simi Valley and mountains in the distance across the valley. Don Barry's confrontation with heavy Arthur Loft in the climax to *Texas Terrors* took place in those rocks, as did portions of *Zorro's Fighting Legion.*

Burro Flats appeared fairly regularly in late 1930s and early

Zorro's Fighting Legion (1939).

1940s titles. For some reason, very little filming was done on the flats from the early 1940s to the early fifties. Toward the end of the B-western era, however, Republic returned often to the area. Publicity material for Rocky Lane's *Marshal of Cedar Rock* (1953) specifically identified the flats as the filming site for that title and even reported that a snowfall in the area had temporarily delayed shooting there. But as usual with studio publicity, that account was at least partially incorrect. Non-studio exteriors for that title were shot at Iverson's, not Burro Flats, but some original footage for Lane's *Bandits of the West* was filmed on the flats.

Several of Rex Allen's titles made extensive and exciting use of the area–not surprisingly, since action master Bill Witney directed all but one of the Allen titles filmed at Burro Flats. Rex's *Iron Mountain Trail* and *Phantom Stallion* used stock footage from Roy Rogers' *Golden Stallion* (1949), shot at Iverson's, while *Iron Mountain Trail* recycled one of the stagecoach chases shot on the flats. But both titles included well-executed original scenes of Rex, Slim Pickens and company racing over the flats. Allen's *Red River Shore* and *Shadows of Tombstone* also made effective use of the area, although the climax to the latter film drew on stock footage originally filmed at the swinging bridge outside Kernville and used in the Three Mesquiteers title *Trigger Trio* (1938), as well as stock footage from another Mesquiteers entry.

As the B-western era came to an end in 1954, Burro Flats' contributions to film history largely ended also. In the golden age, though, the flats provided an impressive alternative to the most frequently used filming sites in the L.A. area.

Directions: To get to Burro Flats, take the Santa Susanna Pass Rd. from Chatsworth west toward the Simi Valley, turn left onto Box Canyon Rd. and follow Box Canyon to the Rocketdyne entrance. Or take Topanga

Burro Flats, overlooking the Simi Valley.

Rex Allen and Slim Pickens before one of the huge Burro Flats boulders.

Canyon Blvd. to Plummer Road in Chatsworth, turn left onto Plummer and follow Plummer and Valley Circle Blvd. up into the hills to the Rocketdyne entrance.

Spahn Ranch

As we have seen, the hills above Chatsworth, in the northwest corner of the San Fernando Valley, boasted the great Iverson Movie Ranch, the oldest, best and most frequently utilized location spread in B-western and serial history. The ranch house, bunk house and western street of the smaller Brandeis Ranch, on the western boundary of the upper portion of the Iverson spread, also appeared in many films. But the Chatsworth locale that achieved the greatest fame, or infamy, was best known not for the movie crews it hosted, but for its dubious distinction as the home briefly of Charlie Manson and his murderous "family."

Located across the Santa Susanna Pass Road from the Iverson Ranch's original entrance, and bordered on the south by the tracks of the Southern Pacific, the Spahn Ranch apparently consisted of 511 acres but only a few acres at most were suitable for filming. Instead, it functioned mainly as a riding stable and supplier of horses and rolling stock to film crews shooting in the vicinity.

George Spahn, a Pennsylvania native, was born in 1889. Before reaching age thirty, he was the owner of a successful dairy farm in Lansdale, Pennsylvania. In the 1930s, however, Spahn gave up the milk business and moved to California, where he raised horses and operated a riding stable, first in Long Beach, later in south L.A., then at the intersection of Orchard and Riverside Drive in Burbank.

Stuntman and stunt coordinator Whitey Hughes knew Spahn and his large family of ten children well, especially his sons Pinto, Jim and Cody, who did some work in films. Hughes often rented horses from Spahn and went riding in the nearby dry wash of the L.A. River bed. Eventually, Spahn expanded the business to include children's pony rides, the rental of horses for parades and fairs, and the provision of horses, wranglers and rolling stock to film makers.

Stuntman Bill Ward, later Clayton Moore's stunt double in "The Lone Ranger" series, also owned a rental stable on Riverside Drive. In 1948, Spahn and Ward bought property in the hills northwest of Chatsworth. The parcel Spahn purchased was along the Santa Susanna Pass Road while Ward's portion was deep in the canyons south of the road. According to Whitey Hughes, Spahn and Ward had plans to open a movie ranch there. Ward, as Hughes put it, "could be a hard man to work with" and he and Spahn soon parted company. But Spahn continued the venture, first constructing the building he would occupy, then adding a small western street and other buildings. The ranch also hosted a stable and one of its buildings, a saloon set with a large, ornate mirror behind the bar, was suitable for interior filming.

The area reportedly had once belonged to silent star William S. Hart and had been used as a movie location site. In fact, profiles of the ranch appearing at the time of the Manson murders claimed that Tom Mix, Johnny Mack Brown and Hoot Gibson, among other oater stars, had once ridden the Spahn Ranch range. Sources even listed Jane Russell's *The Outlaw* (1943) and Bogart's classic *Treasure of the Sierra Madre* (1948) among titles shot there. But none of the settings used in those titles resemble the Spahn Ranch sets or countryside and neither Whitey Hughes nor others familiar with the ranch's history can remember any use of the area in mainstream A and B-westerns or TV episodes.

Whatever the ranch's earlier role in films, moreover, George Spahn attracted few productions of any sort to the site. Instead, divorced from his first wife, Spahn and his ranch manager/girlfriend Ruby Pearl used the ranch, like his Burbank property, primarily as a riding stable and supplier of movie horses and props. Toward

Spahn Ranch in the 1970s.

the end of the period that Jack Wrather's Lone Ranger Corporation leased Corriganville in the mid-fifties, Spahn was also briefly in charge of rental horses at the Simi Valley western theme park. But Spahn's horses were so old and poorly nourished that Charlie Aldrich (real name Aldridge), who staged shows at Corriganville for eleven years, soon had to replace Spahn with another stockman. Veteran stuntman Jerry Vance was Aldrich's assistant at Corriganville. Vance and his friend Bob Bickston shot a number of low-budget–or no-budget–independent films at Spahn Ranch. Bearing such titles as *Joaquin Murietta, Hang Fire* and *Stinking Springs*, they got some overseas play dates, and *Hang Fire*, according to Vance, was a hit in Japan.

Low budget producer-director Al Adamson shot portions of *The Female Bunch (1969)*, with Russ Tamblyn and a pitifully inebriated Lon Chaney, Jr., there, as well as *Hell's Bloody Devils* (1970) (a.k.a. *Swastika Savages*, etc.) and *Lash of Lust* (1974). Spahn Ranch also apparently had roles in Greg Corarito's *Diamond Stud* (1970), *Fabulous Bastard from Chicago* (1969) and *Wanda, the Sadistic Hypnotist* (1969).

Charlie Aldrich remembers shooting one pickup shot for an Alan Jones TV pilot, "Guns of the Lawless West," there. But the closest thing to a real western lensed there in those days was Lash LaRue's *Hard On the Trail*, filmed in late 1969 and released in 1971. Lash (who appeared in none of the film's soft-porn scenes) was about the only redeeming feature in that amateurish effort. Most of the epic's street scenes, including a whip fight sequence early in the film, lensed on the Bell Ranch's western street off Box Canyon

Road, a few miles west of the Spahn spread. Corriganville also appears in several quick action shots. But a ramshackle ghost town featured in several later scenes of Lash's western swan song is indeed the Spahn Ranch.

By that point, though, Spahn's world, like his ranch, seemed to be collapsing around him. Members of the Manson clan, who began showing up at the ranch as early as 1967, had at first been welcome company to the lonely old man–especially the sexually liberated young women in the group. But Charlie and his followers soon became a more menacing presence. When Clayton Moore stopped at the ranch in 1969 to visit his now nearly blind old friend, he was alarmed at the squalid conditions in which Spahn was living, and especially at the motley and hard-eyed assortment of young people living on the spread.

A Spahn worker, Donald "Shorty" Shea, disappeared from the ranch before the murders of actress Sharon Tate and her friends. When Shea's remains were discovered in 1979, a Manson associate was convicted of his murder. Shea apparently had threatened to expose the group's illegal activities.

The ranch's western street was too close to the traffic on the Susanna Pass Road for effective use in filming and once its association with the Manson clan became public, it largely lost whatever appeal it previously had as a film site or riding stable. Film historian Jim Goldrup was a day player in *Hard On the Trail*. During the shoot, he recalled, one of the crew mentioned it was a "little eerie" working in the area where the Manson family had recently roamed. Later, Jim took his brother Tom up to the ranch. "Some folks there," Jim recalls, "said that we looked as though we could be part of the Manson family (I guess because we had long hair and moustaches)." The bulk of the ranch buildings burned in the September, 1970, brush fires that swept through the area, destroying most of Iverson's and Corriganville's sets as well. In fact, in the TV movie version of *Helter Skelter*, the L.A. D.A.'s account of the Manson murders, the once great Paramount Ranch was reduced to impersonating the lowly Spahn spread.

But even before George Spahn's death in 1974, he and his ranch had achieved international notoriety. I first began visiting Chatsworth in the mid-eighties. Few residents were familiar with Iverson's; all knew the Spahn Ranch.

Chapter 3

The Conejo Valley
and Other "TV Lands"

Although Iverson and Corriganville were clearly the favorite filming sites for producers of low-budget oaters, the Conejo Valley northwest of L.A. also played a prominent role in filmdom's golden age. Warner Bros., Fox and Paramount maintained ranch facilities in the Agoura/Calabasas area. Movie heavie Jack Ingram built a western street on his little spread (a former goat ranch) in Woodland Hills. Movie makers often utilized Lake Sherwood and thoroughbred ranches in nearby Hidden Valley, outside Thousand Oaks. The Agoura-Albertson ranch and adjacent Morrison ranch regularly hosted production crews, as did the huge Russell Ranch. As television replaced the Saturday matinee for six-gun shootouts, other Conejo ranches, with their rolling hills and scattered trees, also made regular appearances on the video screen, as did locales in other areas that had previously hosted theatrical fare. In this chapter, we examine the Conejo Valley filming sites, as well as various California locations that became prominent in the production of TV westerns.

The Ingram Ranch

One of our western movie ranches had its beginnings in the efforts of two celluloid cowboy stalwarts to avoid military service! During World War II, prolific western writer/director/producer Oliver Drake worked with Jim Newill and Dave O'Brien on *Border Buckaroos* (1943) and *Trail of Terror* (1943), two entires in PRC's lowly Texas Rangers series. As a ploy to avoid the draft, Drake recalled in his interesting autobiography, Newill and O'Brien bought a goat ranch off Topanga Canyon road in Woodland Hills, a few miles northwest of L.A.

The two stars apparently found getting up at 3 a.m. daily to tend nearly a hundred goats even less appealing than working for PRC. When both received draft deferments, they sold the ranch in 1944 to B-western-serial heavy Jack Ingram, who often appeared in Texas Rangers series entries. Ingram soon enlisted Pierce Lyden and other pals into helping him construct sets for filming on the ranch.

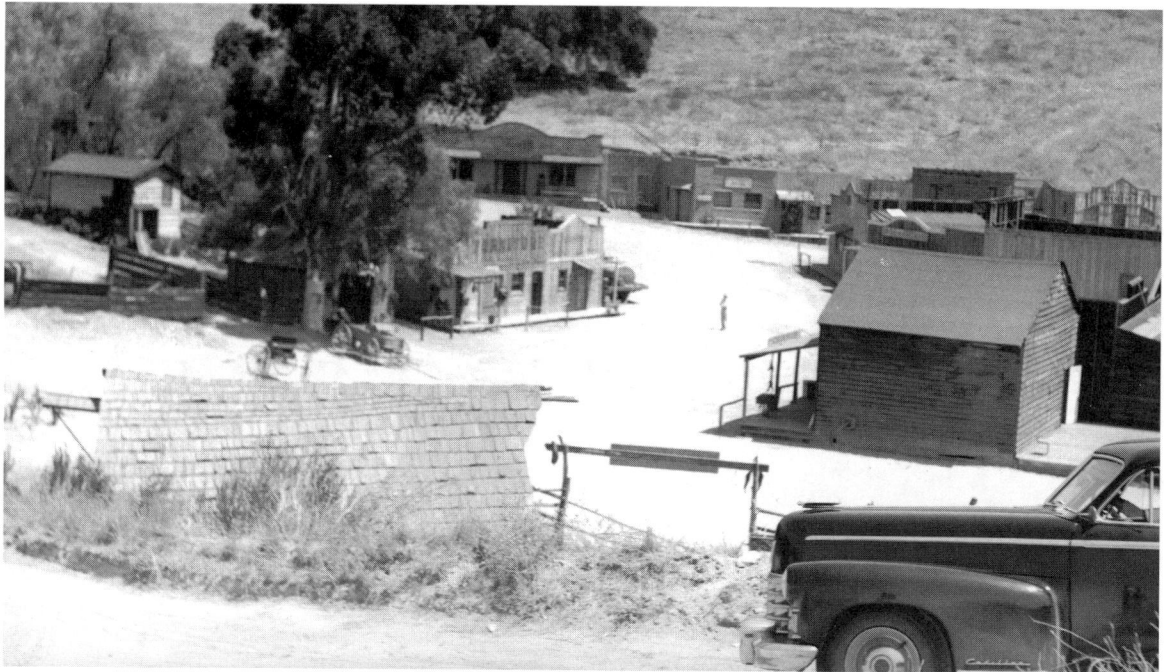

The Ingram Ranch in 1946, with the camera looking down on the street from the entrance road. Photo Bison Archives

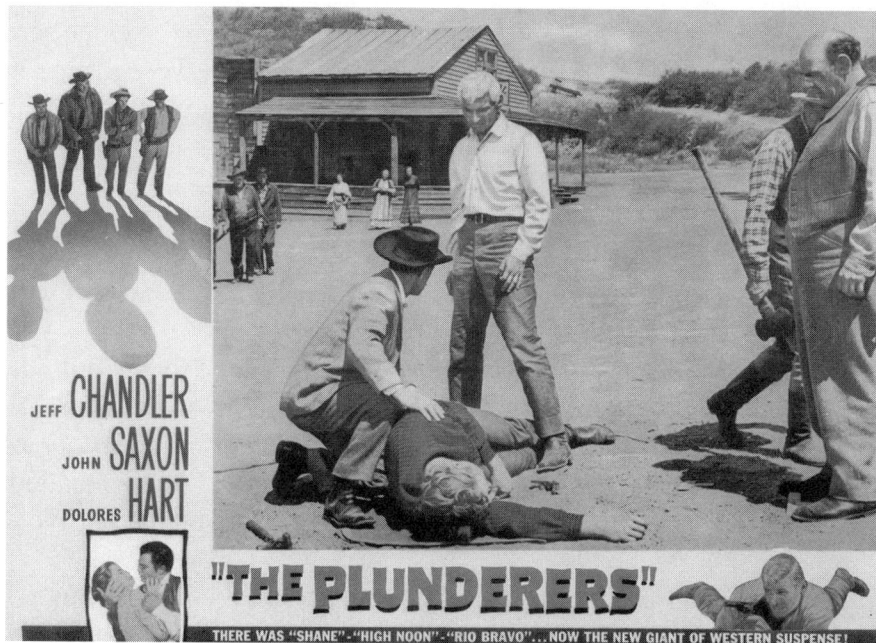

In this scene, the camera looks toward the entrance road. The large building with porch in the background was added after the initial construction of the town set.

Once part of the Charlie Chaplin estate, the property included a well-landscaped house that became Ingram's home and can even be seen in the background of a few scenes in Lash LaRue's *Mark of the Lash* (1948), with a white rail fence separating it from the ranch's western street. The Ingram Ranch served as the filming site not only for several of Lash's titles, but also for such Monogram/Allied Artists features as Bill Elliott's *Kansas Territory* (1952) and Wayne Morris' *The Desperado* (1954), as well as entries for several western TV series, including "The Cisco Kid," "The Lone Ranger" and "Roy Rogers." Ed Wood's TV pilot "Crossroad Avenger: The Adventures of the Tucson Kid" and a number of other lamentable Wood-produced films featuring

Jack Ingram's home can be seen in the background of this production shot (and the final film!) from the collection of beloved western heavy Pierce Lyden.

Tom Keene, Tom Tyler, Bud Osborne and other old-timers were also shot there, as was Johnny Carpenter's *Lawless Rider* (1954), which not even the directorial skills of stunt ace Yakima Canutt could save.

Ingram's ranch was situated in a valley off Topanga Canyon Road, west of Topanga and south of Ventura Blvd. His home faced west overlooking the street sets. The ranch included three street sets arranged roughly in a triangle. One street ran northwest down into the valley from Ingram's home. A second street began north of the house where the curving Topanga Canyon entrance road ran into the valley. That street ran south and slightly west by Ingram's house to connect with the first street at its southeast end. It had buildings on one side and a tree with a surrounding bench could often be seen in the middle of the street. A third street intersected with the first and second streets at their northwest and northeast ends, respectively, completing the triangle formed by the three streets.

A livery stable and corral were located camera left in the curve of the entrance road off Topanga Canyon Blvd. In later years, a saloon-general store and other buildings were situated camera right of the entrance road. That area sometimes served as yet another street set for the ranch, while a large building with a porch on at least two sides, located south of the stable, sometimes served as a stagecoach relay station or ranch. A number of shacks and a large horse stable with doors to each stall rounded out the sets, although the stable was only seen in the background of scenes. Titles shot at Ingram Ranch often used other locations as well, most frequently Corriganville or the Iverson Ranch.

In 1955, Ingram bought a yacht on which he lived until his death. Failing health obliged him to sell the ranch in 1956 to 4-Star Productions, which used the site a number of years in association with Paramount Ranch owner Bill Hertz for "Trackdown," "Zane Grey Theater" and other 4-Star TV series. The sets were eventually destroyed and the little valley is now covered with development. Several years ago, however, the Chaplin-Ingram house still stood on the property.

Directions: During the filming days, as noted, the ranch was reached from an entrance road off Topanga Canyon Blvd. In fact, it was often referred to as the Topanga Ranch. But the easiest way now to see the area that was once used for filming is to take Topanga Canyon south off the Ventura Freeway to Mullholland Drive (which did not extend to the area during the filming days) and Mullholland west about a half mile to the former ranch site on the right, just beyond the gated side driveway entrance to the Chaplin/Ingram house. Unfortunately, the entire ranch site has now been consumed by development.

The Agoura-Albertson Ranch

In Agoura, northwest of L.A. along the Ventura Freeway, could be seen for years the remains of another movie spread, the Agoura-Albertson Ranch. Once part of a 14,000 working ranch, a two-story ranch set on the Agoura served as Gene Autry's "Radio Ranch" in *The Phantom Empire* (1935), as well as the setting for several of the star's later features, including *Home in Wyomin'* (1942), *Sons of New Mexico* (1949) (as heavy Robert Armstrong's gambling den) and *Hills of Utah* (1951), as Denver Pyle's ranch.

Tim Holt saw duty there in several of his post-war entries, including *Target* (1952). It served as the Duchess' ranch in two of the Jim Bannon Red Ryder entries, as Kenneth McDonald's lair in *The Durango Kid* (1940), as Iris Meredith's ranch in the 1938 Charles Starrett starrer *West of Cheyenne* and as the ranch of "Wild Bill" Elliott's screen mother in *Bullets for Bandits* (1942). The ranch and/or surrounding countryside also hosted several Three Mesquiteers entries, such as *Heroes of the Saddle* (1940), some Johnny Mack Brown, Tex Ritter and Bob Baker Universals, several Don "Red" Barry Republics, as well as his Lippert modern western *Tough Assignment* (1949), and a few early Roy Rogers entries, among many other B-western titles. It even hosted some very cheap independent productions, including Lane Chandler's *Guns for Hire* (1932).

But fans of western and non-western A and B+ movies would also remember the Agoura. It was "burned," for example, in an early scene of Tyrone Power's *Brigham Young* (1940), a target of anti-Mormon wrath. It appeared, too, in Scott Brady's *The Law vs. Billy the Kid* (1954).

The Agoura featured a large, two-story main house framed by oak trees, a bunkhouse situated at an angle some distance camera right from the front of the main house, a huge barn located at a great distance camera right from the front of the main house and rolling hills with scattered trees and chase roads.

The main house was a movie set of unknown origin that changed appearance on several occasions over time. It was surrounded by a picket fence in Hoot Gibson's *Sunset Range* (1935) and had a slightly different facade when it played a prominent role in *The Durango Kid*. Later, it underwent a further, extensive facelift, probably initially seen in *The Red Pony* (1946) and *I Remember Mama* (1948), but put to best use in post-war Autry and Tim Holt titles.

Unlike the main house, the bunkhouse, large barn and other outbuildings were authentic, serving as the ranch's headquarters when the spread was not being utilized for filming. The Agoura family owned the ranch, part of a Spanish land grant, until the 1920s, when a land and cattle company controlled by William Randolph Hearst bought the Agoura and several other area spreads, including most of the Russell Ranch,

The Agoura-Albertson ranch set in The Phantom Empire (1935).

As usual, perennial western heavy Dick Curtis is up to no good on the Agoura porch.

In this scene from Bullets for Bandits (1942), *starring Tex Ritter and "Wild Bill" Elliott, the camera looks from the front of the ranch house set toward the large ranch barn. The bunkhouse was camera left between the house and barn.*

which was also used for filming.

In 1943, Fred Albertson, a prominent area rancher and automobile dealer, bought the 30,000-acre Hearst holdings, which extended from the eastern boundary of Thousand Oaks east to Woodland Hills, at the western end of the San Fernando Valley. Jim and Marion Jordan of "Fibber McGee and Molly" radio fame also owned a portion of the property at one time.

The Russell Ranch family leased portions of the spread during the Hearst years. Patricia Russell Miller, daughter of Russell Ranch

The bunkhouse in 2002.

patriarch Joe Russell, worked as an extra in some of the early films shot there, including a Slim Summerville feature and Richard Barthelmess' *The Lash* (1931), which also featured Fred Kohler. For the latter film, she recalls, she, her brother, a sister and her father's wranglers stampeded cattle through a western street set constructed on the Agoura as cameramen for *The Lash* (and other film companies as well) captured on film a scene that was used as stock footage in scores of later features. Sheep that Basque herders grazed in the area could also occasionally be seen in films shot on the ranch, including, I believe, Roy Rogers' *Twilight in the Sierras* (1950).

Finding the ranch's remains was an adventure in itself. *Phantom Empire* producer Nat Levine, interviewed shortly before his death, could not recall its location, nor could Gene Autry or his publicist Alex Gordon. But trade papers listed Agoura as site for a number of titles filmed there. Tim's sidekick Richard "Chito" Martin also recalled shooting at Agoura, as did Peggy Stewart, who co-starred in one of the Bannon Red Ryders filmed there. But she assumed that the property had succumbed to suburban development long ago.

Finally, Boyd Magers put me in touch with actor and location enthusiast Brent Davis, who introduced a group of us to Richard Angullo. Angullo, a Native American of the Agoura area with long connections to the movie/TV industry took us to the "mystery ranch" I had long sought.

Angullo took us to the Chesebro Road exit off the Ventura Freeway, about a half mile north on Chesebro to the Chesebro Park entrance and parking lot on the right. From there, we walked east up a hiking trail about half a mile to a locked, posted, but unmarked entrance gate on the right, then walked south down the entrance road, by then overgrown with weeds, about a half mile to the ranch house area. The main house and barn (except for its foundation) were long gone. But the remains of the bunkhouse (slightly altered in appearance from filming days) were still there. A house trailer then occupied the spot on which the main house set once stood. The large oaks were still there. Initially, I was confused by a large hill that could be seen in the distance from the front of the main house site—a hill not visible in film clips. Angullo explained, however, that the hill was manmade, gradually formed from garbage deposited at a dump site there. Ah, civilization! On subsequent visits, the bunkhouse appeared increasingly more dilapidated. By now, it too may be gone.

In the filming days, the main entrance road to the ranch was about a quarter mile up Chesebro Road from the Ventura Freeway, on the right. It is now closed to traffic. But Gene rode up that road to the main house from camera left in *Sons of New Mexico* and serenaded Fay McKenzie on the road at the end of *Home in Wyomin'*. At the end of the song (and film) Gene and Fay appeared to ride through the ranch entrance archway. But that may have been a prop placed there by the production crew. Real or fake, it was located at a considerable distance from the Chesebro Road cutoff to the ranch.

The Morrison Ranch

Adjacent to the Agoura-Albertson spread, and featuring the same rolling hills dotted with scattered oaks that were so common in the Conejo Valley, was another ranch that often appeared in filming. In 1898, cattle rancher Alonzo Morrison built the main house to his 4,000-acre ranch along what was then the Butterfield stagecoach route on Las Virgenes Canyon Road in Calabasas, east of the Agoura-Albertson spread. The large main house, which was still standing just north of the Las Virgenes exit off the Ventura Freeway several years ago, was rarely, if ever, used for filming. But the countryside was the frequent site for chase scenes and other houses and barns on the property (which over time had been subdivided into several smaller ranches) often appeared in western movies.

The most prominent set of structures on the spread was either a caretaker's house on the Morrison Ranch or the main house of one of the smaller ranches subdivided from the Morrison over the years. It was a relatively small house with a front entrance stoop and a chimney on the right side of the house. It also sported a picket fence, several barns and other outbuildings, and a corral. That collection of buildings served as Sam Flint's ranch in Roy Rogers' *Along the Navajo Trail* (1945) and the corral is featured at the beginning of Johnny Mack Brown's *Son of Roaring Dan* (1940). But the spread was put to best use as the home of MacDonald Carey and Patricia Medina in Bill Witney's favorite of

The Sons of the Pioneers at the Morrison Ranch for
Along the Navajo Trail (1946).

all the fine titles he directed, *Stranger at my Door* (1956). The house with the picket fence, as well as the largest barn on the spread, the corral and the surrounding countryside, received prominent display in that excellent film.

Nor was *Stranger at my Door* the only A or B+ film to visit the Morrison spread. Anthony Perkins' *The Tin Star* (1957) and Joel McCrea's *The Tall Stranger* (1957) also used the ranch. Earlier, *The Lusty Men* (1952), a modern-day rodeo yarn starring Robert Mitchum and Susan Hayward, was filmed on both the Morrison Ranch and at the Agoura-Albertson ranch set.

Other structures on the Morrison property also appeared in films. A small house with a picket fence had roles, for example, in "Wild Bill" Elliott's *Man from Tumbleweeds* (1940) and Don "Red" Barry's *Death Valley Outlaws* (1941), among other titles. That house may also have appeared, albeit in a dimly lit day-for-night scene, in *Belle Starr* (1941), starring Randolph Scott and Gene Tierney, in which a plantation set on the ranch was also burned as part of the storyline.

Unlike its neighbor, the Agoura-Albertson spread, the Morrison Ranch has not escaped suburban sprawl. In fact, the decision to name one of the housing developments there the Morrison Ranch Estates is about the only reminder left of that once beautiful location's ranching and film history. At one time, though, it hosted a multitude of western titles.

The Morrison Ranch barn in 1964. Photo Bison Archives

And as it appeared in Stranger at My Door (1955).

The French Ranch

Hidden Valley, northwest of L. A. near Thousand Oaks and Lake Sherwood., is home to several beautiful thoroughbred ranches and still plays host to movie and television production crews. During the golden age, however, the area's ranches were most frequently used for western and serial filming. Most recognizable of the Hidden Valley filming sites was the French Ranch with its distinctive white Spanish-style main house, surrounding waist–high adobe wall, huge windmill with large adobe base, and stable/bunkhouse area situated across an expansive meadow from the front of the main house. Whether pictured in color or glorious black and white, the French Ranch made a glorious backdrop for film makers. In fact, I can still remember marveling at its beauty–and wondering where it was located–when I first saw it in Columbia's *The Vigilante* chapter play as a Front Row kid in 1947.

Major Leigh French and a friend formed a partnership to develop ranches in Hidden Valley in the 1920s. Over the years, many Hollywood celebrities, including George O'Brien, Ronald Colman, and Robert Wagner, were to own ranches in the lush area. But the French Ranch, nestled in the hills at the south end of the valley, became the favorite of movie-makers. In the early years, Elinore Brown French, the major's wife and first lady of the area, often recruited locals to serve as extras for titles filmed there. Tom Mix's *Destry Rides Again* (1931) was one of the first westerns shot at the ranch, and it appeared in numerous other titles over the years. Another early title putting the spread to effective use was George O'Brien's *Smoke Lightning* (1933). It was the guest

Leigh and Elinore French and their ranch in the early days.

ranch in Tim Holt's pre-war *Dude Cowboy* (1941). In Smith Ballew's *Hawaiian Buckaroo* (1938), it served as a ranch in that future state. It even appeared in the Spade Cooley cheapie *Border Outlaws* (1950).

In later years, several Randolph Scott titles, including the location-rich *Man in the Saddle* (1951), utilized the spread. In the climax to *Conquest of Cochise* (1953), movie magic made it appear that Indians at the famous Vasquez Rocks, north of Newhall, were attacking the ranch–50 miles away. Columbia used

The French Ranch in the 1990s.

the ranch in several of its serials, not only as heavy Lyle Talbot's lair in *The Vigilante*, but also in *Black Arrow* (1944) and *Roar of the Iron Horse* (1951), although many of the latter's exteriors were shot outside Carson City, Nevada. Heavy Lyle Bettger also made the ranch his lair in the 1956 Lone Ranger feature. A number of TV episodes made effective use of the spread as well–most notably the highly entertaining "Bonanza" entry ("Caution: Easter Bunny Crossing") in which Hoss Cartwright impersonated the world's largest Easter rabbit. The ranch was put to most impressive use, though, in Gene Autry's *Sons of New Mexico* (1949) and in Roy Rogers' *Lights of Old Santa Fe* (1944), *Song of Nevada* (1944) and especially *Under Nevada Skies* (1946).

Major French's widow died in 1992, and Hidden Valley is now dominated by mega-bucks horse ranches with surveillance cameras. For several years after Patricia Russell Miller, a descendant of the Russell Ranch family, first directed me to the ranch, my friends and I went out regularly, ignoring the No Trespassing sign and climbing the fence for another visit to this glorious filming location. Then one day, we found the gate open and a construction crew hard at work. The main house had already been razed; the stable and bunkhouse would soon follow. Yet another god-awful looking southern California "MacMansion" would now occupy the site on which one of the most impressive filming sites of the golden age had long stood.

Directions: Take the Ventura Freeway northwest to the Westlake Blvd. exit. Go left on Westlake Blvd. to Potrero Road, turn right onto Potrero and follow it past Lake Sherwood and through Hidden Valley to Hidden Valley Road (at the end of the valley). Turn left onto Hidden Valley Road and follow it to its end. Then, follow the service road of another ranch up to where the French Ranch entrance gate once stood.

The Russell Ranch

Republic studio files listed a "Russell Ranch" in L.A. and Ventura counties as a location for a Roy Rogers title. That bit of information led me to *Tales of Triunfo* (1985), an interesting history of the Russell Ranch that included a 1920s photo of the nearby French Ranch, the beautiful Hidden Valley spread at which the Rogers film was actually shot. The book's gracious author, Patricia Russell Miller, daughter of one of the Russell Ranch's former owners, then directed me to the French Ranch and, through her book and several conversations, also introduced me to the Russell Ranch's significant role as a movie location site.

Originally, the Russell Ranch was part of the huge El Rancho Conejo, in what is now the Agoura/Westlake Village/Thousand Oaks area northwest of L.A. In 1881, Mrs. Miller's grandfather Andrew

Patricia Russell Miller and her brother at the Russell Ranch fort set.

and his brother bought nearly 7,000 acres in the area. A ranch headquarters was established at what is now Westlake lake along Westlake Blvd., and by 1911, Mrs. Miller's father Joseph and his three brothers were running the ranch. About 1925, the brothers sold all but 165 acres of the ranch to William Randolph Hearst, who was then buying up much of the property in the area. Hearst apparently visited the ranch only once, when his companion Marion Davies was filming at Lake Sherwood, and since the publishing tycoon leased the property to the Russell family, the area continued to be known as the Russell Ranch.

The ranch, the nearby Lake Sherwood and Lake Malibu areas, and the adjoining 14,000 acre Agoura Ranch, which the Russells also leased for a time from Hearst, were ideal for filming. They featured rolling hills and plains with scattered oaks, lush woodlands, creeks and lakes, resembling not only the moviegoer's image of the American west, but England, France and other foreign countries as well.

Not surprisingly, they became favorite location sites for major companies and poverty row outfits alike.

Movie sets soon dotted the countryside. Portions of John Wayne's *Flying Tigers* (1942) were shot there. A barn and outbuildings were constructed at the ranch headquarters for the original movie production of *State Fair* (1933) and a fort set south and east of what is now the Ventura Freeway and Westlake Blvd. was left standing for films, including Mascot's *Last of the Mohicans* (1932) serial.

Mrs. Miller, her sister and brother worked as extras in films made on the ranch and her brother often served as a night watchman at the movie sets, becoming a skilled poker player to boot. An elaborate adobe walled ranch constructed on the ranch for the early sound western *The Lash* (1931) was also often used in later films.

Mrs. Miller left the ranch early in the sound era and has few memories of western filming in the area. She did recall, though, that Leo Mahoney, star of one of the first sound westerns, visited the ranch one day while shooting a western along the Triunfo Creek. It was the first time, she later said, that she and her sister had ever seen an intoxicated person.

Lake Sherwood

A great scene in *The Adventures of Captain Marvel*, Republic's superb 1941 chapter play, features a chase through a lush forest area, rescue of the heroine atop a high, curving dam, and Captain Marvel's tossing heavies off the dam and an adjacent steep cliff. Ace director Bill Witney was uncertain, but thought he had shot that scene at Lake Sherwood, near what is now Westlake Village, a 30-minute drive northwest of L.A. on the Ventura Freeway.

Lake Sherwood. Its curving dam can be seen to the left; its cliff is in the lower center of the photograph.

As usual, the action master was right. First formed with the completion of the dam in 1904-05 and originally called Matthiessen Lake (and later Las Turas Lake), Lake Sherwood and the surrounding countryside have been the site for many B-westerns and serials, as well as numerous A titles and TVers. The lake got its current name when the Douglas Fairbanks Sr. silent version of the Robin Hood epic utilized the oak-studded woods at the base of the dam–the same forest through which heroine Louise Currie was pursued

in *Captain Marvel* years later, with the base of the dam clearly visible in the scene's background.

Originally constructed for a Mary Pickford silent, the partially fake cliff at one end of the dam quickly became a favorite filming site. On rare occasions the camera would be directed toward the dam for dives or falls from the cliff, with the tip of the dam visible above the lake waterline. See, for example, the climax to Chapter 1 of *Last of the Mochicans* (1932), one of the earliest sound films to utilize the Lake Sherwood area. But for most cliff shots, the camera was directed away from the dam with part of the cliff serving as a backdrop for the scene.

A rescue on the Lake Sherwood dam, in
The Adventures of Captain Marvel (1941).

Shot from that angle, stunt doubles for "Wild Bill" Elliott and "Gabby" Hayes in *Wagon Tracks West* (1943), Tom Neal and Frances Gifford in *Jungle Girl* (1941), Duncan Renaldo and Pauline Moore in *King of the Texas Rangers* (1941), Roy Rogers and a wagon in *Silver Spurs* (1943) (for a climactic chase scene begun in Kernville), passengers, horses and a wagon in Duke Wayne's *Dark Command* (1940) and a host of other stars hit the chilly waters at the base of Lake Sherwood's cliff.

A Lake Sherwood inlet and surrounding hills also appeared regularly in films. Opening scenes

A future Tarzan jumps from the Lake Sherwood cliff.

for Roy's *Romance on the Range* (1942) featured that area, for example. Woods at the opposite end of the lake from the dam were also stars, appearing in, among other titles, Errol Flynn's *Adventures of Robin Hood* (1938) and Linda Stirling's *The Tiger Woman* chapterplay (although motorboat chases for that fine serial were shot at Lake Elsinore southeast of L.A. rather than on Lake Sherwood). The lake itself appeared in the opening scene of Monte Hale's *Out California Way* (1946) and Republic serial queen Kay Aldridge's *Haunted Harbor*, among other titles.

Unfortunately, Lake Sherwood, like so much of southern California, has fallen victim to suburban sprawl in recent years. A mid-nineties Perry Mason TV movie was shot in part at the then-new Lake Sherwood golf and country club. But that beautiful area's filming days are largely over.

Directions: Take the Westlake Blvd. exit off the Ventura Freeway, go left on Westlake Blvd. to Potrero Road, turn right on Potrero. The lake begins on the left about a mile up Potrero.

Kentucky Park Farm
(Ventura Farms)

Roy Rogers and Dale Evans at Kentucky Park Farm for My Pal Trigger (1946).

A Hidden Valley thoroughbred ranch still used for filming, like other ranches in the Lake Sherwood area, traces its origins back to the 1920s but is still a favorite filming site for TV and commercial producers. In 1923, F.W. Matthiessen, one of the pioneers of the Lake Sherwood area, completed plans for Kentucky

The Kentucky Park Farm stable.

The stable interior, setting for My Pal Trigger'*s happy ending.*

Park Farm, so named because its long rows of white fencing, stable design and rolling hills with scattered trees so resembled the stud farms of the Bluegrass state.

Kentucky Park was put to most prominent use in Roy Rogers' *My Pal Trigger* (1946). Remember the paddock where Dale put Golden Sovereign through his paces, the large brick stable where Trigger's colts were foaled and the track where Roy trained Trigger for the film's racetrack finale? The track has been torn down but the stable and paddock are still there.

Other structures on the ranch appeared in Roy's films as well. The main house and its swimming pool

Kentucky Park's main house and pool.

were featured in *San Fernando Valley* (1944), as were the track and rolling hills. A stable scene for his *Rainbow Over Texas* (1946) was also shot there. But the ranch was not limited in film use to westerns. It also appeared in non-western titles, including Ronald Reagan's *Stallion Road* (1947).

Now called Ventura farms, the ranch's owner at this writing was David H. Murdock, colorful CEO of Dole Food Co., and founder and president of the Sherwood Country Club. The ranch is still devoted to raising thoroughbreds; one had just sold for a million dollars when we were there in the mid-1990s. But the spread–within the 30-mile zone from L.A. and thus excellent for one-day filming trips–has remained a frequent setting for current theatrical releases, commercials and TV series. Sean Connery's *Robin and*

Jean Porter and a would-be beau at the Kentucky Park pool in San Fernando Valley *(1944).*

Marian (1976) was filmed in the woods there and at the time of my visit a mansion set was under construction for a Rodney Dangerfield title. Ventura Farms offers its facilities to production companies and its website features various filming sites on the ranch that are easily recognizable as the locales for a variety of features and TV shows.

Directions: Ventura Farms is not open to the public. But to reach its main gate and gate phone, take the Ventura Freeway northwest from L.A. to the Westlake Blvd. exit, Westlake Blvd. south to Potrero Road, right on Potrero past Lake Sherwood and into Hidden Valley. It is the first ranch on the right upon entering the valley.

TV Ranches

Many of the locales used for filming western features were also regularly seen, of course, in television series, especially such location mainstays as the Iverson Ranch, Corriganville, Jack Ingram's ranch, Gene Autry's Melody Ranch, Walker Ranch and Pioneertown, all examined elsewhere in this volume. More distant locations, including Lone Pine and even Tuolumne County, Kanab, Apacheland and Old Tucson, Arizona, also became video as well as theater stars. And Russell Hayden's low-budget but enjoyable "26 Men" series, chronicling the exploits of the Arizona Rangers, was shot at Phoenix's tiny Cudia City studio and Apache Junction, outside Phoenix.

Janss Conejo Ranch

But several L.A. area ranches were devoted almost exclusively to television productions. The Conejo Valley northwest of L.A. was perhaps the most frequent host of western TV crews during the heyday of "Gunsmoke," "Wagon Train," "The Rifleman" and other adult western series, with the Janss, or Conejo, Ranch the center of much filming. Around 1910, Edwin and Harold Janss, sons of a Dutch immigrant, bought nearly 10,000 acres of what would one day become Thousand Oaks, devoting their holdings to farming and raising thoroughbred horses. From the earliest days, however, the Janss Ranch also hosted moviemakers. A ranch landing strip with hanger, located across the Ventura highway from the ranch headquarters on property now occupied by a golf course, was also often seen in films and displayed most prominently,

The Janss Ranch landing strip appeared in several films.

perhaps, in Roy Rogers' *The Gay Ranchero* (1948), Gene Autry's *Riders of the Whistling Pines* (1949) and the Universal chapterplay *Ace Drummond* (1936).

It was in the 1950's, though, that the Janss Ranch landscape really became familiar to western fans. The spread's stark terrain, dominated by bare rolling hills and distant cliffs, seemed a perfect fit for the often grim themes of the nighttime video fare that reigned supreme on network television in those days. Far too many of those series' episodes relied heavily on studio interiors and sound stage "exteriors." But when production crews ventured out into the countryside, their usual destination was a portion of the Janss Conejo Ranch that now comprises state-owned Wildwood Park outside Thousand Oaks. That section of the ranch consisted of rolling hills and flats set against a distant backdrop of cliffs, called the Stagecoach Bluffs for unknown reasons, but perhaps because they were the frequent site of coach crashes in filmdom's earliest days.

Stagecoach Bluffs.

A small ranch/town set in that area can be seen in Conejo rancher and western star Joel McCrea's *Gunsight Ridge* (1957), Jock Mahoney's *Joe Dakota* (1957) and Elvis Presley's *Flaming Star* (1960). Although much of *Cheyenne Autumn* (1964) utilized spectacular Utah and Colorado sites, John Ford also shot a comic chase scene with Jimmy Stewart for that epic against the backdrop of the Stagecoach Bluffs.

The ranch/town set in Gunsight Ridge *(1957).*

North Ranch

Another Conejo Valley ranch used primarily for video productions was situated closer to L.A., near the northern end of what is now Westlake Blvd. Known as the North Ranch because of its location on the northern boundary of the vast Agoura-Albertson holdings examined earlier in the chapter, this site featured a small western street first constructed for Dean Martin's *Texas Across the River* (1966) and put to excellent use in *Welcome to Hard Times* (1967) and the equally grim *Firecreek* (1968). (Interestingly, the superb character actor Morgan Woodward remembered rather extensive shooting for *Firecreek* in Sedona, Arizona. But in the final

Firecreek (1968).

cut, the Arizona scenes appear only behind the credits; remaining exteriors appearing in the final film were shot entirely at North Ranch.)

Like the Janss spread, North Ranch also regularly hosted TV series. "Vengeance," a two-part color "Gunsmoke" episode, featured, for example, the North Ranch town set, which also had a backdrop of distant cliffs, posing as the town of cattle baron John Ireland. Other color "Gunsmoke" entries, including "Judas Gun" and "Reprisal," also utilized North Ranch, as did many of that fine series' black and white episodes, which often gave prominent play to the spread's humble ranch/farm set.

Big Sky Ranch

Suburban sprawl has largely consumed North Ranch, much of the old Janss Ranch and most other Conejo Valley filming sites. But a spread in the hills northwest of Corriganville and the Simi Valley to date has substantially escaped development and remains relatively active as a location devoted primarily to television and commercial shoots. The 7-8,000-acre Big Sky Ranch, situated at 4927 Bennett Road in Tapo Canyon, was long known as the Patterson Ranch. Leased in the 1880s by a New Mexico company, it was devoted for years to raising cattle and farming. But filming reportedly began on the ranch in the 1930s, when oil tycoon J. Paul Getty bought the property, renaming it the Tapo Ranch. In 1981, Watt Industries of Santa Monica bought the spread from the Getty estate and again renamed it, this time dubbing the property the Big

Sky Ranch.

Filming on the ranch (which would be confined to only about 500 acres on the eastern portion of the property) reportedly began in the 1930s, although I have been unable to locate any feature from that period shot there. Big Sky first began appearing in late-fifties "Gunsmoke" entries, which featured a small ranch

The Big Sky ranch set with multiple fronts in the 1990s.

set with a front porch, a barn camera right from, and perpendicular to, the porch, and two additional "fronts" to the main house to maximize filming angles. Big Sky really came into its own, however, as the principal location for "The Little House on the Prairie" series. In fact, its rolling, tree-dotted hills, as well as the Ingalls family homestead, Walnut Grove town set, school house and other sets became almost as familiar to fans as the "Little House" stars. During its relatively brief run, the "Father Murphy" series, another Michael Landon

The Big Sky barn set was camera right from and perpendicular to the front of the house set.

production, also made extensive use of the ranch. Nor were they the only series utilizing Big Sky. An episode of the nighttime soap opera "Dallas," for example, used the "Gunsmoke" ranch set.

Big Sky also hosted occasional features. *The Trackers* (1971), starring Ernest Borgnine and Sammy

The Big Sky school set, familiar to all fans of "Little House on the Prairie."

Davis, Jr., used the "Gunsmoke" ranch. So too, years later, did Kurt Russell's *Breakdown* (1997). That terrific non-western thriller about a young couple's encounter with a vicious gang of carjacker/kidnappers, offered location fans a veritable feast of exotic Utah, Nevada and California locales. But I was certain that the shots of chief heavy J.T. Walsh's farm had utilized Big Sky's "Gunsmoke" ranch and the surrounding area.

In a 2006 telephone conversation, Heather Hasse, who had recently become ranch manager, confirmed my suspicion, recalling that a crew member on a recent shoot there had mentioned that he also worked on *Breakdown* at Big Sky. When John Leonard and I toured the ranch in the early 1990's, we entered the property with a crew member for a Civil War zombie (!) feature (working title *Gray Knights*) starring Corbin Bernsen of "L.A. Law" fame. Not surprisingly, that title was ultimately released only on video, as *Ghost Brigade*, a.k.a. *The Killing Box* (1993), in which Billy Bob Thornton also appeared.

At the time of my visit, the "Gunsmoke" ranch and a number of other sets were still standing. In the plot for "Little House: The Last

The "Father Murphy" saloon set in the 1990s.

Farewell" (1984), that series' final episode, the townspeople had elected to blow Walnut Grove to bits rather than turn their beloved community over to the robber baron who had recently purchased the property on which the town stood. But a portion of the "Father Murphy" town set was still standing, as were the school house and several other sets.

On two occasions since that time, though, Big Sky has fallen victim to disaster. The January 17, 1994, Northridge earthquake required the dismantling of about half the twenty buildings on the spread and refurbishing of the rest. By that point, the ranch was used primarily for commercial shoots and one of the structures slated for dismantling was a stagecoach depot that had appeared in Wells Fargo commercials. The damage also brought a temporary halt to an annual YMCA fund-raiser and open house at the ranch, the only time each year when Big Sky was open to the general public.

Then, in October 2003, Big Sky was one of several Ventura County film landmarks in the path of a huge wildfire that swept through the area. A news photograph of the scene pictured the charred chandelier of the "Father Murphy" saloon set lying on a bed of ashes. A number of other sets were also destroyed, as well as fences, barns and as many as forty cattle on the working portion of the ranch. Close on the heels of the fire were looters seeking props, period riding tack and other valuable memorabilia. Long-time ranch managers Don and Debra Early estimated the damage at more than $1 million and predicted that the ranch would be out of business for at least a year. *The Aviator* (2004), the Howard Hughes bio-pic, was scheduled to begin production at the ranch but had to move elsewhere. Someone had once termed the Earlys "guardians of a thousand dreams." "I guess now we are the keepers of a thousand memories," Debra Early said.

Far fewer sets now dot the Big Sky landscape. The "Gunsmoke" ranch set is gone, for example. But several landmarks, or at least their replicas, are still in place and the ranch continues to attract film crews, albeit mainly for commercial shoots. It is only a matter of time, though, that this site—one of the most active TV ranches of them all—will also be covered with residential and commercial development.

The Disney Ranch

One TV ranch that continued to remain active in both television and feature productions long after other sites had been subdivided was, of course, the Disney company's Golden Oak Ranch near Newhall. Situated along the left side of the Placerita Canyon Road a couple of miles east of Highway 14 and the old Jauregui Ranch, the Disney property was earlier owned by Lloyd Earl and another thoroughbred rancher. With its mottled bark sycamore trees, live oaks, pasture land and backdrop of green mountains, the area closely resembles in appearance the nearby Walker Ranch, examined in another chapter, and was occasionally used for chase scenes in the B-western and early TV era. Horse ranch scenes for the 1953 "Phantom Rustlers" episode of the Roy Rogers Show appear clearly to have been shot, for example, on the Earl ranch or its neighboring spread.

The Disney company first leased the property in 1955 as the site for Triple R Ranch scenes in the Mickey Mouse Club's "Spin and Marty" series. The Earl ranch stable and caretaker's house, which were still there when this book was being written, appeared regularly in the series. Concerned that residential and commercial development might soon gobble up

The Disney Golden Oak stable.

all the filming ranches, Disney ultimately decided to buy the spread outright, paying a reported $300,000 for the Golden Oak Ranch, which was named for an ancient live oak tree on the property, at the base of which early rancher Francisco Lopez supposedly had discovered gold in 1842, seven years before the Sutter strike outside Sacramento. At the time of the purchase in 1959, the ranch comprised 315 acres but later acquisitions had enlarged the holdings to 691 acres by 2000.

Naturally, Disney continued to use existing ranch structures in its productions and for other purposes. The Lloyd Earl caretaker's house became the residence of the Golden Oak's ranch foreman, another structure the foreman's office. For the "Spin and Marty" series, the latter structure also played the office of the Triple R's manager–perennial B-western heavy Roy Barcroft essaying a rare "good guy" role. The main house on the Earl ranch became a guest house, complete with a terrace and barbeque. Julie Andrews reportedly lived there during filming of *Mary Poppins* (1964), as did Fred MacMurray during the *Follow Me, Boys* (1966) shoot. A swimming pool on a hill above the guest house was another Lloyd Earl carryover. Walt Disney stabled his horses at the ranch as well.

The town set in the 1990s.

New sets were also constructed. A large town set built for "Roots II" (1988) later appeared in Lee Horsley's "Paradise" series, among other titles. A barn and house erected for *Pee Wee's Big Adventure* (1985) became a permanent fixture but a church used in the "North and South" (1985) mini-series was later dismantled, as was a rural church constructed for John Travolta's *Primary Colors* (1998). Yet another house and several mine entrances were built for the Don Knotts-Tim Conway comedy *The Apple Dumpling Gang* (1975). A guard tower, baseball field and other sets were used in Eddie Murphy's *Life* (1999).

The Golden Oak also featured a manmade pond, regularly spread with algaecide to keep it cinematically inviting. Perhaps the most visually memorable set on the ranch, a covered bridge originally constructed for a "Bonanza" episode, later appeared in "Little House on the Prairie" and other titles. When we toured the ranch in 1998 with ranch manager Steve Sligh, who had recently followed longtime manager Pat Patterson into that position, a mansion set was under construction for the 1999 Will Smith movie version of the "Wild, Wild West" series and a scene involving 300-400 extras. A working model for a possible Disney World ride was also being tested on the ranch.

The Golden Oak was used, of course, not only by Disney, but by other companies as well. Crews,

The Golden Oak's covered bridge, most recognizable set on the ranch.

A ranch chase road.

moreover, came not only from the United States, but also from Japan, Italy and other nations. The daily fee in the late nineties was $1,500 on days when a scene was being prepped and $3,000 for each shooting day.

To assure filming sites free of encroaching "civilization," Disney has always been very protective of its Golden Oak property. When nearby Highway 14, the Antelope Valley Freeway, was in the planning stages in the 1960s, studio officials worked closely with the state to assure that the ranch would not be visible from the new road. Years later, when Chevron, owner of the property on which the neighboring Jauregui Ranch had long stood, sold it to a buyer with development plans, the studio quickly intervened, buying that old movie and working spread to protect the Golden Oak's western boundary from developers. Eventually, however, the financial inducement for Disney to sell the ranch or develop the property itself will probably override any incentive to preserve one of the most scenic filming sites of all and the Golden Oak will also succumb to suburban sprawl.

Chapter 4

The Santa Clarita Valley

The Newhall/Saugus area in the Santa Clarita Valley, forty minutes north of L.A., was a favorite filming site from the earliest days of motion pictures. William S. Hart began using Newhall streets and Placerita Canyon locations for filming as early as 1914. John Ford featured Beale's Cut south of Newhall, along what is now the Sierra Highway, in his *Straight Shooting* (1917) long before returning to that location for the beginning (at the area's Beale's Cut) of the famous Indian chase in *Stagecoach* (1939). Tom Mix often filmed in the area, as did Harry Carey, Sr., and Hoot Gibson, who, like Hart, were local ranchers as well.

Newhall's picturesque Presbyterian church and other landmarks regularly appeared in silent films. A stretch of railroad northeast of Saugus in Soledad Canyon was a frequent site for filming (Roy Rogers' *Nevada City*, 1941), as was the Saugus train depot, put on display years later at the William S. Hart ranch/park and seen in the modern thriller *Suddenly* (1954), among other modern titles. Area working ranches, including the Jauregui Ranch, Sable Ranch, Rancho Maria and Walker Ranch, were also mainstays of western films, as were the distinctive Vasquez Rocks a few miles north of Newhall.

Monogram-Melody Ranch

The most famous Newhall/Saugus location of them all was the Monogram/Melody Ranch, located today at 24715 Oak Creek Avenue, near the intersection of Oak Creek and Placerita Canyon Road. Accounts of the Monogram Ranch's origins and early history vary greatly in detail and chronology. Ernest (Ernie) Hickson, often listed as technical or art director in the credits for Monogram titles shot at the ranch, may have owned the property from 1910 until his death in 1952, although some local histories date his connection with the ranch only from around 1922. By some accounts, Hickson built all the original sets on the property and William S. Hart's *The Disciple* (1915) was the first title lensed there. Others have written that Hickson, an inveterate collector of western Americana, imported some of the sets from Nevada and built others, placing them originally on the Rancho Placeritas, owned by producer Trem Carr, with whom Hickson was associated as a technical director, and situated on the current site of the Disney Studio's Golden Oak Ranch, about a mile east of Highway 14 on the Placerita Canyon Road–or, according to yet another account, near or on the Jauregui Ranch, which adjoined the ranches that would one day become the Disney Ranch. According to those versions of Monogram history, when Carr later sold his ranch, Hickson moved the sets to the current ranch site, along with other sets originally built on the eastern portion of the Walker Ranch

The early street.

east of Rancho Placeritas and used in silent films.

Several early Newhall/Saugus newspaper articles appear to support this latter version of the history of the Monogram and Trem Carr spreads and it may well be correct. There are difficulties with this account, however. The original structure on the Monogram Ranch property–a walled, adobe house constructed in the earlier 1920s–appears in several of John

The walled adobe, oldest structure on the Monogram Ranch.

Wayne's Lone Star Monogram titles, which were said to have been shot at the Trem Carr Ranch. But that adobe house, which is still on the property, is hardly a set that could easily have been moved from the Disney Ranch area to its current site. It also appears to be in the same location in the early films as later. Yet it can be seen in shots clearly connected with the western street said to have been on the Trem Carr ranch.

Note also an early scene in Gene Autry's *Red River Valley* (1936), a film that not only used the early western street but also the beginnings of the "new" Monogram street with hotel backdrop at one end. In a cattle herd scene, the wall of the adobe house can be seen, as well as a hill close to the house–the hill on the northern boundary of the Monogram Ranch.

The original street was differently configured and closer to the adobe house than the later Monogram street. But it may well have been on the same property as the Monogram-Melody Ranch rather than on the Trem Carr spread.

Sound westerns shot on the original western street included not only the Wayne Lone Star Monogram titles, but also early Republics (including Gene Autry's *Tumbling Tumbleweeds*, 1935) lensed during the brief period (1935-37) that Carr's Monogram studio and others were combined under Herbert J. Yates' new

Gene Autry at the adobe wall in Red River Valley (1936).

Republic banner. Interestingly, *Way Out West* (1937), the last film to use the original street set, featured not one of our Saturday matinee stalwarts, but Laurel and Hardy!

Whatever the spread's history, the pace of ranch operations really began to accelerate when Monogram separated from Republic in 1937 and signed a long-term lease with Hickson, including a stipulation the ranch would bear the studio's name. Sporting the enlarged and rearranged western street set first seen in, among other titles, Tom Keene's *Where Trails Divide* (1937), Jack Randall's *Danger Valley* (1937) and Tex Ritter's *Starlight Over Texas* (1938), which not only included the enlarged street set but a hacienda set and adobe village as well, the "new" Monogram Ranch quickly became a familiar setting not only for Ritter, Randall and Keene but for such later studio oater stars as the Rough Riders (after their first couple of titles, shot in Prescott, Arizona), the Trail Blazers, Johnny Mack Brown, Jimmy Wakely, the Cisco Kid and Whip Wilson. The first Bill Elliott series (*In Early Arizona*, 1938), independently produced but released by Columbia, several of that studio's western serials (*Deadwood Dick*, 1940, *Valley of Vanishing Men*, 1942), a large number of early PRC features, including *Song of Old Wyoming* (1945) and other Eddie Dean color titles and numerous Hoppy entries (e.g., *Santa Fe Marshal*, 1940) were also shot there. While enlarging its own backlot western street, Republic used the ranch for a number of titles (*Gangs of Sonora*, 1941).

Monogram sets became almost as familiar as the stars shooting there. The walled adobe house, still standing on the northeast corner of the ranch, was seen in Wayne's *Blue Steel* (1934) and *Desert Trail* (1935), among many other titles. The main street at Monogram City, as it became known, ran east-west. Near its west end, it intersected with a smaller side street running north-south. That side street hosted one of the western street set's most familiar buildings–a two-story adobe with a second-floor porch, which often served as a sheriff's or marshal's office.

An early view of the developing "new" street, in Law Comes to Texas (1939).

Originally, a residence with a single gable and picket fence was situated on the east corner of the main and side streets. The Range Busters' *Black Market Rustlers* (1943) has an unusual scene with the camera looking out from the entrance of that house toward the main street. A blacksmith shop and livery stable were located on the opposite (west) corner of main street, where it intersected with the side street. In the late forties, however, the residence was replaced with a storefront and moved to a site farther east on the main street, while the blacksmith shop and livery stable were replaced with a hotel structure and porch.

Initially, a hotel backdrop was situated at the west end of main street on the enlarged western street set. But by the 1948-49 film season (Johnny Mack Brown's *Hidden Danger*, 1948, Jimmy Wakely's *Brand of Fear*, 1949), the hotel had been moved to the south side of the main street at a slight angle, creating an open west end for the main street. In the early days, a small second side street or alley running south off main street near its west end was also occasionally seen in westerns (Jack Randall's *Land of the Six Guns*, 1940).

This scene from Bob Steele's The Feud Maker (1938) *was filmed near the intersection of the new set's main (east-west) street with hotel backdrop (upper left) and the side (south-north) street. The picket fence to the house that originally stood on the corner of the two streets, and the blacksmith/livery stable on the opposite corner, are pictured, as well as part of the two-story building with balcony on the side street, which often served as a sheriff's or marshal's office.*

To the east on main street was another very familiar structure–a small, one-story, "shotgun" style frame building that often served as a newspaper office, but also occasionally as the town sheriff or marshal's office. Beyond the open-ended east end of the street was a walled adobe village and, not always out of camera view, the ranch office. The adobe village appeared in Eddie Dean's *Colorado Serenade* and the Trail Blazers' *Arizona Whirlwind* (1944), among other titles. During the TV filming days on the ranch, the east end of main street also featured a small church set visible in the opening credits gunfight scene of early "Gunsmoke" episodes–and probably put there to block from any view the adobe village, an incongruous set even for a TV version of Dodge City, Kansas.

The main side street also continued to appear in films. Riders headed north on that street out of town encountered another east-west street. A small Mexican set stood on the corner there and a few yards east on that street from the side street was the ranch's elaborate Mexican hacienda/mission set seen, for example, in the Gilbert Roland Cisco Kid entry *Beauty and the Bandit* (1946), but put to best use perhaps in Gene Autry's *The Big Sombrero* (1949) and the 1956 Lone Ranger feature.

Beyond the northern end of the main side street was Monogram's principal ranch set. It featured a small main house surrounded (usually) by a picket fence, a large adjacent barn (that still stands as one of the most

The open-ended west end of the main street in later years, with the house with picket fence and blacksmith/livery stable replaced by other buildings.

The hacienda set.

The main Monogram ranch house.

familiar ranch structures) and several small outbuildings that usually served as bunkhouses but occasionally as separate small ranches. Johnny Mack Brown's *Raiders of the South* (1947) provides a useful view of the main house in relation to the other outbuildings. The barn exterior and occasionally its interior (Eddie Dean's *Wild West*, 1946) as well as the bunkhouses were used in countless titles.

The Monogram barn.

140

The principal Monogram cabin/hideout shack was situated a few yards west of the barn.

The school/church set in its original location on the ranch's northern boundary, in the 1980s.

On a road bordering the ranch's northern boundary was a schoolhouse/church set. The ranch's current owners moved that set, which figured prominently in Jimmy Wakely's *Brand of Fear*, to the western street area. But it remained in the original location for years after its filming days. Occasionally, it could be seen in the distant background of scenes shot on the ranch/barn set. Beyond the west end of the main western street, there was also a train depot set, which dated only from the ranch's later years.

The property included other houses and cabins as well, including one said to have been used in the Mary Pickford silent *Rebecca of Sunnybrook Farm* (1917). The additional structures enabled the ranch to play a rustic community in non-western Monogram titles such as Boris Karloff's *The Ape* (1940).

Toward the end of the B-western era, another ranch set–this one quite elaborate–began to appear in westerns shot at the ranch, including Johnny Mack's *Sheriff of Medicine Bow* (1948). That set featured a large main house with porch, extensive rail fencing, a modern looking barn and other outbuildings. To date, I have been unable to determine the precise location of this ranch, or whether it was a set or permanent nearby spread. In a rare shot for Whip Wilson's *Haunted Trails* (1949), it can be seen situated along a road that could have been the Placerita Canyon Road. It is thus uncertain whether it was part of the Monogram ranch or a neighboring working spread. But it clearly appears to have been in the same general area of other structures on the ranch.

The "Mystery" Ranch.

"Mystery" Ranch Barn.

Most of the Monogram sets were full structures rather than facades, with one building on the western street serving as a dining room for film crews. Actors and crew members working on a film shoot lasting more than a day often slept in the sets; in fact, the late Pierce Lyden, a beloved B-western heavy, had fond memories of the relaxed, friendly atmosphere at the ranch–and perpetual poker games.

Even during its filming days, the Monogram Ranch was often the scene of local festivities. For several years, it hosted the annual roundup of the L.A. Westerners Corral and from 1949-51 played host to Newhall's Old West July 4th celebration, with Monogram renamed "Slippery Gulch" on those occasions and all sorts of entertainment, including a battery of "one-arm bandits," provided for the amusement of visitors.

Nor, of course, did the demise of the B-western feature end the ranch's days as a filming site. Shortly after Ernie Hickson's death on January 22, 1952, Gene Autry, who always said that he shot parts of his first starring feature there, bought the ranch, renamed it Melody Ranch and converted it into a thriving TV factory not only for such Autry Flying A productions as the "Annie Oakley" series, "Range Rider," "Adventures of Champion," "Buffalo Bill, Jr.," the Allan Lane "Red Ryder" pilot and the star's own series, but also for episodes of Hopalong Cassidy's video series, "Wild Bill Hickok," "Wyatt Earp," "Cisco Kid," "Sheriff of Cochise" and "Gunsmoke," among many other series. Somewhat ironically, in fact, the last Monogram/Allied Artists entries with Johnny Mack Brown, Whip Wilson, "Wild Bill" Elliott and Wayne Morris used the town sets at the Iverson Ranch, Corriganville and the Jack Ingram Ranch rather than the Monogram home spread.

Contrary to various published reports, no part of Gary Cooper's *High Noon* (1952) was filmed at

Melody Ranch. Instead, that great film lensed on the Columbia Ranch western street in Burbank and at sites in Tuolumne County, including the historic mining town of Columbia and a railroad stop at Warnerville in the same area.

But the ranch did host a number of B-plus and A-westerns, including Fred MacMurray's fine Allied Artists answer to *High Noon*, *At Gunpoint* (1955). In 1958, the NBC series "Wide, Wide World" hosted a 90-minute western special at the ranch, featuring not only Autry but John Wayne, Jim Arness and dozens of other cowboy players.

Then, tragedy struck. On August 28, 1962, a massive firestorm roared through the Santa Clarita Valley, destroying virtually all the structures on the property except the adobe house, the house reportedly used in the silent *Rebecca of Sunnybrook Farm*, a cabin, the barn , the adobe village, the schoolhouse and the spread's Melody Ranch entrance. Fifty-four structures were burned on the 110 -acre ranch, as well as Gene's extensive collection of western Americana and 17,000 recordings, with losses set at $1 million. "The fire left the terrain so convincingly battle-scarred," Autry later recalled, "that it was used two months later for an episode ['The Celebrity'] of the television war series 'Combat.'"

The inner wall of the adobe house, one of the few structures not destroyed by the 1962 fire.

Following the fire, Autry gave up plans to establish a western museum at the ranch and over the next three decades gradually sold all but twelve acres of the property to developers. Scenes for "Roots II," the TV mini-series, used the ranch's train and depot set, which once included four trains running over 1.8 miles of track. Otherwise, the ranch's filming days seemed clearly over.

But appearances can be deceiving. Not only did Gene Autry's dream of a western museum become a wonderful

The adobe village also survived the fire.

reality, albeit in L.A.'s Griffith Park rather than Newhall. But in 1990, he sold the spread, for a reported $975,000, to Renaud and Andre Veluzat, Santa Clarita Valley natives whose family had operated a film ranch in Saugus since the early 1950s and who hoped to restore the Melody Ranch to its former glory. After winning a battle with developers bent on converting the remaining property into yet another condo eyesore, the brothers painstakingly drew on photographs and videotapes in restoring the western street largely to its appearance during the early television era, with their only sacrifice of historical accuracy a slight elevation of buildings on the street set beyond their original height to eliminate from camera view the blight of condos perched on the hill north of the ranch. Later, other sets, including the magnificent hacienda set, were restored, with only minor alterations from their original locations on the property.

The ranch entrance still welcomes visitors also.

The ranch barn was still there, too, in 2007, but sadly neglected.

Although obliged to modify the sets temporarily for Jeff Bridges' *Wild Bill* (1995) and other features filmed there, as well as HBO's "Deadwood" series, the Veluzat brothers have faithfully maintained the permanent sets' Melody Ranch appearance, as was evident when episodes of the CBS series "The Magnificent Seven," the first TV series shot there under the new owners, began airing. All Front Row kids owe the Veluzat brothers a deep debt of gratitude for restoring this great movie ranch of the golden era.

Directions: To reach Melody Ranch, take Highway 170 north from L.A. to I-5, I-5 north to Highway 14, Highway 14 north to the Fernando Road exit, Fernando Road west into Newhall, past Lyons Avenue to a street on the right that becomes the Placerita Canyon Road and east on Placerita to the Melody Ranch entrance sign. (Previously, visitors could take the Placerita Canyon Road west off Highway 14 to the ranch entrance but that portion of the road is now partially closed to through traffic.) Walking tours are available at the ranch.

The Jauregui Ranch

My favorite Newhall area filming site was the Andy Jauregui Ranch, which first began hosting moviemakers in 1929 and was exactly what it appeared to be--a working ranch. Located off the Placerita Canyon Road a few hundred yards east, in later years, of Highway 14, the Jauregui's small main house and front porch, picket or rail fence (depending on the period and movie company wishes) and large oak tree in the front yard were a familiar setting for countless westerns and TV series as well as some serials, including Ralph Byrd's *The Vigilante* (1947). Perhaps even more recognizable was the spread's large barnyard, located down from the west side of the main house and bordered initially on one side, and later on both sides, by barns, a stable and corral, a blacksmith shop and other buildings. In very low-budget features, the Jauregui outbuildings even served as towns, with a "Sheriff's Office" sign put on one building, a "Bank" sign on another!

The Jauregui Ranch main house in the 1980s.

Ranch owner Andy Jauregui was born and reared in Ventura County's Santa Paula area. In 1928, he and his wife Camile, a native of northern Italy whose family moved to Ventura in 1910, leased the ranch from Standard Oil (now Chevron). According to one account, the oil giant had originally built what would be the Jauregui's main house in nearby Pico Canyon as a dormitory for men working in the Pico oil fields, then moved the house by mule to the ranch in 1925. At first, Clarence "Fat" Jones, who was to develop one of moviedom's major rental stables, worked the ranch with Jauregui, living with his own family in a bunkhouse behind the main house. In fact, for a time the Jauregui spread was apparently known as the Jones Ranch. But Jauregui soon bought Jones' interest in the ranch.

The Jauregui barnyard, with an on-ramp to Highway 14 in the background, where the ranch pasture once hosted cattle rustling and other action scenes.

Roy Rogers in the Jauregui barnyard for The Golden Stallion (1949).

The spread made its most impressive celluloid appearance in Gene's *The Strawberry Roan* (1947), Roy's *Southward Ho* (1939) and a number of Tim Holt features, especially *Arizona Ranger* (1948) and *Pistol Harvest* (1951). But filming began there in 1929, with the Bob Steele silent *Texas Cowboy* (1929) and Tom Tyler's *Call of the Desert* (1930) among the earliest titles shot on the ranch. (For other early views of

Tim Holt and his sidekicks investigate foul play on the Jauregui Ranch.

the ranch, see Tim McCoy's 1932 Columbia entries *Texas Cyclone* and *Two-Fisted Law*.)

Over the years, the Jaureguis and their daughters–Julain, Noureen, Joann and Andreena–hosted nearly every cowboy star in the industry, from Fred Scott to Ken Maynard and Bob Steele (individually, and as the Trail Blazers), to Eddie Dean and Lash LaRue (in their *Song of Wyoming*, 1945), to Buck Jones, Dick Foran, Johnny Mack Brown and Charles Starrett, to Joel McCrea, Randolph Scott and "Duke" Wayne.

Non-western A-features shot at the ranch included the Claudette Colbert-Fred MacMurray hit *The Egg and I* (1947), which launched the careers of "Ma and Pa Kettle." Among TV series shooting there were "Stoney Burke," "Scarecrow and Mrs. King," "The Fall Guy," Dennis Weaver's short-lived 1987-88 medical series "Buck James" and "Gunsmoke," plus some of the kiddie westerns of TV's early days. (Spotted dozing between takes on a "Gunsmoke" shoot, a groggy James Arness explained to Mrs. Jauregui that his wife had presented him with a baby the previous night!)

Film companies occasionally made changes to the ranch's appearance. The crew for Autry's *The Strawberry Roan* (the Ken Maynard version was also shot there) added, for example, a back porch to the main house. (For a pre-back porch view of the main house's rear, see Fred Scott's *In Old Montana*, 1939.)

Advancing civilization also brought change to the ranch. Originally, the Placerita Canyon Road had a dirt surface and actually ran by the ranch's barnyard and front of the main house, then east toward what was later to become Disney's Golden Oak Ranch, examined in the previous chapter. In one unusual scene for *Black Market Rustlers* (1943) in the Ranger Busters series, George Chesboro and another heavy in a roadster shoot from the road into the front of the Jauregui main house. Later, a two-lane, paved road was constructed that ran about 300 yards south of the ranch and a new entrance road was installed that ran from the new road to the rear of the Jauregui's main house and two bunkhouses, leading some fans to confuse the back porch to the main house with its front porch.

Like many other titles, *Black Market Rustlers* also made extensive use of the spread's beautiful meadow west of the barnyard for its story of World War II cattle rustling by truck. But construction of Highway 14 through much of that beautiful meadowland in the 1960s ended the filming days of that part of the ranch.

The Jauregui remained exactly what it was, though, a working ranch rather than a movie set. Even the rooster (a critic perhaps) crowing in the background of scenes there was authentic, not the product of studio special effects.

Films shot at the ranch thus had a realistic look about them, even if their plotlines were often pure fantasy. In fact, although Andy Jauregui, like his brother Edward, stunt-doubled for a number of stars, including Richard Dix and Tom Tyler, he left much of the day-to-day dealings with movie companies to ranch hands, devoting most of his attention over more than fifty years to his work as a rodeo performer and stock contractor, providing horses and cattle to rodeos. He also sold horses to members of the film community, including Will Rogers, Robert Taylor and Barbara Stanwyck, Glenn Ford and Harry Carey, Sr. and Jr., as well as rodeo star Casey Tibbs. On an early visit to the ranch, for example, we encountered both Carey, Jr. and Tibbs.

Eventually, though, "progress" took its toll. Although Andy Jauregui died in 1990, his dear widow continued to live at the ranch for a number of years. In 1996, Mrs. Jauregui died and wealthy invester Arnold Cattani purchased the property from Chevron, presumably for development purposes. Shortly thereafter, however, Disney bought the Jauregui from Cattani, seeking to protect its adjacent Golden Oak Ranch. But that move delayed cruel fate only briefly. Disney razed the outbuildings, although at this writing the main house still stood. Now, little remains of the Jauregui except, fortunately, its many cinema appearances.

Walker Ranch

One of the smallest yet most scenic and recognizable western film sites was the Walker Ranch, east of Newhall along the Placerita Canyon Road. Frank Evans Walker, owner of the ranch during its filming years, inherited the spread from his mother in the 1890s. Filming took place on both an upper and a lower portion of the ranch but the lower ranch is most familiar to filmgoers.

The lower spread featured mottled-bark sycamore trees and a creek running east-west across the property, sometimes filmed in the rainy season with a small stream running through its bed (Johnny Mack Brown's *Law Comes to Gunsight*, 1947, Roy Rogers' *Springtime in the Sierras*, 1947) but more often seen dry and dusty. The only structure on that portion of the Walker Ranch was a tiny cabin once occupied by the Walker family during the winter months and seen in countless movies.

The front of the cabin, which initially lacked a porch but later was supplied one by a production

The most familiar Walker Ranch cabin in the 1990s.

The Walker cabin was usually the setting for action but sometimes hosted romantic interludes. Here Eddie Dean serenades pretty Shirley Patterson.

company, was the portion most used in films. But the rear of the cabin also appeared in a few titles, sometimes as a separate ranch or hideout shack. Both entrances were seen in the Trail Blazers' *Blazing Guns* (1943), in which chubby Hoot Gibson appears to climb up the cabin's stone chimney Santa-style to elude the heavies.

At an angle behind the cabin, embedded in a hill, was a small mine entrance seen in Jimmy Wakely's *Across the Rio Grande* (1949) and a few other titles. An insert chase road perhaps 150 yards long ran east-west by the front of the cabin. The cabin could often be seen in the background of chase scenes shot on the road–frequently, in fact, several times in the same chase, much to the dismay of Front Row kids!

In the trees across the creek bed from the insert road and cabin was another east-west road sometimes used for filming. At a point near the east end of the chase area, that road curved north across the creek bed to connect with the insert road. A bridge across the creek bed could also sometimes be seen in the background of Walker Ranch scenes (*Under California Stars*, 1948). Wooded hills surrounded the filming area, although a partially treeless peak could sometimes be seen in the distance between two wooded hills at the east end of the filming area.

Andy ("Jingles") Devine in the Walker creek bed.

Although Walker Ranch appeared in many films, the spread was perhaps given most impressive display in several of Roy Rogers' post-war Trucolor films, including not only *Under California Stars* and *Springtime in the Sierras*, but also *On the Old Spanish Trail* (1947), *Eyes of Texas* (1948), *Down Dakota Way* (1949), *The Far Frontier* (1949) and *Sunset in the West* (1950). *Springtime in the Sierras*, one of my all-time favorites, made particularly effective use of the insert road and creek bed. The sense of speed and distance director Bill Witney and his cameraman created on the Walker Ranch's cramped quarters for the climactic chase in that little gem was truly amazing.

Other Republic stars, including Don Barry (*Desert Bandit*, 1941), the later Three Mesquiteers (*Outlaws of the Cherokee Trail*, 1941), Bill Elliott (*Bordertown Gunfighters*, 1943), Rex Allen (*Silver City Bonanza*, 1951) and Allan Lane as Red Ryder (*Oregon Trail Scouts*, 1947), also rode the Walker range. Columbia cowboys fought there (Charles Starrett in *Lawless Empire*, 1945, Gene Autry in *Saginaw Trail*, 1953) as did RKO stars (Tim Holt in *Pistol Harvest*, 1951), PRC's (Eddie Dean in *Colorado Serenade*, 1946) and virtually every other western feature and TV cowboy star.

But Walker was only a few miles up the Placerita Canyon Road from Newhall's Monogram/Melody Ranch and the spread was home mainly to such Monogram cowboy heroes as Jack Randall (*Wild Horse*

Roy Rogers and Republic heavy Roy Barcroft, in the exciting Walker Ranch climax
to Springtime in the Sierras *(1947).*

Range, 1940), Tom Keene (*Lone Star Lawmen*, 1941), the Rough Riders (*Forbidden Trails*, 1941), the Trail Blazers, Johnny Mack Brown (*Law of the Valley*, 1944), Jimmy Wakely (*Springtime in Texas*, 1945) and Whip Wilson (*Shadows of the West*, 1949). Johnny Mack's first Monogram series entry opened, in fact, with the star riding the Walker Range behind the credits to *Ghost Rider* (1943).

Not surprisingly, given its compact size, Walker Ranch also hosted its share of unscripted goofs. Watch the heavies chase Fred Scott past the Walker cabin during *In Old Montana* (1939), for example, and you will surely spot a modern auto house trailer parked behind the cabin. A Kit Carson TV episode included a Buick convertible in the background of one action scene ("Hi Yo, Roadmaster!").

Although the lower Walker spread, its cabin and trees were most familiar to Front Row kids, the upper portion of the ranch was also used for filming. Its main house stood on the edge of a grove of trees about a mile east of the lower ranch. The area also hosted an impressive natural bridge that created a doorway through an earthen embankment. That doorway often appeared in films, frequently serving as the entrance

The Upper Walker natural bridge.

Hopalong Cassidy at the natural bridge for Texas Trail *(1937).*

to the heavies' hideout. In the opening scene of Whip Wilson's *Gunslingers* (1950), payroll robbers Riley Hill and Carl Matthews race beneath the bridge in an effort to elude our hero. It also served briefly in Whip's *Range Land* (1949) and Jack Randall made regular use of the site, which served as the entrance to

Iron Eyes Cody's Indian encampment in Randall's *Overland Mail* (1939) and as a hideout for horse thieves in *Wild Horse Canyon* (1938) and *Wild Horse Range* (1940).

The top of the natural bridge, which also appeared in Bob Steele's *Wild Horse Valley* (1940) and had a cameo in Hopalong Cassidy's *Texas Trail* (1937), has collapsed over time. But its remains, now hidden by foliage, are situated next to the south side of the Placerita road about a mile east of the main filming area on the lower spread.

The upper ranch's cabin, which no longer stands, was accessible only in the summer during the early days. The Walker family called this structure the summer cabin and

Walker family members at the upper cabin.

used the cabin on the lower spread for lodging in the winter months until 1938, when the family began occupying the summer cabin year-round. The cabins on the lower and upper spreads were similar in appearance, often causing confusion for moviegoers interested in filming sites. But the summer cabin on the upper spread was wider and had a step leading up to the front porch, while the winter cabin's entrance was flush with the ground. Adjacent to the summer cabin were three small bunkhouses and a separate garage, which resembled a cabin and also made some film appearances.

I first began noticing the summer cabin in films while watching Whip Wilson's *Range Land* several years ago, initially mistaking it for the more familiar cabin on the lower spread, but then noticing a smaller cabin or bunkhouse in the background of the scene–a structure not visible in films featuring the lower ranch cabin. Ultimately, George Starbuck, a Walker family descendant, came to my assistance, providing me with photographs and information regarding the upper Walker spread.

Like certain other locations, including the nearby Jauregui Ranch, the upper Walker spread sometimes even posed as a "town." The main cabin and outbuildings played that role, for example, in Fred Scott's *Songs and Bullets* (1938). (Oh, the indignities of low-budget film-making!)

Directions to the lower Walker Ranch, which is now a state park: Take Freeway 170 from L.A. north to I-5, I-5 to Highway 14, Highway 14 north to the Placerita Canyon Road exit and the Placerita road several miles east to the park entrance on the right, not far beyond the Disney Golden Oak Ranch entrance on the left. The upper spread's structures and the top of the natural bridge disappeared long ago. They were located about a mile east of the lower spread on the right side of the Placerita Canyon Road.

Sable Ranch and Rancho Maria

Sable Ranch main house in the 1980s.

Along Sand Canyon Road near Newhall are two interesting filming sites still in use today. Area rancher Frank Sentous built the Sable Ranch around 1920. Purchased in 1940 by Ralph Wagner, and later owned by George White, among others, the spread received its current name when chickens advertised as "smooth as sable" were raised on the ranch. The Sable Ranch features a large stone main house with a high front

Sable Ranch stable.

porch and circular stone terrace situated camera right from the front porch. A stable with individual horse stalls is located camera left down from the front porch and the property also includes other outbuildings.

The ranch played a prominent role in *Ride 'Em Cowboy* (1940), with Johnny Mack Brown and Dick Foran playing straight-men to Abbott and Costello. It received its most impressive B-western display as Roy's ranch for a brief early scene (with character actors Ed Cobb and John Hamilton on the Sable's circular terrace) in *Bells of Coronado* (1950), for which most exteriors were shot at Littlerock Dam outside Palmdale and elsewhere in the Palmdale and Lake Los Angeles area. (Establishing shots for the Sable Ranch scene in *Bells of Coronado* including the entrance road, it should be noted, were filmed elsewhere.)

The Sable Ranch actually has been used more as a filming location in recent years than during the golden era. It was Jim Garner's ranch in "Bret Maverick," the 1981-82 television series based on the 1950s hit. A ranch set was constructed in the field between Sand Canyon Road and the main house for Beau Bridges' 1993 TVer "Harts of the West" and the main house was also used occasionally in that short-lived series. Mel Brooks also constructed a medieval castle/village in the field for his spoof *Robin Hood: Men in Tights* (1993). The main house was also featured in Bruce Boxleitner's *Diplomatic Immunity* (1991) and the Shelley Long-Lindsey Wagner TV movie *A Message from Holly* (1992). In more recent years, it appeared in episodes of "24," among other series and features.

Two hundred yards or so east of the Sable Ranch is Rancho Maria, originally known as the Riley Ranch and later as the Brooks Ranch, as well as by other names. Rancho Maria may also have been owned at one time by B-movie producer Philip N. Krasne and known as the Circle-K. At least, a 1938 trade item indicated that Krasne was then filming *Trigger Pals* (1939) on his Circle-K

Rancho Maria pool.

ranch and the barnyard and stables used in that Lee Powell Grand National title closely resembled those at Rancho Maria.

The most interesting feature of this little ranch was not its modest main house or outbuildings, but its patio swimming pool, an excellent site for dude ranch scenes. Rancho Maria and its pool played that part in Jimmy Wakely's first starrer, *Song of the Range* (1945), which Krasne also produced, and in Gene Autry's *Big Sombrero* (1948). Elena Verdugo's comic swimming pool scene with Autry was filmed at Rancho Maria, according to western film researcher Richard Smith, when inclement weather forced a cancellation

Rancho Maria stable.

of shooting plans at Tucson's Arizona Inn pool.

Rancho Maria also included a fence-lined entrance road, visible in *Song of the Range,* and several barns that can be seen very briefly in *Big Sombrero*. In later years, sets also included a small western street, first

The town set.

constructed, according to a caretaker, for the Kenny Rogers TV movie "Gambler III: The Legend Continues" (1987). (Rumors that the western street was formed from buildings brought over from the Bell Ranch, when it was dismantled in 1989, may be correct, but appear to conflict with published reports that the Bell buildings were donated to the Wilderness Institute.)

Modern productions, including "Harts of the West," have sometimes included scenes shot on both the Sable Ranch and Rancho Maria. This is not surprising since both ranches have been jointly owned, and accessed by the same entrance road, in recent decades.

Directions: To reach the Sable Ranch and Rancho Maria, take Freeway 170 and I-5 north from L.A. to Highway 14, Highway 14 north to the Placerita Canyon Road exit, right (or northeast) on Placerita to Sand Canyon Road, right on Sand Canyon about 100 yards to the ranches on the right. The entrance gate to the Sable Ranch, as noted above, serves both spreads.

Mentryville

A Newhall area community not only played a significant role in California's oil-drilling history, but also appeared in at least two western features. In 1876, transplanted Pennsylvania oil man Charles Alexander Mentry sank Pico No. 4 at the west end of Pico Canyon. The first commercially successful oil well in the western United States, the gusher attracted teams of oil workers and their families to the area, which was soon named Mentryville. In 1898, Mentry built a 13-room Victorian mansion there. He died in 1900 and

The Mentryville "Big House," without front porch, as it looked in the 1990s.
It has since been restored largely to its original appearance.

the community soon lost virtually all its population as the richest oil deposits were depleted. But Pico No.

4 was reportedly the world's longest running oil well when it ceased operations in 1990. Moreover, Mentry's "Big House," as it was called, played a major role in John Wayne's *The Lonely Trail* (1936). Later part of Warner Bros.' Newhall ranch property, the area also appeared in episodes of the "Dukes of Hazzard" TV series. Directions: To reach Mentryville, take I-5 to the Pico Canyon exit and go west on Pico Canyon Road.

Beale's Cut

The chase across the salt flats in John Ford's classic *Stagecoach* (1939) remains one of the most exciting scenes in western filmdom. Contrary to frequent reports, that riveting sequence was filmed on the Lucerne dry lake near Victorville, California, not in Monument Valley, on the Utah-Arizona border, site for other visually stunning shots in what is perhaps John Wayne's finest film. The establishing scene for the chase–a quick shot of the stagecoach rolling through a deep, narrow pass–was filmed even closer to Hollywood, at Beale's Cut a few miles north of L.A.

First chiseled through the Santa Susanna mountains by General Phineas Banning in 1854, the cut was initially only thirty feet deep. Used mainly for carrying supplies through the mountains from L.A. to Fort Tejon, northwest of what is now Newhall, the cut was first known as Fremont Pass and Newhall Pass. But in 1863-64, it began to acquire its current name when General Edward Fitzgerald Beale, a veteran of California's Mexican-American war and surveyor-general of California and Nevada, had a crew of workers

Beale's Cut.

from Fort Tejon enlarge the pass to a depth of ninety feet. Soon, Beale began charging fees for the cut's use–fifty cents for a horse and wagon, twenty-five cents for a horse and rider, etc. In 1910, L.A. County bore a narrow tunnel through the mountains, eliminating the need for the cut as a passage to the San Fernando Valley, and in 1938-39, the Sierra Highway, connecting Los Angeles and the Newhall area north, was completed.

By that point, however, Beale's Cut had also long been a filming site. More than two decades before *Stagecoach*, John Ford became one of the first directors to feature the cut–first in *Straight Shooting* (1917) with Harry Carey, Sr., and Hoot Gibson, and later in Tom Mix's *Three Jumps Ahead* (1923), in which the star and Wonder Horse Tony appear to jump across the cut. Stunt ace Richard Talmadge took credit for the feat, while Mix chronicler Robert S. Birchard credits Nevada horse trainer and stuntman Earl Simpson, aided considerably by a wooden ramp. Others suspect "camera magic," especially since the whole scene has an unreal look to it and horse and rider appear smaller in scale than surrounding objects. Whatever the truth about *Three Jumps Ahead*, a scene of Frankie Darro jumping Rex across the cut in Episode 2 of *The Devil Horse* (1932) appears clearly to have been a process shot, unless Rex had suddenly learned to fly.

Straight Shooting (1917).

Contrary to various sources, shots of a horse and rider jumping a chasm in various Republic chapter plays, including Episode 6 of *King of the Texas Rangers* (1941), were obvious process shots that did not rely on Beale's Cut at all.

Other titles that did use the site included Ford's *The Iron Horse* (1924), with the cut playing Brandon's Pass for a scene in which heavy Cyril Chadwick nonchalantly cuts the rope with which star George O'Brien is climbing down the wall of the gorge, sending our hero to (almost) certain death. The 1943 Columbia chapterplay *The Phantom* utilized the cut in Episode 8. But only the most sharp-eyed location fans would realize it, since that scene included no shots of the full cut.

One of the more elaborate (if unintentionally hilarious) film uses of Beale's Cut occurred, surprisingly enough, in an independent cheapie. Jack Hoxie's *Via Pony Express* (1933) has our hero racing along at breakneck speed until roped off his steed by two heavies lying in wait on opposite sites of the cut. While the hapless and slightly ridiculous looking Jack dangles helplessly in midair near the top of the cut, a baddie rifles through Hoxie's mail pouch, finds the dispatch he is after and rides off, instructing his henchies to leave Jack hanging, since he was not worth the bullet it would take to kill him (a comment, perhaps, on Hoxie's thespian talents, or lack thereof). When the outlaws depart, Jack takes out his trusty pocket knife and cuts not one but both ropes, then, as required by the laws of gravity, drops heavily, quickly and with a loud thud to the gorge floor below and walks off camera, limping noticeably. A choice scene!

For years, an historic marker along the Sierra Highway directed tourists to the cut. But our reel west is fast disappearing. A rockslide in the spring of 1998 filled the cut to half its depth, making the area hazardous for hikers. At least when Lake Isabella was created, flooding Old Kernville and much of the surrounding area, Kernville's famed Wofford Ranch, star of so many oaters, was moved intact to a new location near the local airstrip, where it remains today. Even the old church that once stood at the end of Kernville's western street set was relocated to the town's post-Isabella site. It also still stands, sans its familiar steeple and substantially modified in appearance. But Beale's Cut may soon have disappeared completely–except in our favorite films. Directions: To reach Beale's Cut, take Freeway 170 north from L.A. to I-5, I-5 north to Highway 14, Highway 14 to the San Fernando Road exit, left on San Fernando across Highway 14 to the Sierra Highway and left on Sierra Highway. A marker once stood on the right side of the highway about a mile down Sierra back toward L.A.. It is now gone but the shoulder widens where the marker was once placed. Park there and walk across the highway and down the steep hill. At the bottom of the hill, what remains of the cut is still visible.

Vasquez Rocks

The distinctive Vasquez Rocks.

Although the filming days of many of our favorite locations are long past, one impressive natural setting seems almost as busy today as it ever was in the golden era. Geologists tell us the huge Vasquez Rocks along Highway 14, a few miles north of Newhall, rested on the floor of a prehistoric ocean over 20 million years ago. As the salt water receded, repeated floods washed away the soil around the sandstone and violent earthquakes tilted the rocks upward into the sky at a sixty-degree angle like giant rockets poised for take-off.

The Tataviam Indians occupied the area from 200 BC until the late 18th Century. But the rocks derived their popular name from the notorious bandit Tiburcio Vasquez, who hid with his gang there until he was captured and hanged for murder in 1875. The first film may have been shot at Vasquez Rocks in the early

Rex Allen and Koko race through the rocks for The Last Musketeer (1952).

20ᵗʰ Century but we know the area best as the setting for numerous westerns, serials, non-western actioners and science fiction-horror titles.

The rocks and surrounding area hosted a horse race in Roy Rogers' *Rainbow Over Texas* (1946). Roy's trusty steed Trigger easily thwarted heavy Roy Barcroft's barrage of oil drums in *The Far Frontier* (1949) and Roy was also there for several other titles, including *Sunset on the Desert* (1942) and *Jesse James at Bay* (1941).

An exciting chase on horseback took place in the rocks in Rex Allen's *The Last Musketeer* (1952) and Monte Hale stalked a baddie there at the beginning of his *Along the Oregon Trail* (1947). A futuristic land-cruiser raced over the area in the Universal serial *Tim Tyler's Luck* (1937) and heavy Bill Henry fell to his just demise there in a wind-swept climax to the Jungle Jim epic *Fury of the Congo* (1951), while stagecoaches rarely made it through the Vasquez Rocks without being overturned or held up by bandits.

Some B-western heroes never made it to the rocks. "Rocky" Lane's titles were there, for example, only in stock footage (*Bandits of Dark Canyon*, 1947), PRC's not at all, to my knowledge, and Monogram's rarely (Jack Randall's *Trigger Smith*, 1937, Tex Ritter's *Song of the Buckaroo*, 1939).

160

The advent of TV brought an onslaught of western video crews to the rocks. Adult TV westerns, from "Wanted Dead or Alive" and "Tall Man" to "Bonanza," "Cimarron Strip" and "Hondo," lensed at the rocks, as did big-budget futuristic adventures and such non-western TV series as "Murder, She Wrote." On my first visit in 1985, a gas station set had been constructed there for an episode of Robert Blake's "Helltown" series. The area even played "Bedrock" in Steven Spielberg's 1993 feature version of "The Flintstones." Commercials for Taco Bell, Energizer batteries, MasterCard, Wrigley's chewing gum, Hanes underwear and many other products are regularly shot there, as was Michael Jackson's "Black on White" video.

Acquired by Los Angeles County in the 1960s, the 745-acre area became a park in 1970. With a $400 daily filming fee and $100 for each day of preparation, the area as of 1993 was providing L.A. county's parks and recreation department $30,000 annually for commercial permits.

Directions: To reach the great Vasquez Rocks area, which, despite parking spaces, picnic benches and rest facilities, still looks today almost exactly as it did in the western-serial days, take Freeway 170 north from L.A. to I-5, I-5 north to Highway 14, Highway 14 north to the Agua Dulce exit and left on Agua Dulce. Follow the signs to the rocks, which are also visible from Highway 14.

Other Santa Clarita Filming Sites

Movie crews went to other Santa Clarita locales as well. Towsley Canyon, now the Ed Davis Park accessible off I-5, hosted, for example, the silent cliffhanger *Hawk of the Hills* (1927) in the early days, as well as one of Republic's later B+ titles, *The Last Stagecoach West* (1957). According to director Bill Witney, a steep gorge often used as the entrance to the outlaws' hideout was also located between Newhall and Los Angeles. It can be seen in

The "Mystery Gorge" in Shine On Harvest Moon (1939).

Tom Tyler's *Deadwood Pass* (1933), among many other titles, and last appeared, as original footage, in Roy Rogers' *Shine On Harvest Moon* (1938). Witney and his co-director Jack English checked out the site but decided against using it. When parts of the mountains separating Santa Clarita from the San Fernando Valley were dynamited to make way for the Sierra Highway in 1939-40, that interesting location also disappeared.

Chapter 5

Trails North

Traveling north from the Santa Clarita Valley, first on Highway 14 and then on Highway 395 and other roads, we find a veritable feast of familiar California, Oregon, Washington and Canadian filming sites.

Lake Los Angeles

The Joshua tree groves in the Palmdale-Lancaster area north of Newhall are fast falling victim to the relentless L. A. suburban sprawl, with housing developments, shopping centers and new freeway exits seemingly springing up all over. During the western era, however, movie crews regularly went to Palmdale and Lancaster for titles requiring the look of Old Mexico, including Gene Autry's *South of the Border* (1939). Production companies sometimes chose the area for non-western shoots as well, among them the sci-fi classics *It Came from Outer Space* (1953) and *Them* (1954). In fact, *The Night Holds Terror* (1955), set both in plot and actually in and around Lancaster, was based on the true story of a local family kidnapped and terrorized by vicious thugs.

Several of Sunset Carson's lamentable post-Republic Astor releases were filmed at nearby Pearblossom, on director Oliver Drake's ranch. At least one title was also shot on the Beery Ranch outside Valyermo, thirty miles or so southeast of Palmdale. Built in the 1920s by the scene-stealing Beery brothers, Wallace and Noah, Sr., as a 145-acre playground for their Hollywood friends, complete with luxury hotel, huge ballroom, swimming pool and trout ponds, most of the facility burned in 1930. But the stone archway that led to the ballroom can still be seen, just as it appeared when Ken Maynard's *In Old Santa Fe* (1934) was filmed there and in the area countryside of Joshua trees. Owned by the Beery family until 1938, the site now hosts a youth camp.

An area east of Palmdale, characterized by Joshua trees and scattered rock formations, became a favorite filming location for Republic director Bill Witney. All exteriors for his Roy Rogers entry *Trigger, Jr.* (1950) and most for his *South of Caliente* (1951) used this site, as did some exterior shooting for Roy's last Republic starrer *Pals of the Golden West* (1951) and Rex Allen's *The Last Musketeer* (1952), another Witney-directed oater.

Lake Los Angeles rock formations.

The area featured a large dry lake as well as the Joshuas and rock formations. In the far distance beyond the dry lake could be seen a large hill and three progressively smaller hills camera right of the largest hill. The rock formations were prominently displayed in action scenes for *Trigger, Jr.*, and Roy rode Trigger in the direction of

Lake Los Angeles' backdrop of hills. Unfortunately, the area is becoming another victim of suburban sprawl.

the dry lake and distant hills at the end of that picture. The hills and rock formations are also seen in the exciting horse-naping scene in *South of Caliente* as well as portions of chases in *The Last Musketeer*, although most action shots for that title were filmed at the Vasquez Rocks north of Newhall.

Witney said that he shot *Trigger, Jr.* at Lake Los Angeles, a few miles east of Palmdale. His memory for filming sites was excellent. And action scenes for Roy's *The Far Frontier* (1949) and *Bells of Coronado* (1950), which Witney had also directed, had been shot at Littlerock Dam near Palmdale. *Bells of Coronado* also used a dry lake in that area. But a couple of other film location fans who had visited Lake Los Angeles doubted it was the site for *Trigger, Jr.* and thought that, in any event, residential development there had made any comparison with the sites for the Rogers titles difficult.

I then forgot about Lake Los Angeles for several years until I began checking locations for Merrill McCord in connection with his fine biography of Bob Livingston and Jack Randall. That research convinced me that several Randall Monogram titles (*Mexicali Kid*, 1938, *Trigger Smith*, 1939, *Overland Mail*, 1939) had been shot in part of the same area where the Roy Rogers titles were later filmed.

Finally, on a 1997 trip to California, friends and I drove out to Lake Los Angeles. As we approached the area, I realized that Bill Witney had been correct as usual. The large hill and three smaller adjoining hills seen in the distance in *Trigger, Jr.* and other

Roy Rogers and his last movie sidekick Pinky Lee (or Pinky's stunt double) at Lake Los Angeles.

titles gradually became visible in the distant haze. Using the hills as landmarks, we also located the spot where the final scene for *Trigger, Jr.* was shot as well as some of the other rock formations used in that film and the other Republic and Randall titles shot at Lake Los Angeles. In fact, the area still looked much as it had in the filming days.

On comparing video and photos of the area with films set there, I also realized that the road we took from Palmdale to Lake Los Angeles, paved by that point, was the dirt road on which the horse-naping took place in *South of Caliente* (1951), with the landmark hills clearly visible in the distance.

Directions: To reach Lake Los Angeles, about an hour's drive from L.A.,take Freeway 170 north to I-5, I-5 north to Highway 14, Highway 14 north to the Palmdale Blvd. exit, and the Blvd. east through town until the road curves sharply to the right (southeast). At that point, leave the main road and continue east a few miles to Lake Los Angeles.

Red Rock Canyon

Red Rock Canyon, on the edge of California's Mojave desert, was another favorite western filming site. Located along Highway 14 a hundred miles north of L.A., Red Rock Canyon's cathedral cliffs and other sites furnished moviemakers with the most spectacular Highway 14 backdrops of the golden era.

The canyon is part of the Ricardo Formation, a 6500-foot thick deposit of white clay, red sandstone, dark brown lava, and pink surface volcanic rock from which the area gets its vibrant, contrasting colors. Native Americans inhabited the area long before other settlers, who first arrived in search of gold in the mid-19th century. By 1862, the canyon had begun to appear on maps.

The cathedral cliffs of Red Rock Canyon.

In 1896, Rudolph Hagen settled there, acquired water rights, and filed for mineral and homestead rights. By 1913, Hagen had obtained nearly complete control of the canyon and some of the surrounding area. His Ricardo Land and Water Company also operated a general store near where the visitors' center for Red Rock Canyon State Park is now situated. (The Ricardo camp is featured in Jack Randall's *Danger Valley*, 1937, among other titles.) As early as 1920, the canyon's scenic wonders had begun to appear on many picture postcards–more than fifty, in fact, before 1950. Those postcards may have first attracted moviemakers to the area. A shot of the canyon's distinctive Camel Rock formation that appeared in the 1936 version of *Three Godfathers* was virtually identical, for example, to a postcard photo of the area.

But whatever the movie crews' initial incentive, by the mid-1920s at the latest they were filming in the canyon and elsewhere in the desert, with Hagen charging fees for the use of his property and imposing production guidelines on moviemakers. By 1930, just before the first paved highway was completed through the canyon, at least five films had been shot there. Hagen left the area that year but in his absence Barney Wolfe, a Hagen assistant, ran the Ricardo camp gas station/outpost and dealt with movie crews.

Following Hagen's death in 1937, his second wife Nora inherited the property. She and her heirs continued the family's arrangements with production companies into the 1960s, directly and at one point through Frank Slingerland, who leased portions of the property for rental to the studios.

Although outside the thirty-mile zone of L.A. area locations most favored by movie crews, Red Rock Canyon proved a reasonably popular filming site, even for low-budget productions such as Ken Maynard's *Tombstone Canyon* (1932), particularly because of its convenient proximity to the highway. Bill Witney, who shot *Zorro Rides Again* (1937) and the Roy Rogers Trucolor feature *Grand Canyon Trail* (1948) there, recalled fondly that a film crew could simply drive into the canyon, "get out and shoot from the road." Nor was Witney the only Republic director attracted to the area. Several other Rogers titles, including *Colorado*, 1940), were filmed there; and Republic made excellent use of the canyon in two titles with the same stolen train plotline–the big-budget Bill Elliott entry *The Last Bandit* (1949) and the little Bob Steele gem *The*

Ken Maynard, pictured here with perennial heavy Charles King (far left) in a rare good-guy role, often filmed at Red Rock Canyon, as did Buck Jones and other stars of their era.

Great Train Robbery (1941).

Red Rock also played the moon in the studio cliffhanger *Radar Men from the Moon* (1952), with actor George ("Commando Cody") Wallace sweating through his scenes in the sweltering heat of the canyon, and Universal made effective use of the area in several of its chapter plays, including *Buck Rogers* (1939) and *Riders of Death Valley* (1941), as did Gene Autry for his color feature *The Big Sombrero* (1949). Such A titles as *The Mummy* (1932), Bogie's *Petrified Forest* (1936), *The Big Country* (1958) and *Westworld* (1973) also featured Red Rock, as did "Hondo" and many other TV western series. *The Big Country* also made effective use of the winding Jawbone Canyon nearby.

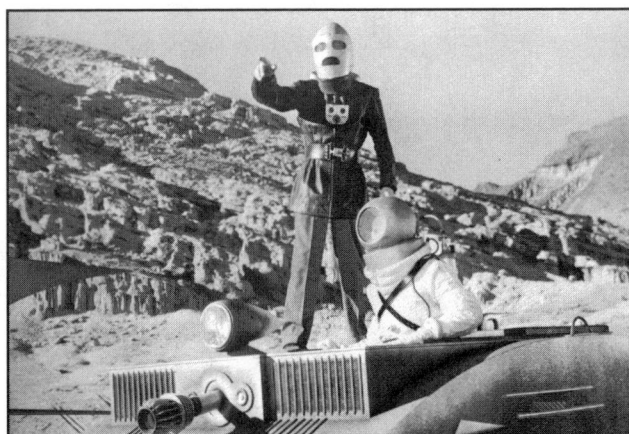

Red Rock Canyon even played the moon in Republic's Radar Men from the Moon *(1952).*

Red Rock has long been a state park with parking areas and a campground. But the area remains largely

The Three Mesquiteers (and their stunt doubles) were there for Pals of the Saddle *(1938).*

Red Rock also provided a backdrop for Gary Cooper's Man of the West *(1958).*

unmarred by "civilization" and even appeared in a few recent features, including *Jurassic Park* (1993) and

I'll Be Home for Christmas (1998). The canyon will be best remembered, however, for its roles in the westerns, major and minor, of the golden age.

Directions: To reach Red Rock Canyon, take Freeway 170 north from L.A. to I-5, I-5 north to Highway 14, Highway 14 north to Highway 395 and 395 north to the canyon, which is approximately 100 miles from L.A.

Kernville

The Kern River Valley, three hours north of L. A., furnished one of the more realistic settings for westerns and serials. Film crews may have begun shooting in the area as early as 1916 but Yakima Canutt's *Branded a Bandit* (1924), the climax to which was set at the Kern River lagoon and cliffs, seen in many later titles, was apparently the first film of record to be shot in the area.

Other silents quickly followed and in 1931, two early Mascot sound serials, *Lightning Warrior* and *Vanishing Legion*, lensed there, with the former using an area mine as well as what were to become familiar Kernville filming sites of the golden age. Bob Steele's *Man from Hell's Edges* (1932) and several of John Wayne's early Monogram Lone Star productions (*Sagebrush Trail*, 1933, *Riders of Destiny*, 1933) were among the first sound westerns filmed there.

Other cowboy heroes soon followed. Hopalong Cassidy shot over 20 titles in the Kern Valley (*Heart of the West*, 1936, *Stagecoach War*, 1940, and his first, *Hop-A-Long Cassidy*, 1935, although most of that film utilized the Alabama Hills and other Lone Pine settings). Gene Autry occasionally filmed there (*Public Cowboy No. 1*, 1937), as did Tex Ritter (*Mystery of the Hooded Horsemen*, 1937), the Three Mesquiteers (*The Three Mesquiteers*, 1936, *Trigger Trio*, 1938), Jack Randall (*Gun Packer*, 1937) and Roy Rogers (*Silver Spurs*, 1943, *Lights of Old Santa Fe*, 1944, *Roll On Texas Moon*, 1946, *On the Old Spanish Trail*, 1947), among other stars. Several Bill Elliott Republic A's (*In Old Sacramento*, 1946, *Wyoming*, 1947) were also set there, as were many other A-westerns (Audie Murphy's *Drums Across the River*, 1953, Tab Hunter's *The Burning Hills*, 1956), non-western titles and serials (*The Vigilantes Are Coming*, 1936, *Oregon Trail*, 1939, *Jack Armstrong*, 1947).

Although the original village of Isabella (now beneath man-made Lake Isabella) was specifically referred to in Canutt's *Branded a Bandit* and may have been the community actually seen in that title, most area filming was done in the original Kernville town (also now under Lake Isabella), in the hills northwest of Kernville along the raging Kern River (and Highway 190), on Kernville ranches, along the river bottom by and south of town and in the lagoon area farther south (now south of the Lake Isabella dam, along Highway 155), as well as in the surrounding hills of rocks and scattered pines.

Several western street sets were apparently constructed in the valley during the early filming days. But Kernville's street set was clearly the most enduring and frequently used. It ran parallel to Kernville's actual Main Street, which ran north-south to the east of the movie street. The origins of Movie Street, originally called Granite Street, are somewhat obscure but Prudential Studio, which leased the property in the 1920s, may have developed the first sets on the street. At the western street's northwest end was the actual Kernville Community Church, which was seen in many titles and played a key role in the plot of Buck

Kernville's western street with its familiar church and steeple.

The Hopalong Cassidy company made many visits to Kernville.

The street looking in the opposite direction from the church.

Jones' *Boss of Lonely Valley* (1937). A 1938 news clipping claimed that the Hoppy production company had recently donated the church, said to be a movie set, to the community for a church. But the church (a Methodist congregation) actually dated from 1898. A community school, visible rarely and only in the background of movie scenes, occupied the property across the street from the church.

One side of the street set included facades for a general store, assayer's office, jail and livery stable, while a blacksmith shop, saloon, dance hall, hotel and harness shop comprised much of the other side of the street. A barn and corral, once used by Wells Fargo for stagecoach teams, could be seen at the south end of the street. Owned by Andrew Brown, local rancher and general store proprietor (who also owned the western street), the barn, corral and a small house were also sometimes used, especially in early Kernville films.

The principal Kernville ranch used for filming was the Wofford Ranch, located about a mile southwest of town and owned by Irven Wofford, a forest ranger turned rancher and developer, who was principally credited with bringing movie companies to the valley. Portions of Roy's *Roll On Texas Moon*, Hoppy's *The Showdown* (1940) and even Jimmy Wakely's *Rainbow over the Rockies* (1947) used the Wofford Ranch. Other area ranches used for filming *Roll On Texas Moon* and other titles included the Doyle Ranch, located about ten miles east of Isabella along Highway 178.

Kernville itself was also sometimes featured in movies. The first episode of Mascot's *Vanishing Legion* included a rare early glimpse of the town's real main street. During a fight between star Harry Carey Sr. and Joe Bonomo, a sign for "Brown's General Merchandise" can be seen in the background. A quick shot of the Mountain Inn, Kernville's only hotel, is visible in the same scene. Early in *Roll On Texas Moon*, Dale Evans drives a buckboard into town from the south, passes the Kernville Garage (formerly Cook's Livery Stable) and pulls up in front of Andrew Brown's general store.

In the hills 20 miles northwest of Kernville on the road to Johnsondale (Highway 190) were a waterfall and the Johnsondale bridge (which still stands, next to a more modern bridge), also used for filming. The bridge and surrounding area furnished the setting for an exciting ambush scene between Roy Rogers and heavy Hal Taliaferro in *Silver Spurs*. The waterfall was put to prominent play in the climax to Hoppy's *The*

The Wofford Ranch provided the backdrop for this scene from the Columbia serial Brick Bradford (1947).

The relocated Wofford house in the 1990s.

"Gabby" Hayes confronts Dale Evans and Elizabeth Risdon at Brown's General Store in a humorous scene for Roll On Texas Moon (1946).

The Mountain Inn.

Johnsondale Falls.

Johnsondale bridges.

Showdown. And autos sometimes plunged (in miniature) into the raging Kern River near town (*Lights of Old Santa Fe*).

South of town (and now southwest of the Lake Isabella dam) was the lagoon into which so many heroes and heavies dived or fell. And just beyond the lagoon was another familiar Kernville filming site–a

The swinging bridge in Buck Jones' Black Aces (1937).

swinging bridge seen in many titles (*Trigger Trio*, 1938, Harry Carey Sr.'s *Aces Wild*, 1936). (The bridge is no longer there but the holes into which bridge spikes were embedded are still visible in the rocks.)

The rolling hills of the area furnished the setting for countless chases, including terrific stagecoach and wagon chases in *On the Old Spanish Trail* and *Silver Spurs*, although the chase in the latter climaxed with

The lagoon and swinging bridge site during a high water period in the 1990s.

Buck Jones on the Kern River.

the wagon plunging into Lake Sherwood near Thousand Oaks rather than the Kern River lagoon. Although dismantled and closed long ago, area mines also made appearances in our films. Arguably the most exciting scene in *Lightning Warrior* was an Episode 2 fight (only a small part of which utilized process photography) between the heavy (The Wolf Man), Frankie Darro and Rin-Tin-Tin on mine ore buckets suspended from parallel cables supposedly high above the ground. Later Columbia serials (*Brick Bradford*, 1947, *Bruce Gentry*, 1949) also made use of Kernville mines.

Relations between film companies and local citizens were generally quite good. A drunken Ken Maynard once was jailed after riding through town, shooting out street lights and windows. But citizens usually found the movie folks friendly and cooperative. Crews and players lodged in private residences or at the Mountain Inn. They frequently participated in community activities and occasionally even fielded a baseball team on which, it was reported, "Roy Rogers could pitch a baseball as straight as he could fire a six shooter." Once the Sons of the Pioneers singing group played for a benefit dance at Kernville's old Bechtel Hall, giving the proceeds to a local family in distress. Bill (Hoppy) Boyd once treated soldiers passing through town to a free meal at the Mountain Inn.

But nothing lasts forever. In 1943, the army bought the Movie Street sets from Andrew Brown's son, Sumner, for $1,500 and transported them to Camp Santa Anita for training exercises. But not before the street made one last appearance, as a ghost town in Roy's *Silver Spurs*.

In the early 1950s, a dam was constructed, flooding the valley, creating Lake Isabella and requiring the transplanting of the original Kernville and Isabella to their current locations. The old community church, now refurbished, stands in the new Kernville. And the old Wofford Ranch? It was moved to a site near the local airport but still looks much as it did in the filming days.

Some filming continued to take place on ranches that had escaped burial beneath Lake Isabella and along the rocky banks of the Kern River southwest of the dam (*The Burning Hills*, 1956). Episodes of such golden age TV series as "Tales of Wells Fargo," "Gunsmoke," "Wagon Train" and "Bonanza," as well as later series ("MacGyver," "Airwolf"), also lensed there. Even today, the valley still plays host to an occasional TVer, commercial or feature. But Kernville's movie heyday is long past. Mention of Lake Isabella is more likely to remind one of water-skiing and fishing than "Lights, Camera, Action!"

Directions: To reach the Kern River Valley from L. A., take Freeway 170 north to I-5, I-5 north to Highway 14, Highway 14 north past Red Rock Canyon to Highway 178 and Highway 178 west into the valley.

Lone Pine

Developers are destroying many of our favorite filming sites but to date glorious Lone Pine has been largely spared. That terrific location at the base of snow-capped Mt. Whitney, 200 miles north of L.A., looks today almost exactly as it did in Fatty Arbuckle's *The Round-Up* (1920), apparently the first film shot there, as well as Ken Maynard's *Fiddling Buckaroo* (1933), Hoot's *Lucky Terror* (1936), Buck Jones' *Sandflow* (1937) and over 300 other titles.

The area's most famous rock formations, of course, are in the Alabama Hills off the Whitney Portal Road about a mile west of town. Movie crews shot memorable running inserts along the Alabama Hills' Movie Road, not least among them heavy Roy Barcroft's helicopter chase after Rex Allen and his horse

The cucumber-shaped Gene Autry Rock with Mount Whitney in the background.

Roy Rogers and the Sons of the Pioneers one very cold morning in the Alabama Hills, during production of Song of Texas *(1943).*

Rex Allen in a Movie Road chase for Under Mexicali Stars (1950).

Koko in the climax to *Under Mexicali Stars* (1950). The cucumber-shaped Gene Autry rock (*Boots and Saddles*, 1937), the deep wash at the north end of the insert road (Gene's *Guns and Guitars*, 1936, Roy's *Under Western Stars*, 1938), the ambush site for *The Lone Ranger* (1938) serial and countless other Alabama Hills locales made appearances as well.

Scenes were also shot in an area south across Whitney Portal Road from the Alabama Hills, along what is now Horseshow Meadow Rd. A flat there beneath "The Mittens" rock formations, to cite but one example, hosted the climax to *Westward Ho* (1936), John Wayne's first Republic starrer. Owens Dry Lake, south of town, also appeared in that title as well as the superb climax to Jack Randall's first

Another shot of the Alabama Hills with Mount Whitney in the distant background.

starring film, *Riders of the Dawn* (1937) and many other flicks, as did the sand dunes at Olancha about ten miles south (Wayne Morris' *Desert Pursuit*, 1952, *Tarzan's Desert Mystery*, 1943).

Crews occasionally filmed along the winding Whitney Portal Road itself, high above Lone Pine. The dusty musical/comic interlude in *Boots and Saddles* was shot up there. So also was a scene for Hoppy's *Law of the Pampas* (1939), as well as such exciting non-westerns as Bogart's *High Sierra* (1941) and its Jack Palance remake, *I Died a Thousand Times* (1955), with the lead in each chased up the Whitney Portal by police in hot pursuit. The falls, woods and glacier lakes near the upper end of the road also had roles in our movies, including Gary Cooper's *Springfield Rifle* (1952), Randolph Scott's *Man in the Saddle* (1951) (a routine oater, to be sure, but one of the most beautifully filmed Lone Pine titles ever) and the George Montgomery version of *Riders of the Purple Sage* (1941).

Tom Mix's silent rendition of the latter title used the town of Lone Pine itself, as did Mix's *Flaming Guns"* (1932) and Bob Steele's *Hidden Valley* (1932), in which the town's Dow Hotel played a courthouse. Lone Pine's train depot made its most prominent appearance in *Boots and Saddles*, with Republic not even bothering to change the name of the station.

Although now long gone, the depot, outbuildings and track at nearby Keeler had roles in Gene's *The Blazing Sun* (1950) and, as "Wheeler," in Hoppy's *Sinister Journey* (1948), among other titles. The station at Owenyo, north of Lone Pine, also appeared in a number of films. See Chapter 11 for photographs of the Lone Pine and Keeler depots.

Permanent Lone Pine structures and studio-built sets made appearances, too. A cabin with a well, situated along what is now Tuttle Creek Road, even became known as the "Hoppy Cabin," not only because the star typically stayed there during Lone

Whitney Portal falls.

The Hoppy Cabin in the 1990s.

Pine shoots, but also because it appeared in at least six Hoppys (including *Renegade Trail*, 1939). But the cabin was a familiar setting in many other stars' flicks as well, among them Steele's *Demon for Trouble* (1934), Bill Cody's *Frontier Days* (1934), Tim Holt's *Guns of Hate* (1948) and Scott's *Man in the Saddle*. Also still standing in a residential area south/southeast of the Hoppy cabin is the "Tim Holt Cabin," used

The Hoppy Cabin hosted this comic scene in a Three Mesquiteers title.

The Tim Holt Cabin.

in *Arizona Ranger* (1948) and other post-war Holts.

But the Alabama Hills ranch set first seen in Hoppy's *Pirates on Horseback* (1941), and later used for such titles as Gene's *Down Mexico Way* (1941), Hoppy's *Bar 20* (1943) and Roy's *Utah* (1945), is long gone. So, too, are a stage station set first constructed in the Hills for Tyrone Power's *Rawhide* (1951) and *Young* (1940) were still visible along Moffatt Ranch Road north of Lone Pine.

The most frequently used sets were those on Russ Spainhower's Anchor Ranch about a mile south of town. For years, Spainhower was Hollywood's principal Lone Pine

Alabama Hills cabin.

contact, scouting filming sites and providing movie folks with livestock and props. Originally, Spainhower leased the Lucas Ranch, renting its large corrals and barns (used for at least one of Wayne's Lone Star titles, Tom Mix's *Just Tony*, 1922, and Guinn "Big Boy" Williams' *Rough Trails*, 1935) to movie companies as early as the twenties. In the 1930s, he bought neighboring rangeland, which he named the Anchor Ranch. Spainhower moved his family to the Anchor in 1940. Earlier, however, he had used portions of the massive *Gunga Din* (1939) sets to construct a large, walled adobe hacienda/mission there for movie use, with Hoppy's *Range War* and *Law of the Pampas*, both released in 1939, the first of many titles filmed on the new site.

The hacienda set quickly became the most familiar in Lone Pine. Spainhower's Anchor brand found its way into titles as well. Gene Autry combined his Flying A logo with the Anchor logo to make the brand for the hacienda in his *Trail to San Antone* (1947).

The fort set built for *King of the Khyber Rifles* (1953) along Moffatt Ranch Road served the next year as Edward G. Robinson's Anchor Ranch in Glenn Ford's *The Violent Men*. (The set for Ford's own ranch in that film was constructed southeast of the intersection of Whitney Portal Road and Horseshoe Meadow Road on the south side of Lone Pine Creek.)

In 1947, Russ Spainhower, joined by a local lumber dealer and William Boyd's production company, added Anchorville, a western street running west-east from the east wall of the hacienda/mission set. But the street, seen first in *Borrowed Trouble* (1948) and *Sinister Journey* (1948), saw limited use. A town set was constructed by the railroad tracks south of town for Spencer Tracy's fine *Bad Day at Black Rock* (1955), which also used the Alabama Hills, and *Bad Day* director John Sturges built a small street over there three years later for his *The Law and Jake Wade* (1958). Audie Murphy's *Hell Bent for Leather* (1960), as well

Spainhower hacienda/mission set.

Anchorville town set, with hacienda wall in the background.

as *Nevada Smith* (1966), *Waterhole No. 3* (1967) and other titles utilized a Dolomite mine and outbuildings southeast of town. The dam scene in Roy Rogers' *Under Western Stars* was shot at the Tinnemaha Dam near Independence, north of Lone Pine. Independence's Winnedumah Hotel served as an exclusive resort in the same title.

Although Lone Pine was home primarily to feature films, it also hosted a number of serials, including

The Winnedumah Hotel at Independence, north of Lone Pine, played an exclusive resort in Roy Rogers' first starring feature Under Western Stars *(1938).*

The nearby Tinnemaha Dam also made an appearance.

Allan Lane's great *Daredevils of the West* (1943) and Columbia's *Jungle Raiders* (1945) and *Brick Bradford* (1947).

Nor are Lone Pine's filming days over. In recent years, it has appeared in *Tremors* (1989), *Gladiator* (2000), *Gone in Sixty Seconds* (2000) and the I-MAX production *Adventures in Wild California* (2000), among other features and many commercials.

Thanks largely to the efforts of the late Dave Holland, the preeminent Lone Pine film historian, the community, in 1990, began hosting a wonderful annual film festival and other events honoring the area's significant role in motion picture history. The recently established Beverly and Jim Rogers Museum of Lone Pine Film History, a wonderful collection of exhibits, thoroughly documents the town's cinema experience.

Death Valley

West of Lone Pine lies the Death Valley National Park, one of the most inhospitable, yet starkly beautiful, spots on earth. According to legend, Death Valley got its name when a weary pioneer woman, survivor of an 1849 wagon trek through the area, bade "Goodbye, Death Valley" to the sweltering expanse. When promoters began advertising it as a tourist attraction at the turn of the 20th century, a local newspaper quickly lampooned their efforts with a mock sales pitch: "All the Advantages of Hell without the Inconveniences."

Tourists did come, of course. On February 1, 1927, Clark Gable's birthday, the luxurious Furnace Creek Inn opened its doors. In 1939, Gable and Carole Lombard honeymooned there following their elopement and Arizona marriage.

Movie crews also came to Death Valley. Certain titles said to have been filmed there (such as Tom Mix's *The Rider of Death Valley* (1932) were actually shot in the Coachella Valley south of Palm Springs or in the Imperial sand dunes on California's southern border. Location research Carlo Gaberscek lists *Chimmie Fadden Out West* (1915), with Victor Moore and Raymond Hatton, as perhaps the first title filmed there.

Death Valley's Zabriski Point.

Over the years, others followed, including George O'Brien's *The Border Patrolman* (1936), in which the Furnace Creek Inn played a prominent role, Wallace Beery's *Twenty Mule Team* (1940), Wayne's *Three Godfathers* (1948), Randolph Scott's *The Walking Hills* (1949), William Holden's *Escape from Fort Bravo*

Three Godfathers (1946).

(1953) and *The Professionals* (1966).

Among Death Valley landmarks featured in such titles were the Devil's Golf Course (clumps of crystalized salt spread across a dry lake), the Devil's Cornfield (weed stalks from which the soil around their roots had gradually been depleted), the magnificent Zabriskie Point and the Death Valley Canyon Natural Bridge. As noted elsewhere in this book, the nearby Nevada ghost town of Rhyolite also had a part in Death Valley's film history. According to one report, over 40 motion pictures were filmed in Death Valley. Borax, sponsor of the Death Valley Days series, also featured a 20-mule-team pulling its cargo across a Death Valley flats. But most episodes for that series were filmed elsewhere, including Apacheland, outside Phoenix.

Bishop, Mammoth Lakes and Bridgeport

A good deal of filming was also done north of Lone Pine, between Bishop and Bridgeport, California. For B-western fans, the magnificent Mammoth Lakes north of Bishop are best remembered for scenes in Gene Autry's *Melody Ranch* (1940) and *Sierra Sue* (1941). *Hawk of the Wilderness* (1938), the fine 1938 Republic cliffhanger starring Herman Brix, also put the lakes to excellent use. Although most Mountie films were shot at Big Bear Lake, southeast of L.A., Robert Kent's *King of the Royal Mounted* (1936) made excellent use of the Mammoth Lakes.

One of the most picturesque Mammoth Lakes area sites was along Hot Creek Road, just north of the local airport. The hot springs or creek running through that area hosted a cabin seen in *True Grit* (1969) and is also seen in Wayne's *North to Alaska* (1960), Steve McQueen's *Nevada Smith* (1966) and Gregory Peck's *Shootout* (1971).

This giant outcropping could be seen often in films made at Mammoth Lakes.

Director Bill Witney took cast and crew to the lakes for Hawk of the Wilderness *(1938).*

A distant shot of the lakes.

Gene Autry and Ann Miller at Mammoth Lakes for Melody Ranch (1940).

These hot springs along Hot Creek Road, south of Mammoth Lakes, appeared in several John Wayne titles, including True Grit (1969)..

Other area sites also appeared in pictures. Henry Fonda's *The Return of Frank James* (1940) reportedly used Convict Lake, among other Bishop area sites. Clint Eastwood's *High Plains Drifter* (1973) was set largely along huge Lake Mono and the Lake Crowley area appeared in exciting cattle stampede scenes (reportedly featuring livestock provided by Bishop ranchers) in a number of titles. Parts of Roy Rogers' *My Pal Trigger* (1946) were also filmed in the Bishop area against majestic backdrops.

Convict Lake.

The large ghost town of Bodie, located south of Bridgeport, seemed ideal for western filming. But titles other researchers have cited as films made there appear clearly to have used other sites. Buck Jones' *Desert*

Remains of the Bodie mine.

Vengeance (1931), for example, was filmed at Rhyolite, Nevada, not Bodie. A short film starring John Dehner as a lonely prospector did lense at Bodie, though, and Tom Keene's *Ghost Valley* (1932) used the Hornitas ghost town in Mariposa County.

A sheep ranch outside Bridgeport was the setting for Tim Holt's *Storm Over Wyoming* (1950), not Agoura or other sites typically mentioned for that title. Parts of Rod Cameron's *Stampede* (1949) were also shot at Bridgeport. But that community's main claim to cinema fame was use of the local courthouse in the Robert Mitchum-Jane Greer *film noir* classic *Out of the Past* (1947), which, although not a western, included much more outdoor scenery than many a talky, studio-bound A-western.

The Bridgeport courthouse.

Tim Holt and Richard (Chito) Martin in beautiful Bridgeport for Storm Over Wyoming *(1950).*

Tuolumne County

Westerns and serials featuring railroad scenes utilized several locations near L.A. But Tuolumne County near Yosemite in north-central California was undoubtedly the most frequently used and scenic setting for such sequences.

Tuolumne's film history apparently dates from 1919, when Universal shot the final episodes of its serial *The Red Glove* there. Since that time, the county has played in more than 300 films and TV shows, as well as countless commercials and industrial entries. Titles reportedly lensed there include western silents (William S. Hart's *Toll Gate*, 1920, *The Covered Wagon*, 1923), portions of such sound classics as Gary Cooper's *The Virginian* (1929) and *High Noon* (1952), Errol Flynn's *Dodge City* (1939), Joel McCrea's *Wells Fargo* (1936), Gregory Peck's *Duel in the Sun* (1946) and Clint Eastwood's *Pale Rider* (1985) and *Unforgiven* (1992). Tuolumne hosted hilarious western spoofs (the Marx Brothers' *Go West*, 1940, and the

Mae West/W.C. Fields starrer *My Little Chicadee*, 1940), many B and B+ titles (Hoppy's *North of the Rio Grande*, 1937, Rod Cameron and Johnny Mack Brown's *Stampede*, 1949, and Sterling Hayden's *Kansas Pacific*, 1952), and such popular Tvers as "Tales of Wells Fargo," "Rawhide," "Legend of Jesse James," "Bonanza" and "Little House on the Prairie."

Tuolumne druggist and insurance agent Henry Ruoff was the prime force in attracting film crews to the county, even arranging at one point to bring a special train of producers, directors and location managers in for tours of filming sites. With virtually every type of scenery available, from rolling hills with scattered trees and rock outcroppings, to expansive plains, woodlands and streams, Tuolumne furnished a superb setting for outdoor epics.

But its Sierra Railway was perhaps its principal attraction for film companies. Built in 1897 to transport lumber from the Tuolumne mountains to major rail connections in Oakdale, the 57-mile-long railroad has appeared in many titles. Even after the company converted to diesel in 1955, it retained several steam locomotives and an assortment of antique

Outlaws attack one of the trains of the Sierra line.

A robbery on the line in Randolph Scott's Rage at Dawn *(1955).*

passenger and freight cars at its Jamestown yard for studio use. Over the years, two of the company's locomotives, No. 3 and No. 18, became true stars. No. 18, the most popular engine in the 1930s and 1940s, appeared in *Dodge City* and *Duel in the Sun*, among other titles. No. 3 became the "star" on No. 18's retirement in 1951, appearing in such films as *High Noon*.

First used for a TV series in 1956, when "The Twisted Track" episode in the Lone Ranger series filmed in Tuolumne, No. 3 was a regular cast member in Alan Hale, Jr.'s "Casey Jones," Dale Robertson's "Tales of Wells Fargo" and "Iron Horse" and the long-running "Petticoat Junction." No. 3 also appeared in episodes of "The Big Valley," "Gunsmoke," "Death Valley Days" and "The Wild, Wild West," among other TV series. "Petticoat Junction" gave prominent play to the water tower at the Jamestown station, while the Jamestown yard and roundhouse

The Jamestown depot in the 1990s.

The roundhouse.

were featured in an exciting shootout for Audie Murphy's *The Cimarron Kid* (1952).

The depot (now long gone) and track on the plains of Warnerville, about 20 miles west of Jamestown, also saw service in *High Noon*. Robert Wilke and Sheb Wooley met chief heavy Ian McDonald (as Frank

The Warnerville depot in High Noon *(1952).*

The Warnerville depot site in the 1990s.

Miller) there with plans for revenge against Gary Cooper's Marshal Kane.

The historic mining community of Columbia, a few miles north of Sonora, was another star. A quaint Columbia residence with picket fence and shrubbery appeared in a brief scene for *High Noon* and Columbia's streets joined the famed western street at the Columbia studio's Burbank ranch for the final shootout in that fine film. The church seen in *High Noon* was a church at Tuolumne City, near Columbia. Columbia's streets and stores, as well as a picturesque Tuolumne covered bridge over the

This Columbia house had a bit part in High Noon.

Columbia's main street.

The Knight's Ferry covered bridge appeared in Rage at Dawn.

Stanislaus River at Knight's Ferry, were also featured in Randolph Scott's *Rage at Dawn* (1955). Columbia's streets saw extensive use, too, in the underrated *The Return of Jack Slade* (1955).

Murphys, a village about an hour's drive north of Columbia, was in the movies, too, given its most prominent role in the underrated *Texas Lady* (1955), in which Gregory Walcott stole the picture from stars Claudette Colbert and Barry Sullivan. When I visited Murphys in 1996, it looked almost exactly as it had forty years earlier, when *Texas Lady* was shot there.

In 1989, Universal built its Hill Valley western town of 27 old west buildings in Tuolumne's Red Hills area a few miles southwest of Sonora and Jamestown for Michael J. Fox's *Back to the Future III* (1990), which also featured Locomotive No. 3. Although used in several later features

In the 1990s, this Murphys store looked much as it had in Texas Lady (1955).

and episodes of "Briscoe County Jr.," that set, then known as Red Hills Ranch, burned in 1996.

The citizens of Tuolumne Country are justly proud of its real and reel history. Columbia today features guided tours and looks much as it did in the gold rush days. Sonora and Jamestown have also maintained a traditional appearance. From 1971 to 1979, the Sierra Railroad ran steam-powered excursions on its narrow-gauge line. But in 1979, the company offered to sell the Jamestown yard to the California park system, provide trackage rights and donate its old-time rolling stock, including No. 3, to the state. State officials agreed and in July 1983, the facilities reopened at Railtown 1897 State Historic Park, with tours of the facilities and train rides for tourists.

But the Sonora area was not the only area movie site. Kennedy Meadows at Sonora Pass, high in the mountains 55 miles east of Sonora, made infrequent appearances as well. A production crew went there for Hoppy's *Eagle's Brood* (1935). It may also have been used in Rod Cameron's *Frontier Gal* (1946) and Bill Elliott's *In Old Sacramento* (1946), although much of the Elliott title was filmed along the Kern River near Johnsondale, which, to further confuse the issue, also hosts a Kennedy Meadows.

But *Eagle's Brood* was clearly filmed at Sonora Pass and its Kennedy Meadows–a fact that long-time Hoppy property manager Henry Donovan confirmed for me several years ago. Those scenes of Kennedy Meadows, with its large, half-dome shaped rock at one end, as well as shots along the Sonora Pass road, with steep mountain slopes in the distance, and on a cliff above the rushing stream at one end of the meadow, made *Eagle's Brood* a special title for location buffs, although much of that film was shot at Newhall's Monogram Ranch, including its walled adobe ranch.

Kennedy Meadows at Sonora Pass.

Oregon, Washington and Canada

Occasionally, of course, western movie crews venture north of California into Oregon, Washington and, especially in recent years, even into Canada. A number of silent titles were reportedly filmed in Oregon, including not only portions of such major productions as *The Covered Wagon* (1923) but also a number of Hoot Gibson oaters and even *The General* (1927), Buster Keaton's version of the Civil War story about Union efforts to sabotage the Confederate railroad. Walt Disney's sound version of that episode, *The Great Locomotive Chase* (1956), was actually filmed in Georgia, where the story was set. But the Keaton version reportedly was shot in part at Oregon sites near Cottage Grove and along the McKenzie River. Among early sound westerns, George O'Brien's *Park Avenue Logger* (1937) used Grants Pass. *Canyon Passage* (1946), with Dana Andrews and Susan Hayward, lensed at beautiful Diamond Lake, while the Eugene area hosted Robert Mitchum's *Rachel and the Stranger* (1948). Robert L. Lippert's directorial debut, *Last of the Wild Horses* (1948), was shot at Jacksonville. In fact, before the opening credits for that last title, a shot of 1948 Jacksonville dissolves into a picture of the same street in period dress. Years later, Hollywood returned to Jacksonville for *The Great Northfield, Minnesota Raid* (1971).

The low-budget but beautiful Eagle-Lion title *Rogue River* (1950), a rustic crime yarn starring Rory Calhoun and Peter Graves (in his film debut), was shot at Grants Pass and on the Rogue River, with the assistance, as indicated in the credits, of the Josephine County Mounted Sheriff's Posse. Jimmy Stewart also went to Oregon for *Bend of the River* (1952), shot against the spectacular snow-covered backdrop of Mount Hood and other northeastern Oregon sites. Considered the star's most physically demanding film, that production required the bulldozing of mountain paths and the use of steel cables to prevent wagons from sliding off cliffs.

Arthur Kennedy and Jimmy Stewart at Mount Hood for Bend of the River *(1952).*

Not surprisingly, Oregon was also the setting for Cavalry and other films about frontier expansion and Indian wars. *The Great Sioux Uprising* (1953) was reportedly shot in Pendleton and Portland, with local Native Americans cast as Sioux for that shoot. Kirk Douglas shot his *The Indian Fighter* (1955), for which he was both star and producer, in Bend, Oregon, which also later hosted *Oregon Passage* (1958). Jeff Chandler's *Pillars of the Sky* (1956) was shot in northeastern Oregon in the LeGrande and Wallowa areas. *Tonka* (1958), the Disney production starring Sal Mineo and Philip Carey, utilized magnificent sites in the northern and central parts of the state. *Tonka*'s version of the Battle of Little Big Horn was shot on the Warm Springs reservation and on an Indian village set constructed for the film along the Deschutes River. Reportedly, portions of the Kirk Douglas-Robert Mitchum-Richard Widmark starrer, *The Way West* (1967), were also shot in Oregon. Scenes for *Mackenna's Gold* (1969) were shot in the Medford area, as well as at Utah and Arizona locales.

The scenery of Washington state enhanced a number of westerns and other outdoor pictures but rough weather at times lengthened shooting schedules on those productions. A company of eighty left Hollywood in January 1934 to begin filming *The Call of the Wild* (1935), starring Clark Gable and Loretta Young, at Mount Baker. Blizzards soon forced their return to California and filming did not resume at Mount Baker until mid-February. A cameraman suffered a heart attack during filming, apparently a consequence of Mount Baker's high altitude.

Two 1937 productions took no such chances. Harry Sherman's company filmed *The Barrier* for Paramount release in July at Mount Baker and Mount Ranier, with publicity boasting that the final film included no process shots. George Brent's *God's Country and the Woman*, filmed at Longview, was also a summer production.

Since the 1930s, few outdoor productions have gone to Washington. In the summer of 1954, John Wayne's production company shot portions of *Track of the Cat*, a fine little film about the hunt for a deadly mountain lion, at Mount Ranier. And Gary Cooper's *The Hanging Tree* (1959) was filmed in the Yakima area. In more recent years, however, movie companies motivated by a desire for "new" scenery and cheaper production costs have been more likely to choose Canada as a filming site. Silent titles shot there included Hoot Gibson's *The Calgary Stampede* (1925). At least one source says that part of Buck Jones'

The Far Country (1955).

sound title *McKenna of the Mounted* (1932) was filmed in British Columbia but much of that title was filmed at Lake Hemet, southeast of Los Angeles. Charles Starrett's *Undercover Men* (1934) reportedly was filmed at Brampton, west of Toronto, while his *Secret Patrol* and *Stampede*, two 1936 productions released by Columbia, were shot at Victoria, in British Columbia. Eagle-Lion's *Northwest Stampede* (1948) was one of the first titles to feature the Banff National Park and Lake Louise, followed the next year by Randolph Scott's *Canadian Pacific* (1949), although the latter title relied unduly on process shots and sound stage "exteriors."

Over the years, films have been set in various Canadian locales. *McCabe and Mrs. Miller* (1971), for example, was filmed in Vancouver. But movie crews generally have preferred Alberta and British Columbia sites in the vicinity of Calgary. *Bronco Buster* (1952) included rugged shots taken at the Calgary Stampede rodeo. Marilyn Monroe's *River of No Return* (1954) featured the Jasper and Banff national parks, as well as scenes shot on the Bow and Snake rivers. Locales for Jimmy Stewart's *The Far Country* (1955) included the Columbia ice fields and Anthabasca Glacier in the Jasper National Park. *Saskatchewan* (1954), starring Alan Ladd, was also filmed at Banff. Years later, Joel McCrea went to Banff for his fine little film *Mustang Country* (1976).

Alan Ladd's Saskatchewan (1954) also benefitted from Canadian locales.

One Calgary area attraction for film companies has been the CL Western Studio and Backlot, located only a few miles west of Calgary. First used in films in 1970, when parts of Dustin Hoffman's *Little Big Man* were shot there, the CL boasts not only 2,000 acres of rugged landscape, but more than thirty buildings, nineteen of which have finished interiors for filming. Included in the facility are a complete town, a sod hut, a trapper's cabin, an abandoned mine, an abandoned ranch and a circa 1900 farm with a barn, corrals, windmill and outbuildings.

The CL has hosted fashion photo and commercial shoots as well as feature and TV productions. Theatrical and TV movies shot there include *Shanghai Knights* (2002) and *Shanghai Noon* (1999), starring Jackie Chan and Owen Wilson, the TV movie versions of "Monte Walsh" (2002), with Tom Selleck, and "High Noon" (2000), starring Tom Skerritt, as well as Selleck's "Crossfire Trail" (1999).

In fact, several of the best-received theatrical and television westerns of the past decade and a half were partly filmed in Alberta. Clint Eastwood's *Unforgiven* (1992) was shot, for example, outside Calgary, Longview and Drumheller. And the 2005 mini-series "Into the West" featured the Hoodoo rock formations near Drumheller, east of Calgary, as well as Santa Fe sites.

Chapter 6

Trails South

Although western film crews most frequently ventured north and west for exterior shoots, a variety of locales were also available south and southeast of Los Angeles. On occasion, production units even went south of the border, especially to Durango, Mexico.

San Bernardino Mountains

Mountie films and other titles with a forest setting were shot at many locations. Rex Allen's *Redwood Forest Trail* (1950) was filmed, for example, at Barley Flats along the Angeles Crest highway north of Pasadena. Most western and serial producers, however, headed southeast of L.A. three or four hours to Big Bear Lake, originally developed in 1884 from Bear Creek, a tributary of the Santa Ana River. At an elevation of more than 6,000 feet, the lake itself was perfect for motorboat chases in Republic's *King of the Royal Mounted* (1940) and *King of the Mounties* (1942), as well as such later imitations as *King of the Forest Rangers* (1946), *Dangers of the Canadian Mounted* (1948) and *Canadian Mounties vs. Atomic Invaders* (1954). Adjacent hills, woodlands, grassy plains and chase roads played host to those and other cliffhangers, including Jock Mahoney's *Gunfighters of the Northwest* (1954), as well as many westerns and outdoor releases going back to silent days, when DeMille's *Call of the North* (1914) was shot there. Producers of "The F.B.I.," "Bonanza" and other TV series also made regular use of the site.

In the early days, movie crews generally lodged at the Highlander Hotel or the Navaho. But several stars, including Hoot Gibson, built plush cabins in the area. Big Bear's dam, constructed in 1911 to replace a smaller original dam, apparently appeared only in a chapter ending for *King of the Royal Mounted*. But nearby Cedar Lake, with its dam (built in 1914), mill house, water wheel and cabins, was a familiar western, serial and TV setting. Constructed initially for Paramount's Technicolor epic *Trail of the Lonesome Pine* (1936) and utilized in such later A-features as John Wayne's *Shepherd of the Hills* (1941), Cedar Lake's sets also starred in many B-films and TV shows.

In *North of the Great Divide* (1950), Roy Rogers battled fur thieves on Cedar Lake and chased them across the plains area east of Big Bear Lake. Cedar Lake cabins served as the hideout for Christmas tree rustlers in *Trail of Robin Hood* (1950). In the climax to that final Rogers color starrer, Roy chased heavy Cliff Young across the dam, then watched him lose his footing and fall from the water wheel to his well-

Allan Lane at Big Bear Lake for King of the Royal Mounted (1940).

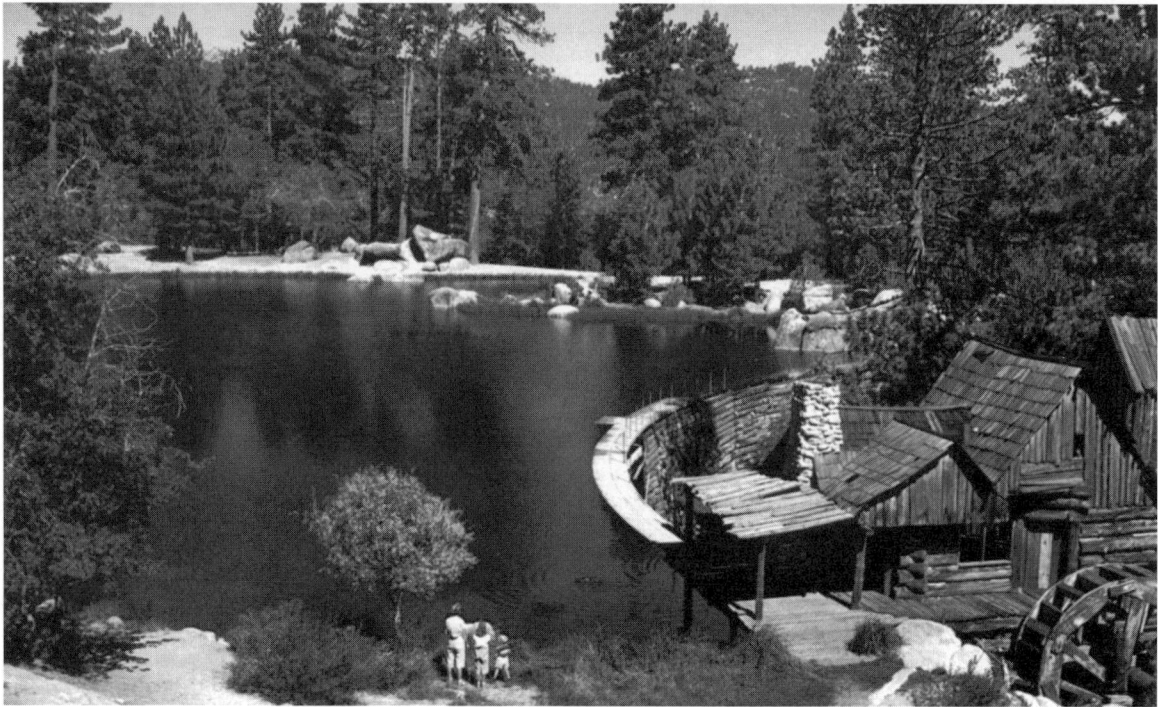

The Cedar Lake dam, house and water wheel in an historic post card.

deserved demise.

Gene Autry saw post-war service at Cedar Lake in *Riders of the Whistling Pines* (1949), *Blue Canadian Rockies* (1952) and *Gene Autry and the Mounties* (1951). Russell Hayden was there in *Riders of the Northwest Mounted* (1943), Hoppy in *Lumberjack* (1944) and *Riders of the Timberline* (1941), while Rex Allen overcame a heavy on the lake (and in the underwater tank on the Republic lot) for *Silver City Bonanza* (1951). Kirby Grant's "Chinook" series, including such titles as *Yukon Vengeance* (1954) and *Yukon Gold* (1952), was filmed almost entirely on the lake and in the surrounding hills, as were many episodes of such TV series as "Wild Bill Hickok."

Kirby Grant and "Chinook" on Cedar Lake.

In fact, with all the movie action that took place there, visitors are surprised to learn that Cedar Lake is not much larger than a stock pond and any celluloid trip on that waterway was over almost before it started! It is truly a beautiful spot, so scenic, in fact, that Roy Rogers reportedly once considered buying it. The religious organization that beat the "King of the Cowboys" to the checkbook tore down the dangerously dilapidated mill house and water wheel in the 1980s but replaced it with a reasonable facsimile.

Another favorite Big Bear filming site was the Shay Ranch, located in a clearing with scattered trees

The Shay Ranch cabin set.

east of Big Bear Lake. Shay Ranch shooting sites included its main house, torn down in the 1970s, and a studio-constructed cabin set. First used in *Brigham Young*, the cabin was seen briefly in Gene's *Blue Montana Skies* (1939). It also served as the ranch luscious June Vincent and her henchman Fred Graham schemed to steal from Mary Ellen Kay and Slim Pickens in Rex Allen's outstanding *Colorado Sundown* (1952). Barns at the I. S. Ranch in Big Bear Lake Village appeared in *Trail of the Lonesome Pine* and other titles, too.

Other San Bernardino locations also appeared in films. Much of Roy Rogers' *Don't Fence Me In* (1945) was shot at Lake Arrowhead and Kermit Maynard's outstanding series of Mountie and straight western features used Crestline, including sets constructed there years before for a title featuring silent star Leo Maloney.

The I. S. Ranch barn.

*The Crestline western street, which dated back to silent days, may also have used
in the Kermit Maynard Mountie films.*

The area continues to attract commercial, feature and TV producers even today. But we shall always remember the Big Bear area best as the scenic backdrop for western and Mountie films.

Directions: From Victorville, take Highway 18 to Big Bear. From Redlands, situated along I-10 southeast of L.A., take Highway 330.

The Garner Ranch

Nestled in the beautiful Garner Valley across the San Jacinto mountains from Palm Springs is the Garner Cattle Ranch, site for the filming of many B, A and TV westerns. First developed in the 1860s by California pioneer Charles Thomas, the ranch was purchased in 1905 by Robert F. Garner Sr. Over the years, it would pass first to Robert F. Jr., then to his son Jack.

After World War II, the Garner Ranch encompassed almost ten thousand acres and even by the 1990s was still running nearly a thousand head of cattle. The ranch featured a white main house with broad veranda as well as a modern, upscale home constructed after the main filming days), a foreman's house off the left side of the main house, assorted barns and corrals, and huge expanses of pasture land bordered by pine trees

Garner Ranch main house in the filming days.

The Garner Ranch in Melody Trail *(1935). Strangely, the mailbox still carries the Thomas name, although the ranch had passed to the Garner family many years earlier.*

*Lake Hemet, across from the Garner Ranch, appeared in the
background of this scene.*

and hills scattered with rock formations. A small movie set also remained on the ranch for years, serving
as a ranch house, bunkhouse, even as a school (in Hoppy's *The Frontiersman*, 1938).

Lake Hemet, across from the ranch entrance, was also used in films, such as Gene Autry's *Gold Mine
in the Sky* (1938) and the Three Mesquiteers entry *Heart of the Rockies* (1937). Those titles featured a small
cabin situated near the lake. Another, more substantial house, also located by the lake, appeared in several
of Tim Holt's post-war films, among other titles.

The Garner spread was featured in many B-westerns, including such cheapies as Bob Steele's
Tombstone Terror (1935) and Tex Ritter's *Arizona Days* (1937). The ranch was displayed most
prominently perhaps in Gene Autry's *Colorado Sunset* (1939), *Springtime in the Rockies* (1937) and *Guns
and Guitars* (1936), as well as in several Hoppys (e.g., *Santa Fe Marshal*, 1940) and post-war Holts, most
notably *Brothers in the Saddle* (1949). In fact, the climactic fight between Tim and heavy Steve Brodie in
the latter film took place in the hills immediately behind the main house.

Several Audie Murphy titles, including *The Kid from Texas* (1950), were also filmed there, as well as
episodes of "Bonanza" and "Rawhide." Early episodes of the popular kids' TV series "Fury" were also shot
there. But the Garner Ranch, posing as the series' Broken Wheel Ranch, was burned to the ground in the

plotline to "Scorched Earth," its fifth episode, after which the "Fury" production company and its stars began making exclusive–and decidedly more economical–use of a ranch set constructed for the series on the upper portion of the Iverson Ranch outside Chatsworth. In more recent years, the Garner spread also provided the backdrop for television commercials.

Jack Garner, who often rode as an extra in cattle-drive scenes filmed on the ranch in order to protect his father's stock from the Hollywood cowboys, had fond memories of those days. Bill (Hopalong Cassidy) Boyd, with whom he became friends in later days, was deathly afraid of horses, he recalled. Garner and his mischievous friends filled their blank pistols with paper wads to spook the star's steed. "It scared the sh–out of Hoppy," he said. The eccentric Audie Murphy, Garner remembered, "didn't say much. He just sat behind a rock and fired his gun." Tim Holt's sidekick Richard "Chito" Martin, who first directed me to the ranch, remained a good friend of the Garner family until his death.

Directions: From L.A., take I-10 toward Palm Springs to Banning, Highway 243 across the mountains and through Idylwild to Mountain Center, and left on Highway 74 for several miles to Lake Hemet. The ranch entrance is on the left just beyond the Lake Hemet Market.

Keen Camp

Gene Autry's terrific *Colorado Sunset* (1939) was filmed in part at the Garner Ranch. But an item in one of the trade papers of the period listed a "Keen Camp" as the Autry filming site. When I asked Garner Ranch owner Jack Garner about the discrepancy, he informed me with a smile that Keen Camp was an area "cat house," then explained that the former hunting and fishing camp located several miles from his ranch had become a haven for abandoned animals. In its day, though, the camp often played host to film companies.

In 1905, the camp's original owners John and Mary Keen moved their resort from nearby Strawberry Valley to a meadow a mile east of what is now the village of Mountain Center, at the base of the San Jacinto mountains. In 1911, the Keens sold the camp to Percy and Anita Walker. Following Percy Walker's drowning in Lake Hemet, Anita married Robert Elliott in 1919 and built Keen Camp's main attraction, the Tahquitz Lodge, named for the surrounding mountains.

A popular hostelry until destroyed by fire in 1943, the camp featured not only the lodge, but the Keen Camp store, a school, other buildings and a beautiful meadow bordered by pines, scattered rock formations and mountains. Gene Autry's *Gold Mine in the Sky* (1938) gave prominent display to the lodge and surrounding countryside. Some scenes from Gene's *Springtime in the Rockies* (1937), among them a quick distant shot of the school doubling as a fine ranch house, were shot in the area. The camp's other buildings were featured in several Republic rustics, including *Grand Ole Opry* (1940), *Jeepers Creepers* (1939) with Roy Rogers, and *Citadel of Crime* (1941), in shots mixed with scenes filmed on the Log Cabin or Brazos Street section of the Republic back lot, which was originally built for Richard Dix's *Man of Conquest* (1939). In opening scenes for the Weaver family's *Grand Ole Opry*, for example, the Keen Camp store served as the local school house.

The camp was perhaps given most extensive display, however, in Tex Ritter's *Take Me Back to Oklahoma*. That 1940 Monogram oater, probably the best from Tex's Grand National/Monogram days,

Tahquitz Lodge.

The Keen Camp Store.

featured Garner Ranch buildings and meadowland. But Keen Camp's store, the front porch of the Tahquitz Lodge, other buildings and countryside were also prominently displayed.

The San Jacinto mountains regularly played host to the major movie companies. A local history notes, for example, that Mary Pickford, Katharine Hepburn, Paulette Goddard and other stars often stayed at the Idyllwild Inn during filming there. But we remember the area best as host to western stars.

Pioneertown

The Jack Ingram Ranch outside L. A. was not the only B-western and serial site to have its beginnings in the ambitions of a movie heavy. Dick Curtis spent most of his career menacing the likes of Charles Starrett. But like Ingram, Curtis also attempted to supplement his meager movie earnings with real estate investments.

In the mid-1940s, Curtis visited Yucca Valley in California's high desert, a 4,500-foot elevation 30 miles northeast of Palm Springs and a two and a half hour drive southeast from L.A. Convinced the location would make an excellent site for homes, resorts and dude ranches of the Palm Springs variety, as well as an ideal motion picture filming site, Curtis soon corralled 17 investors, including Roy Rogers, the Sons of the Pioneers singing group, Russell Hayden, B-western directors Frank McDonald and Tommy Carr, badman Terry Frost and comedian Bud Abbott. In 1946, each invested $500 in the project, formed a corporation, established an office on Ventura Blvd. in Studio City and acquired 32,000 acres, encompassing the entire valley.

Curtis soon left the venture, with Russell Hayden replacing him as corporation president. Several restaurants and other businesses, configured so that they could double as the buildings on a western street, were constructed and dubbed "Pioneertown," after the songsters–although investors had initially considered calling the development "Rogersville" in honor of "The King of the Cowboys."

A 1950 appraisal of the properties showed a value in excess of $1.5 million. But there was one major problem–a water supply entirely inadequate for a desert vacation paradise.

For a time, it appeared that the venture would be a complete failure. Then, Philip N. Krasne, a Nebraska-born lawyer turned low-budget movie producer, spent a weekend in Pioneertown. Krasne was producing "Cisco Kid" westerns for United Artists and he and his star, Duncan Renaldo, scouted the area, finding a variety of scenic settings.

Krasne arranged for production of future series entries in and around Pioneertown. He also built, on the town's "Mane Street," as it was called, a 60 x 100-foot sound stage that later posed as a stable in movies and TV episodes.

By the end of 1949, four Cisco Kid titles and Gene Autry's *Cowboy and the Indians* had been filmed there. That same year, Columbia began location shooting for the studio's latest serial, *Cody of the Pony Express*, starring Jock Mahoney and former child actor Dickie Moore in the title role. As usual with Sam Katzman's Columbia serial productions, the budget was tight. For a fort scene, for example, only an entrance gate was shown, with Lone Pine's rustic motel serving as the fort's headquarters. But the area's beautiful landscape was effectively displayed.

Production also began on additional Cisco Kid and Autry titles, while independent producer Niven Busch scouted the area for a movie featuring his actress wife, Teresa Wright. Wright's *The Capture* (1950) and the exciting Barbara Stanwyck thriller *Jeopardy* (1953), both directed by John Sturges, were filmed

A wide shot of Pioneertown in 2007.

The Red Dog Saloon, a Pioneertown landmark seen in many western titles.

there.

But the Pioneertown landscape, with its arid rolling hills, sparse vegetation and distinctive rock formations resembling huge mounds of giant pebbles, was best suited for westerns. The dirt road (now paved) running by the town made an excellent insert stretch for chases. Although far wider than the typical western street set, "Mane Street," with its "Red Dog Saloon" and other buildings, had the reel-authentic look of a dusty trail town–even if hitching posts, Autry sidekick Pat Buttram later explained, were sometimes placed in the center of the street to minimize just how wide it was.

Pioneertown became a frequent television location, especially for such series as "The Cisco Kid" and

Veteran heavy and stuntman George DeNormand ambushes Duncan (The Cisco Kid) Renaldo on the Pioneertown street in Satan's Cradle *(1949).*

Gene Autry's various Flying-A productions, including "Range Rider," "Annie Oakley," "Buffalo Bill, Jr." and Gene's own show. In fact, Autry spent so much time in Pioneertown that his room at the Spartan local motel–dubbed "Club 9"–became a favorite after-hours watering hole for actors and crew.

Russell Hayden even settled there. The original corporation eventually lost the property to the finance company but Hayden was able to purchase acreage for a ranch across the road from the town. He and wife Mousie built their own modest sets and shot his "Judge Roy Bean" TV series there (although episodes of "26 Men," another Hayden-produced series, were filmed at the Cudia City movie facilities in Phoenix).

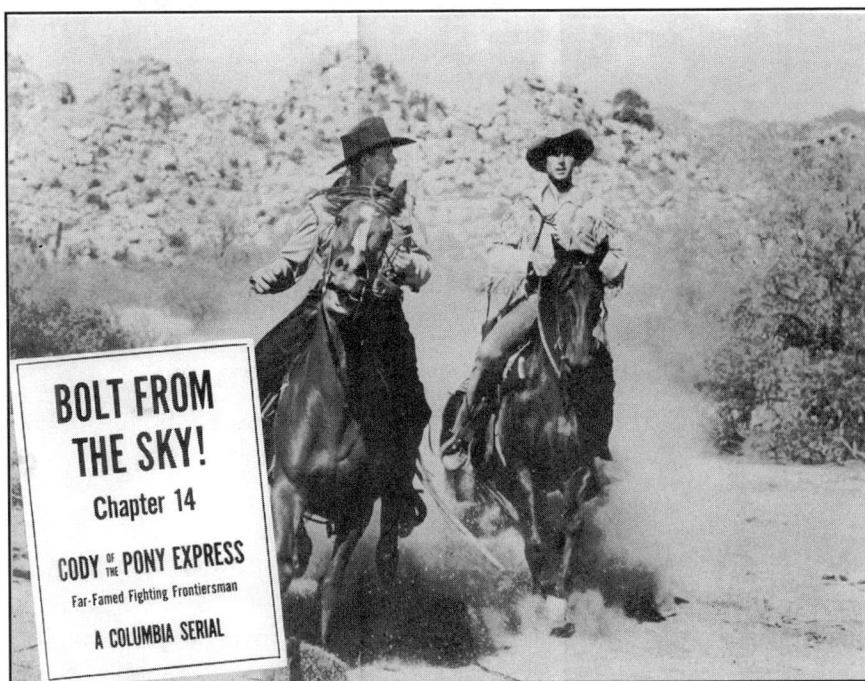

Dickie Moore and Jock Mahoney in the Pioneertown rocks.

After the 1956 auto accident death of his daughter Sandra (from his previous marriage to actress Jan Clayton), Hayden and Mousie moved to Arizona. But they returned to Pioneertown in 1966. At his death in 1981, they were living in the building that had served as Judge Roy Bean's general store and court in that TV series, amidst the ramshackle sets that comprised the Hayden Ranch and Western Museum. His widow continued to live there until her death in 1997. Most of Hayden's memorabilia, including props, guns and scripts were sold to either the Gene Autry museum in Griffith Park or to collector Boyd Magers. But area residents continue to promote Pioneertown's film heritage.

Directions: To get to the area, used now mainly for commercial filming, take I-10 southeast from L.A. to Highway 62, Highway 62 left (northeast) to Yucca Valley, left at the sign onto the road to Pioneertown, which is about nine miles up the road on the right.

The Coachella Valley

For years, I wondered where desert scenes were filmed for *Riders of the Whistling Skull* (1937), one of my favorite Three Mesquiteers titles. The opening credits for that film were superimposed over a shot of Red Rock Canyon, situated along Highway 14, a hundred miles northeast of L.A. I initially assumed that desert scenes for *Riders of the Whistling Skull* were also shot in that vicinity but was unable to locate the specific sites.

No wonder! I was just a mite off-course—more than a couple hundred miles, in fact—as I learned when western film researcher Richard Smith alerted me to a vintage trade paper item indicating that *Riders* heavy Roger Williams was then at work on that title near Indio in the Coachella Valley, southeast of Palm Springs and about a three-hour drive from L.A.

On my next trip to California, I found the *Riders* filming sites along Box Canyon Road near the village of Mecca, a few miles southeast of Indio. But the desert, cliffs and hills of the Mecca area were not the only

This scene from Riders of the Whistling Skull (1937) *mixed movie magic with desert landscape.*

attractions for film companies. Mecca and neighboring communities also host the Salton Sea, a huge inland expanse of high saline content that had been a dry lake until the waters of the Colorado River basin flooded 350,000 acres (some of which has since been reclaimed) early in the century, making this inland site, ironically enough, an excellent locale for sea epics.

By mid-morning, the summer heat along Box Canyon Road reaches 120 degrees.

Extending more than forty miles along the eastern edge of the valley in a band averaging five miles in width, we also find the Imperial Sand Dunes (Mecca is in Imperial County), host to such modern A-titles as *Star Wars* (1977), *Stargate* (1977), *Patriot Games* (1992) and *Dune* (1984), among others.

Veteran director Earl Bellamy remembered working on *Sahara* (1943) and *Ten Tall Men* (1951) in the Imperial dunes. He also noted, however, that the Columbia cliffhanger *The Desert Hawk* (1944), starring Gilbert Roland, had used dunes northeast of San Diego rather than those near Mecca.

The Imperial County Film Commission continues to attract production crews to the Mecca area for feature, TV and commercial shoots. Nor was *Riders of the Whistling Skull* the only western shot there in the golden era. *The Professionals* (1966) with Burt Lancaster was filmed partly in the valley, as was the exciting cattle stampede for Jimmy Stewart's *The Rare Breed*, another 1966 release. During filming of the Stewart title, according to articles in the local press, ace stuntman Hal Needham and two stuntwomen suffered minor injuries in a scripted Box Canyon buckboard crash gone awry.

The extreme summer heat of the Coachella Valley must be a continuing concern for moviemakers. A 1966 article from a local newspaper indicated that film crews for both *The Rare Breed* and *The Professionals* praised filming conditions in the area. A spokesman for the latter company even noted it lost no filming days there because of the weather, in contrast to the crew's experience with extreme heat and sandstorms in Death Valley, and bitter cold and snow in Nevada's Valley of Fire, near Las Vegas, where portions of the film were also shot.

But the article also mentioned that *The Professionals* company had arrived shortly after Christmas and departed at the end of January. I strongly recommend that time of year for any location buff's visit also. *Riders of the Whistling Skull* began filming on Halloween, 1936–an appropriate date given that title's spooky theme, but one more likely dictated by the temperate fall climate in the Mecca area! When we were there in August one year, civil engineers working in the area warned us to get an early start the next morning; the heat, they said, would be unbearable by mid-morning. They were right!

Directions: To reach the area, take I-10 southeast from L.A. to Indio and Highway 111 to Mecca. Box

The Professionals (1966).

Canyon Road, where most filming was done, runs east from Mecca and other filming sites cover a large area south of Mecca, bordered by Highway 86 on the west, Highway 78 to the south and mountains to the east.

Durango, Mexico

Production companies venturing south from L. A. did not always stop at the U. S. border. Mexico has long been a favorite filming site of Hollywood movie makers. In his exhaustive list of titles shot there, Italian location expert Carlo Gaberscek includes, among many other films, Mickey Rooney's *My Outlaw Brother* (1951), shot in and around Mexico City; many titles shot in Cuernavaca, among them *Vera Cruz* (1954), starring Gary Cooper and Burt Lancaster, *Treasure of Pancho Villa* (1955), starring Rory Calhoun and Gilbert Roland, and Jock Mahoney's *Last of the Fast Guns* (1958); Clint Eastwood's *Two Mules for Sister Sara* (1969), shot at Morelos; the Paul Newman-Robert Redford mega-hit *Butch Cassidy and the Sundance Kid* (1969), shot partly at Taxco; and Sam Peckinpah's incredibly bloody *The Wild Bunch* (1968), filmed at several Mexican sites.

But Durango, in the Mexican interior, was the locale most closely associated with western titles. Long known as "La Tierra del Cine," the Land of the Cinema, the area has hosted over 140 productions. The remains of the many sets constructed for shoots there still dot the countryside. And movie-savvy visitors immediately recognize the area's varied landscape of desert, lush Sierra Madre mountains, cool streams shaded by overhanging trees, waterfalls and impressive buttes dominated by giant rock outcroppings that closely resemble organ pipes or castle turrets, as the setting for many of their favorite films.

The story of Durango's role as a major western filming location hardly had an auspicious beginning. In the summer of 1954, producer Leonard Goldstein's Panoramic Productions, an arm of Twentieth Century-Fox, shot *White Feather* there. A routine Cavalry epic starring Robert Wagner, Debra Paget and Jeffrey Hunter, it quickly disappeared from theater marquees after its release in February 1955.

In May, Goldstein released *Robber's Roost* (1955), yet another retelling of the Zane Grey epic, which he and his twin brother Robert had made in Durango through their own production company for United Artists release. Although *Robber's Roost* starred the reliable George Montgomery and always interesting Richard Boone, it too was a routine oater. But that title, like *White Feather*, at least featured some spectacular scenery not often seen in low-budget western programmers.

Inevitably, such "runaway" productions produced howls of protest in the United States. In the summer of 1955, independent producer Albert Gannaway brought another movie crew to Mexico. This time, mountains south of Mexico City, which boasted a frontier fort set built for Victor Mature's *The Last Frontier* (1955) and later seen in Randolph Scott's *Seventh Cavalry* (1956), doubled for Kentucky in *Daniel Boone, Trail Blazer* (1956), with Bruce Bennett–who was also a member of the *Robber's Roost* cast–in the title role.

Randolph Scott's Seventh Cavalry (1956) *was shot not in Canada or the U. S. northwest, but near Mexico City.*

Incensed that a film about one of the U.S.'s early pioneer heroes would be made in a foreign country, a Kentucky congressman attempted to organize a boycott of this latest venture in runaway productions, which Gannaway released through Republic Pictures. The AFL-CIO also launched a boycott as a means of teaching "a lesson to any American employer who ran away to a foreign country [and thereby] escaped paying American union wage rates to American workmen." Gannaway responded that inclement weather prevented shooting in Kentucky and also claimed that some of the film's financing had originated in Mexico. According to a April 16, 1956, *Los Angeles Times* report, the boycott was ultimately lifted when the producer agreed to avoid runaway productions in the future.

In those days of skyrocketing Hollywood budgets, however, labor union complaints were no match for the significantly cheaper production costs luring movie makers to foreign locales. As noted above, Randolph Scott's *Seventh Cavalry* (1956) used the fort set constructed for *The Last Frontier*. And Durango also became a primary beneficiary of Hollywood's growing penchant for foreign locations, with Dana Andrew's *Comanche* (1956), another independent released through United Artists, one of the earlier titles shot there following *White Feather*.

Soon, major stars and big-budget features were also shooting in the Durango area. Much of Burt Lancaster's *The Unforgiven* (1960) was shot there, as well as Gable's *The Tall Men* (1955), Chuck Connors' turn as a blue-eyed *Geronimo* (1962), Chuck Heston's *Major Dundee* (1965), the suspenseful Robert Mitchum-Dean Martin thriller *Five Card Stud* (1965), Glenn Ford's *Day of the Evil Gun* (1968), Richard Harris' *A Man Called Horse* (1970), and Sidney Poitier's *Buck and the Preacher* (1972).

But John Wayne was to be the western star most closely identified with Durango. Portions of the Duke's *Hondo* (1953) were shot just below the Texas border. Beginning in 1965, however, Wayne made at least portions of seven features in Durango–*The Sons of Katie Elder* (1965), *The War Wagon* (1967), *The Undefeated* (1969), *Chisum* (1970), *Big Jake* (1971), *The Train Robbers* (1973) and *Cahill, U.S. Marshal* (1973).

When Wayne began shooting *The Sons of Katie Elder* in January 1965, Durango was a remote, primitive mountain village, a town, his daughter Aissa later recalled, of "dirt streets with no names, one horseshoe-shaped motel, and one hole in the wall that everyone called a diner." Aissa took one look at her temporary new home and "began counting the days" until she could leave. The Duke's wife Pilar was equally unimpressed. "All the things urban men and women take for granted were unheard of luxuries in that community. . . . [It] seemed to have been caught in a time warp." Asked about his memories of Durango, stuntman Neil Summers remembered only the extreme poverty of the area, the filth, the starving dogs wandering about the village, then sneered, "You don't want to go there."

John Wayne's first Durango filming experience was physically exhausting as well. Only four months earlier, he had undergone surgery for lung cancer and Durango's 6200-foot altitude required him to take oxygen much of the time. Action scenes, especially a plunge into the icy Rio Chico river for one strenuous sequence, were extremely taxing–leaving him gasping for breath and spitting up phlegm for most of the shoot.

But the Duke loved Durango's magnificent landscape as much as he admired Mexican women. He realized, too, that movie audiences were no longer satisfied with routine westerns filmed against familiar backdrops; they wanted new, exotic locales. Most important, Mexico offered an abundance of cheap labor and escape from the union wages required in the U.S. film industry. John Wayne may have been a super-patriot. But his Batjac productions shot most of the films he made in Durango and he appreciated the financial advantages of filming south of the border. Somewhat astonishingly, he had even planned to make his beloved *The Alamo* (1960) in Panama or South America, dropping his plans only after Texans complained that such a move would be a gross affront to the heroes of the Alamo.

However stressful and tiring his work schedule, the Duke also enjoyed the company of cast and crew after hours. Andrew McLaglen, who directed most of his Durango titles, said, "Both Wayne and I love Durango. People say to us, 'Why are you going to that horrible hole?' But there are some beautiful houses where we always live when we go there. In the evenings we eat something of a specialty out there which is a little suckling goat roasted over a spit that they butterfly, and with it you drink a little tequila to keep you relaxed."

Wayne and Dean Martin certainly knew how to relax. They had remained friends since working together at Old Tucson on *Rio Bravo* (1959). Late one night during shooting for *The Sons of Katie Elder*, Aissa Wayne was awakened by a loud racket outside her hotel room. "Down below in the dirt street, my father and Dean Martin marched arm-in-arm, singing their booze-soaked lungs out." Despite his homophobic reputation, Wayne also became good friends with Rock Hudson during filming of *The Undefeated* (1969) in Durango and outside Baton Rouge, Louisiana. The Duke thought Hudson's private life was his own and enjoyed having another avid chess and bridge player on the set.

Wayne won an Oscar for *True Grit* (1969), filmed mainly in Colorado, and his last film, *The Shootist*, shot at Carson City, Nevada, also garnered considerable acclaim. For the most part, though, his Durango titles were mediocre at best. "By the time we were doing those films," Ben Johnson said, "it was all pretty much the same film. . . . I think if there'd been no 'True Grit,' there might not have been such a thing as a John Wayne western anymore– . . . they weren't good pictures." Rock Hudson was grateful for the role Wayne gave him in *The Undefeated*. "The guy is an angel," he later said of the Duke. "He saved my life back then when no other filmmaker wanted to know me." But Hudson dismissed *The Undefeated* as "crap."

Wayne was determined, however, to keep making old-fashioned westerns and using Durango as a film site. In 1972, his production company even built a western street set on property purchased from farmer Antonio Lozoya in the village of Chupaderos, along Highway 45, a few miles north of Durango. Years later, a woman living in a house behind the set's barbershop facade still vividly recalled seeing Wayne there for the first time thirty years earlier, when he stepped out of his trailer to begin shooting a scene. "He was so tall, and so handsome, and so nice to all of us," she remembered. Realizing immediately that the Duke was *The Star*, she was "awestruck" when the smiling film icon walked over to talk with the children and give them candy.

Nor was Chupaderos the site of the only Durango western set. Nearer to town on Highway 45 was Villa del Oeste, which was originally constructed as a western street set but later occupied by squatters until it eventually became an actual village. Between Chupaderos and Villa del Oeste, another collection of decaying western sets still stands as well.

A number of non-western sets remain also. For *Fat Man and Little Boy*, the 1989 Paul Newman film about development of the atomic bomb, the producers built a large set to represent Los Alamos, New Mexico. Still intact from that set, located 29 km south of Durango on the road to La Flor, are several structures, including wooden military barracks and a water tower.

But Durango's natural wonders were the most impressive feature of films shot there. The organ pipe-shaped buttes of the Los Organos Valley enhanced *Geronimo*, *The Undefeated*, *The War Wagon* and *Cattle Annie and Little Britches* (1981), among other titles. And the El Saltito waterfalls, some 20 miles south of Durango along Highway 45, appeared in such films as *Major Dundee* and Burt Lancaster's *Lawman* (1971).

Over the years, however, the steady decline in western film production has made movie crews an

The organ pipe-shaped buttes of the Los Organos Valley provided a dramatic backdrop for action scenes in John Wayne's The War Wagon (1967).

increasingly rare sight in Durango. Bill Witney directed the low-budget *Showdown at Eagle Gap* (1982) there with a largely Mexican cast and crew. Gregory Peck and Jane Fonda were there for *Old Gringo* (1989). The John Candy spoof *Wagons East* (1994) also utilized Durango's scenery. But *Blueberry*, a 2004 title that included U.S. actors (e.g., Ernest Borgnine) in its cast was, alas, a French production. And when HBO shot a 2003 Antonio Banderas movie about Mexican revolutionary hero Pancho Villa, the producers chose filming sites elsewhere in Mexico, even though Villa was born in Durango state. "When I heard they were making a movie about Villa in Guanajuato," grumbled the current owner of John Wayne's Chupaderos western set, "I wanted to cut my throat." Producers of other recent American titles, including *Frida* (2002), have also gone elsewhere in Mexico for filming, as have Mexican directors themselves. Indeed, after no member of the Wayne family had visited the Duke's Chapudaros western set for 20 years, a local court awarded ownership to the original owner of the property.

Durango leaders are doing their best to attract movie makers and film fans to the area. Road maps prominently display the location of "Movie Sets" and western fans can still enjoy the scenic beauty of Durango filming sites, as well as the decaying remains of familiar sets. They can also visit the Campo Mexico Motel, where the Duke always stayed in Suite 22A, its only two-story room; drink tequila in the hotel bar, just as the Duke and other actors did every evening during shoots; peruse the entire wall of autographed star photographs in the lobby; and check out the stars' handprints and bootprints (as well as Wayne's famous fist) embedded in cement tablets that still stand in the grass next to a line of parking places. Best of all, they can remember the favorite movies of their past, when heroes and heavies rode over the Durango countryside.

Chapter 7

Utah

Outside California, more western movies were filmed in southern Utah and along the Utah-Arizona border than in any other location. Of those locales, Monument Valley, Moab and Arches National Monument offered the most spectacular scenery. But Kanab, in southern Utah near the Arizona border, clearly deserves its reputation as the "Little Hollywood" of non-California western filming sites.

Kanab

Everyone agrees that Kanab, county seat of Kane County, owes its significant place in film history largely to the efforts of three men–Chauncey (Chaunce), Gronway and Whitney (Whit) Parry. Chaunce, the eldest of the Parry brothers, and Gronway first attracted outsiders to the area in 1916, when they began hauling tourists by bus from Cedar City to Bryce Canyon, Zion National Monument, the north rim of the Grand Canyon and other scenic wonders of the region.

Eventually, the Union Pacific took over the Parrys' tourist franchise but the brothers then turned to the ultimately more lucrative venture of bringing movie-makers to the area. Tom Mix reportedly starred in the first title, *Deadwood Coach* (1924), filmed at Kanab. According to local lore, Mix convinced the Parrys to induce other production crews to come there also.

Armed with many photos, including aerial shots, Chaunce Parry eventually went to Hollywood for meetings with studio executives, persuading them that he and his brothers could not only provide them splendid vistas and unusually varied terrain, but also livestock, wagons and other rolling stock, ample lodging, a large company of willing extras, even Paiute and Navajo Indians from nearby reservations.

Soon, movie crews were beating a path to Kanab. Portions of John Wayne's *The Big Trail* (1930) are said to have been filmed there, although it is difficult to spot distinctive Kanab locales in that title. And while usually listed among early Kanab titles, Buster Crabbe's *Forlorn River* (1937) was shot entirely at Kernville, California. But MGM took a crew to Kanab and Zion for the Wallace Beery-Dennis O'Keefe entry *Bad Man of Brimstone* (1937). The same studio did some Kanab shooting for Robert Taylor's *Billy the Kid* (1941), although much of that film used Monument Valley and Sedona, among other locales, and the actors' scenes were mainly shot in front of a process screen rather than on location.

Earlier, Fox carried a crew to Kanab for George O'Brien's *Dude Ranger* (1934). And in the late thirties and early forties, Kanab played host to a number of other B-westerns, including Bob Steele's *Feud of the Range* (1939), for which Chaunce and Whit Parry, albeit with their nicknames misspelled, are listed in the credits as associate producers; Tim Holt's *Wagon Train* (1940) and early scenes for his *The Fargo Kid* (1940); Tex Ritter's *Westbound Stage* (1940) and *Roll, Wagons, Roll* (1940); Bill Elliott's outstanding chapterplays *The Great Adventures of Wild Bill Hickok* (1938) and *Overland with Kit Carson* (1939), even low-budget independent producer Denver Dixon's *Mormon Conquest* (1941).

Initially, movie companies came to the area by motor caravan. In 1942, World War II gas shortages obliged them to take their crews by train to Lund, Utah, then by truck and car the last hundred miles to Kanab. But wartime strictures hardly dampened Hollywood's enthusiasm for the area. Republic brought a crew to Kanab for John Wayne's *In Old Oklahoma* (a.k.a. *War of the Wildcats*) (1943) and Fox filmed exteriors there for Joel McCrea's *Buffalo Bill* (1944).

By that point, the community was well-equipped to handle the movie companies' needs. In 1930-31, the Parrys built Parry Lodge. About that same time, Guy Chamberlain, whose family later purchased Moqui Cavern, a filming site north of town, opened the Kanab Hotel. Other motor courts and private homes were also available for film crews. An abandoned gasoline station was converted into a casting office, complete with lists of available extras, stunt doubles and livestock.

When Chaunce Parry was killed in an automobile accident on Kanab's main street, Gronway and Whit continued as Hollywood's principal Kanab contacts. Gronway provided transportation and food for casts and crews, while Whit ran the lodge. At times, Gronway also supervised construction of replicas of period rolling stock, such as those used in Joel McCrea's *The Outriders* (1950). Fay Hamblin, whose father Walt played many minor parts in Kanab films, was largely responsible for acquiring livestock and other Kanab residents often appeared in films shot there.

During one of my visits, Kanab native Lee Mace recalled that his father Charles played one of the "Black Raiders" in *Overland with Kit Carson*, while his brother Wayne impersonated an Indian in the same title–and spent hours each evening painfully removing the dark "Indian" makeup he was obliged to endure on location. Dan Frost, town barber and local Mormon bishop, played bit parts. The nephew of the Kane County sheriff was stand-in for Roddy McDowell during filming of *Thunderhead, Son of Flicka* (1945). Guy Chamberlain's daughter Bonnie had a part in *Mormon Conquest*. Della Pugh, an accomplished horsewoman, was stand-in for Maureen O'Hara in *Buffalo Bill*. And Lee Mace doubled Wally Cassell in a wagon chase shot for Rod Cameron's *Oh! Susanna* (1951).

Jackie Hamblin Rife, another Kanab native, made her screen debut at age 6, playing a child scalped by Indians in *Drums Along the Mohawk* (1939), filmed largely at Duck Creek in the mountains northwest of Kanab. She went on to become an expert stunt double for the stars, regularly "eating dirt," as she put it, in Kanab productions. "I basically did anything that might cause an injury to the actresses," she once recalled. "They were too valuable to the studios to get hurt. That included riding horses, being in fights and being on run-away wagons!" For Rife, *Yellow Tomahawk* (1954), in which she doubled Peggy Castle, "was definitely the most fun to do. . . . There was never a dull moment. It was just an all-around good movie." It had become a tradition that when a movie was completed and the production company was leaving town, all those involved in the film would jump into the Parry Lodge pool. When *Yellow Tomahawk* wrapped, Peggy Castle was already dressed for an early departure, wearing a mink stole and high heels. "We all teased and taunted her," Rife said, "until she jumped in too. . . with all her clothes on."

The stunt woman had fond memories of all the actors who worked in Kanab–with the exception of Tony Curtis. "Oh, my, was he in love with himself."

Some Kanab residents even got involved in movie production. Not only were Chaunce and Whit Parry associate producers on Bob Steele's *Feud of the Range*, but a local outfit called Security National Pictures Corp. of Kanab was involved, according to 1939 newspaper reports, in the making of *Mormon Conquest*. In the late forties, moreover, state senator Lewis H. (Dude) Larsen formed the Kanab Motion Picture Corp. and produced a low-budget oater starring Ken (Festus) Curtis there. Originally entitled *Wild Horse Range*, it was released by Astor in 1949 as *Stallion Canyon*. Larsen was included in the cast.

Locally produced films were hardly money-makers. Guy Chamberlain reportedly lost his hotel in a movie investment gone sour. But as actors, stand-ins, stunt doubles, or providers of lodging, livestock and props, Kanab's populace reaped regular financial benefits from the movie companies. For Joel McCrea's *The Outriders* (1950), MGM brought in a company of 100 for a thirty-day shoot, but also hired 120 locals, including fifteen women, as extras. Robert Taylor's *Ride, Vaquero!* (1953) brought in a company of 75. Columbia Pictures not only imported a sizable Hollywood company and hired many locals for *Overland with Kit Carson*, but also imported two busloads of Navajo Indians. A buffalo herd supervised by the Arizona game department was brought in for the Kit Carson chapter play and *Buffalo Bill*, among other titles.

In 1943, by one estimate, Hollywood left $300,000 in the community; the next year, the Parry brothers alone netted $30,000 from their movie-related operations. By 1949, movie companies were spending an estimated $20,000 a day on Kanab shoots. Cowboys were getting $55 daily, citizen extras $35 and children $10.

Kanab's natural wonders, of course, were its major attraction. Much filming was done in area canyons, especially winding Kanab Canyon, a few miles north of town off Hwy 89, with its overhanging house rock

The Lone Ranger (Clayton Moore) and Tonto (Jay Silverheels) in
Kanab Canyon for their 1956 feature.

formations and other familiar settings. A small, unnamed slot canyon seen in Randolph Scott's *The Desperadoes* (1943), among other titles, was also located in Kanab Canyon.

The unnamed slot canyon that appeared in The Desperadoes (1943).

Another frequent site was Johnson Canyon, about five miles east of Kanab, which featured more even terrain bordered by beautiful white cliffs. Paria Canyon, farther east from Kanab and surrounded by hills and cliffs of brown, red and white hues, includes at one point a winding narrow canyon floor bordered by steep cliffs. Paria was put to extensive use. On rarer occasions, movie crews also ventured into beautiful Cottonwood Canyon.

About a mile off Johnson Canyon Road to the right is a distinctive natural landmark that western and serial fans would find especially familiar, although film companies rarely put it to use. Eagle Gate, an arch rock used first perhaps in O'Brien's *Dude Ranger*, as the entrance to a cattle rustling hideout, was also featured in Episode 4 of *The Great Adventures of Wild Bill Hickok*, as well as Episodes 6 and 7 of *Overland with Kit Carson*. The Eagle Gate shots of lead heavy Trevor (Pegleg) Bardette in *Kit Carson* are visually stunning, especially for a relatively low-budget cliffhanger. The arch also had a role in Grant Withers' *Lure of the Wasteland* (1939), an independent cheapie produced in color. A Johnson Canyon ranch also played a major role in *Dude Ranger*.

From a distance, the Eagle Gate Arch looks small and insignificant. But up close, it is a majestic sight.

Arch villain "Pegleg" made several visits to the arch in Overland with Kit Carson *(1939).*

Paria Canyon's wide, flat creek bed was put to good use for many scenes, including the burning oil wagon chase for John Wayne's *In Old Oklahoma* and the terrific battle between the Indians and Cavalry in *Buffalo Bill*. So also were Paria's narrows, bordered by steep cliffs and several distinctive rock "windows," as well as a huge, cockscomb rock formation visible in the distance of scenes shot in the Paria creek bed.

In Old Oklahoma (*aka* War of the Wildcats, 1943).

The most prominent Paria Canyon cockscomb

The Paria Canyon narrows. Note the "windows" at lower right.

Denise Darcel and Robert Taylor ride through another part of the narrows in Westward the Women (1952).

224

Bill Elliott's Overland with Kit Carson (1939) *was filmed not only in Paria Canyon, but all over the Kanab area.*

Cavalry productions made regular visits as well.

The overhanging (or house rock) formations in Kanab Canyon, as well as similar ones in Paria Canyon and House Rock Valley east of Kanab, also figured prominently in the Elliott serials and other titles. Kanab Canyon's most distinctive house rock formation and an adjoining corral were given prominent play not only in the Carson serials but also in Rod Cameron's *Ride the Man Down* (1953), which includes a rare overhead shot of the corral area.

According to a June, 1939, newspaper item, the Kit Carson crew was preparing to dynamite the ledge of a Kanab Canyon cliff down onto a wagon train. Another cliff overlooking Kanab Canyon furnished the setting for the opening scene of Clayton Moore's *The Lone Ranger* (1956), while the canyon itself hosted exciting fight scenes in that title as well as many other films.

Clint Walker and Virginia Mayo at the Kanab Canyon house rock corral.

The corral, with its barn, in the 1990s.

The Coral Pink Sand Dunes northwest of Kanab were another filming site, whether for a desert epic such as Jon Hall's *Arabian Nights* (1942), or westerns, including *The Outriders*, *Ride the Man Down* and

The Coral Pink Sand Dunes.

Three Lakes.

One Little Indian (1973). Three Lakes, a collection of tiny lakes on the left side of Hwy 89 a few miles north of Kanab, was yet another area star. In one episode of *The Great Adventures of Wild Bill Hickok*, Bill Elliott's stunt double jumps from a high cliff into one of the lakes. Three Lakes also provided the setting for a nighttime romantic interlude with *Yellow Tomahawk* (1954) stars Rory Calhoun and Peggy Castle, although closeups for that scene were actually filmed in the Parry Lodge swimming pool!

Nearby Cave Lake was used for filming, too. A settlement set constructed there appeared in *Overland with Kit Carson* and Tim Holt's *Wagon Train,* among other titles. The set is long gone and the lake flooded its banks several years ago. But in 2006, the lake was again filled with water.

The most beautiful lake in the area, however, is the Aspen Mirror Lake at Duck Creek, an hour or so drive northwest of Kanab. Mirror Lake, as well as the area's white-barked aspen trees, meadows and nearby Strawberry Point and Navajo Lake, probably made their first film appearance in *Drums Along the Mohawk* (1939). But they were also

Tex Ritter at Cave Lake for Roll, Wagons, Roll *(1940).*

A Black Bart (1948) *scene at Duck Creek.*

put to scenic use in *Black Bart* (1948), *Oh! Susanna* (1951), *My Friend Flicka* (1943), *Best of the Bad Men* (1951) and *The Outriders,* among other titles–although scenes with the principal actors in *Black Bart* seem to have been shot entirely in California, with only second unit work in Utah.

According to stuntman and former Kanab resident Neil Summers, the tiny village of Alton, north of Kanab near the entrance to Zion National Park, appeared in Joel McCrea's *Ramrod* (1947). Elderly residents could recall neither McCrea nor the picture's title but one man remembered *Ramrod*'s pretty blonde co-star, Veronica Lake. An Alton family also provided at least one of the horses used in *My Friend Flicka*, portions of which were also filmed at the Ward Esplin Ranch on Cedar Mountain in the Duck Creek area.

Duck Creek cabin remains from
Drums Along the Mohawk *(1939).*

Other sites in the Kanab vicinity appeared in pictures, too. *Overland with Kit Carson*, for example, used the Kaibab Forest and Jacob Lake near the north rim of the Grand Canyon (which appears itself in the climax to *Dude Ranger*), as well as an area east of there for buffalo herd and other scenes. Until enclosed and converted into a gift shop, Moqui Cavern, north of Kanab, also appeared in features and episodes of such TV series as "Death Valley Days." A wooded canyon north of the current site of the Holiday Inn Express was the setting for a cabin set and gun battle seen in *Ride in the Whirlwind* (1965), in which Neil Summers had a featured role. The area's Virgin River was seen in *Ramrod* and other titles. And a dam was constructed on the Virgin in Long Valley north of Kanab for a scene in the Hickok serial. Bottom land just north of Kanab on the left side of Hwy 89 served as a military encampment for *Bugles in the Afternoon* (1952).

Kanab streets and other sites made occasional film appearances as well. Main Street had a brief role in *Dude Ranger*. The local rodeo grounds with bleachers embedded in a hillside (now the site of the local hospital) was used in *Calamity Jane and Sam Bass* (1949) as well as *Red Canyon* (1949). Parry Lodge itself, sporting its actual name, appeared in *Girl in Black Stockings* (1957), a Howard Koch-produced mystery with Lex Barker, Mamie Van Doren and Anne Bancroft, in which a principal character was also named Parry. One scene for that title was shot at Moqui Cavern, another at Three Lakes. Kanab's Pink Poodle shop provided the wardrobe for women in the cast. But Parry Lodge was the real star of that title. In fact, most scenes were set in and around the lodge rather than at Kanab's familiar natural sites.

Production companies did not rely entirely, of course, on natural locales and permanent structures. They also built a variety of movie sets. Among the first were the fort set, houses and outbuildings constructed at Duck Creek and Strawberry Point for *Drums Along the Mohawk*. Remains of that fort were later used for *Oh! Susanna* fort exteriors, while most scenes shot inside the fort for that title were filmed at Corriganville's Ft. Apache set outside L.A. Structures originally built for *Drums Along the Mohawk* also appeared in *My Friend Flicka* and other Duck Creek area titles.

The Buffalo Bill (1944) *fort in Johnson Canyon.*

The fort at Strawberry Point, however, was hardly the only stockade set in the Kanab area. Another fort, first built for *Buffalo Bill*, was situated in Johnson Canyon, on the left side of the current road there (in fact, the current road may run through the former fort site), about a mile north of the only remaining Kanab area street set. That fort was burned for Victor Mature's *Fury at Furnace Creek* (1948).

The remains of Fort Kanab.

The Kanab fort set perhaps most familiar to movie and TV fans, though, was Fort Kanab itself. First built for Heston's *Pony Express* (1953) and situated on private property southwest of town, it also appeared in *Yellow Tomahawk* (1954), *Fort Yuma* (1955), *Quincannon, Frontier Scout* (1956), *Fort Bowie* (1958), Glenn Ford's *The Long Ride Home* (a.k.a. *A Time for Killing*) (1967) and Don Knotts' *The Apple Dumpling Gang Rides Again* (1979), among other features, as well as in numerous TVers (e.g.,

"Daniel Boone," "Boots and Saddles"). At this writing, the remains of Fort Kanab could still be seen southwest of town.

The locations of Kanab town and settlement sets are generally more difficult to pinpoint. A 1939 item from a local newspaper referred to a "main street" at the "studio grounds" that was soon to be enlarged with five additional storefronts. Elderly locals did not recall that set but it may have been the settlement/lake set situated at Cave Lake and seen in *Overland with Kit Caron* and in Tim Holt's *Wagon Train*, as well as Tex

Remains of the Johnson Canyon town set in 2006.

Ritter's *Westbound Stage* and *Roll, Wagons, Roll*. Lee Mace also remembered that a small town set seen in *The Badge of Marshal Brennan* (1957) and *Raiders of Old California* (1957), two Albert Gannaway-produced cheapies featuring country-western singers, was located at the east end of town near the current site of the Holiday Inn Express.

The set's assembly hall.

Two area town sets are easily identified, however. A western street set in Johnson Canyon, first constructed for Robert Taylor's *Westward, the Women* (1952), also appeared the next year in *Pony Express*. It was later enlarged and remains relatively intact. One of its owners erroneously identified the Johnson Canyon site as the Dodge City set for "Gunsmoke," earmarking various structures as the Long Branch Saloon, Doc Adams' office and other series landmarks. On the rare occasions when the "Gunsmoke" crew ventured out of the L.A. area for color series entries, they sometimes did use the Johnson Canyon set–but not as Dodge City. Other features and TV series, including color episodes for the Lone Ranger show, John Russell's *The Dalton Girls* (1957) and Don "Red" Barry's *Convict Stage* (1965), also used that set. South of the town set is the site where the Macahan Ranch for the "How the West Was Won" TVer, another James Arness project, once stood.

A town set stood for years in Paria Canyon as well. It was first built for and appeared prominently in Frank Sinatra's *Sergeants 3* (1962). It also appeared in the James Garner-Sidney Poitier title *Duel at Diablo* (1966) and Jack Nicholson's *Ride in the Whirlwind* (1965) and *The Shooting* (1966), but most notably in the climax to Clint Eastwood's *The Outlaw Josey Wales* (1976). Unused apparently after the Eastwood shoot, the Paria set became so dilapidated it was finally torn down and replaced with several replicas of the original buildings, which were themselves also later dismantled.

The Paria Canyon town set at dusk in the 1990s.

Interestingly, a very similar town set situated in what seems to be Paria Canyon also appears briefly in the 1939 Kit Carson serial. Paria Canyon structures can also be seen in *Western Union* (1941) and *Pony Express*. The remains of Old Pahreah, a Paria Canyon ghost town, may also have appeared in some titles. Individual log and adobe cabin sets dotted the countryside during the filming days as well. Ruins of several remain on their original sites but some were moved and rebuilt for display at Kanab's Frontier Movie Town, a local tourist attraction.

Found mainly in Kanab Canyon, the origins of many such sets remain obscure. A barn still standing at the base of one of Kanab Canyon's overhanging house rocks was apparently originally built for *Fort Dobbs* (1958) but another barn on the same site can be seen earlier in *Ride the Man Down*. The production crew for *The Outlaw Josey Wales* probably constructed the several cabins used in that title. But adobe cabins very similar to those can be seen in the background of scenes for *Ride the Man Down*, shot years before. A house with a high porch seen in the latter title and also in earlier films, including Tex Ritter's *Westbound Stage*, is of equally uncertain origin.

Whatever confusion exists regarding the construction of certain sets, residents abound with anecdotes about the stars who worked in Kanab. Joel McCrea was much beloved. Returning in his Cadillac one evening from filming for *Buffalo Bill* in Paria Canyon, the star and his driver spotted a cow stuck in a bog. Over the driver's objections, McCrea insisted they pull the animal out.

WW II hero and western star Audie Murphy, who made *Sierra (1950)* in nearby Zion Canyon, is remembered as quite a gambler. The Black Cat, a log cabin behind Parry Lodge, was off-limits to locals, but a popular drinking and gambling spot for the movie folks. Audie was a frequent patron of the Black Cat. The star also befriended Dee Crosby—one of Utah's top three WW II soldiers and a patient with Murphy in an Italian hospital—often inviting the Panguitch resident and his German wife to Parry Lodge for dinner.

Clark Gable sometimes visited Kanab for mountain lion hunts. Arriving at Parry Lodge in the middle of the night on one such occasion, Gable had difficulty rousing Whit Parry. When a gruff and sleepy Parry finally responded through the lodge door, the star shouted, "I'm Clark Gable and I want a room." "Well, I'm Shirley Temple!" Parry shot back, and refused to open the door. The next morning, the lodge owner apologized profusely to the star.

During filming of Duke's *In Old Oklahoma*, Kanab resident Lee Mace was working briefly for Parry Lodge, driving the catering truck to sites used in that title, including an oil rig set constructed west of Fredonia, a community south of Kanab. One day some of the crew took more than one lunch box, leaving others without a meal and, under union rules, on "golden time" the rest of the day—infuriating tight-fisted Republic studio executives.

The next day, Mace was unloading boxes of lunch and wafer cookies onto the tailgate of the catering truck when he heard someone opening one of the wafer packages. Giving the tarpaulin covering the rear of the truck a sharp whack, Mace ordered the culprit away. But when he pulled back the tarp, he was face to face with star John Wayne. Mace immediately began apologizing, explaining that the studio probably did not mean to limit its star to one lunch. But Wayne smiled, said he would follow the rules and walked off without his cookies. "A nice guy," Mace remembered, as were McCrea and Bill Elliott, among movie folks visiting the area in the early filming days. Mace also had fond memories of Walter Brennan, who regularly entertained folks with his juggling feats and hilarious (if at times unprintable) practical jokes.

The actors could also be the source of unintended amusement for the locals. During filming of Tim Holt's *Wagon Train* in Paria Canyon, heavies were perched on a high cliff, preparing to ambush a wagon. The scene had to be reshot time after time as lead heavy Bud McTaggart repeatedly flubbed his line, telling a henchie, "Get a *lead* on that *bead* team." Nor were the locals above a little horseplay on the set. Ordered to drop his gun during filming of the Kit Carson serial, Black Raider Charles Mace did just that—on another Raider's boot!

Accidents and near mishaps were also relatively common. One of the buffalo used in the Kit Carson serial had to be put down after a horse fell on it. During filming of *Oh! Susanna*, a serious accident was narrowly avoided in a wagon chase to the fort set at Duck Creek.

Like the locals, movie and TV folks generally have fond memories of filming in the area. But producer Howard Koch was perhaps most closely associated with Kanab's film history. Koch first visited the area while scouting locations for Gable's *Lone Star* (1951). That title ultimately was filmed elsewhere but Koch returned to Kanab in 1954 for *Yellow Tomahawk* and shot a total of ten titles there between that year and 1962, when *Sergeants Three* was produced. In 1990, the community declared a "Howard Koch Day." The emotional producer said that tribute to him was "greater than getting an Academy Award." Koch once told an interviewer he was "smitten" with the area's beauty. We location fans know exactly what he meant.

Eventually, Norman Cram replaced Whit Parry as owner of the Parry Lodge and Kanab's principal Hollywood contact. As westerns fell out of favor with movie-makers, film crews became an increasingly rare site in the community.

But when the town, several years ago, began its Western Legends Roundup, an annual three-day celebration of things western and especially the area's historic role in film history, public response was tremendous–clearly demonstrating that Kanab and its scenic wonders will always be "Little Hollywood" to fans.

Monument Valley and Moab

Asked to name just one location used in western movie-making, most fans immediately mention Monument Valley on the Utah-Arizona border. For many, the Mittens and other massive Monument Valley formations personify the "Reel West" and other filming sites pale by comparison. As a percentage of total western film product, of course, the number of titles lensed there was small. But the list includes several true classics, especially the John Ford-John Wayne collaborations for *Stagecoach* (1939), two entries in their Cavalry trilogy (*Fort Apache*, 1949, and *She Wore a Yellow Ribbon* 1950), and *The Searchers* (1956).

Stock footage from *Stagecoach* also regularly appeared in other westerns, even Saturday matinee oaters. The title and credits for entries in Monogram's "The Rough Riders" series, for example, were superimposed over a Monument Valley scene from *Stagecoach*. And the entire climax to Charles Starrett's Durango Kid entry *Laramie* (1949) was lifted from *Stagecoach*'s great Indian-stagecoach chase sequence. When our hero suddenly appeared in an unusual outfit (to match John Wayne footage) rather than his typical garb, we Front Row Kids just knew we were in for a heap of stock. But at least it came from one of the most thrilling scenes in all western filmdom!

The Totems.

On one occasion, a Monument Valley B-western appearance was not limited to stock footage. In an aerial scene for *Trail to San Antone* (1947), one of the titles Gene Autry made for Republic before beginning his post-war association with Columbia Pictures, a plane flies past the Totems, among Monument Valley's most distinctive edifices. Since exteriors for *Trail to San Antone* were filmed at Lone Pine, California, one can only surmise that the Monument Valley footage was shot while Gene, or his production company, was scouting possible locations for his upcoming Columbia series, portions of early entries for which were ultimately filmed in Old Tucson (*The Last Round-up*, 1947), Sedona (*The Strawberry Roan*, 1947) and the Valley of Fire outside Las Vegas (*The Big Sombrero*, 1949).

Not surprisingly, given his strong cinematic ties to the area, John Ford is often credited with "discovering" Monument Valley for the motion picture industry. Actually, though, the valley made its first film appearance in the silent epic *The Vanishing American* (1925), starring Richard Dix and directed by George Seitz. And appropriately so. For Monument Valley was part of the huge Navajo reservation that encompassed three states and *The Vanishing American* was, for its time at least, a sensitive story of Indian abuse at the hands of whites, vividly portrayed in the picture by Noah Beery as a ruthless Indian agent.

Credit for Monument Valley's prominent part in western films must go, however, to Harry Goulding, who first visited the area in the early 1920s, then later returned with his wife to build a trading post at the base of Big Rock Door Mesa, one of the valley's largest monuments. When the Depression of the 1930s exacted a heavy toll on the Navajo reservation, Goulding hit on a possible solution to the area's desperate economic plight. Taking his cue from Kanab, Utah, which would become known as "Little Hollywood" for its success in attracting movie productions, Goulding sought to convince film moguls that Monument Valley also offered a perfect backdrop for outdoor pictures. When his brother, a California resident, told him that United Artists was seeking an unusual location for a western film, Goulding and his wife, armed with a couple of dozen black and white photographs, went to Hollywood, eventually meeting with UA production chief Walter Wanger and John Ford. Albeit with some hesitation based on financial concerns, Wanger and Ford ultimately decided to shoot their film–*Stagecoach*–in Goulding's valley.

One of the most familiar Monument Valley scenes in Stagecoach (1939).

Despite the close association of *Stagecoach* with Monument Valley, very little footage in the final film was actually shot there. John Ford did take his crew and a number of cast members to the valley. But arguably only one Monument Valley scene in the final cut–a brief close-up of Tim Holt playing a cavalry officer–included any of the picture's principal players. The admittedly stunning shots of the Mittens and other formations, as well as El Capitan Rock at nearby Kayenta, appear to have been entirely second unit work. The same approach was used for scenes featuring Saguaro cactus, shot at Mesa, Arizona, near Phoenix.

In fact, the actual locales for much of *Stagecoach* could have been taken right out of any B-western title. The Tonto town scenes early in the picture were shot on RKO's Encino western street in the San Fernando Valley, home mainly to that studio's B-western series. John Wayne ostensibly makes his first appearance in the film in Monument Valley, but actually in front of a studio process screen. Most of the scene of the actor meeting the stage was actually shot in the familiar "Garden of the Gods" section on the famous Iverson movie ranch outside Chatsworth, examined elsewhere in this volume.

After passing through some more second unit Monument Valley scenery, the stage arrives at Dry Fork–actually the Iverson ranch fortress set first constructed for Shirley Temple's *Wee Willie Winkie* (1937). Additional Monument Valley second unit process shots follow–indeed, some of the same locations seen earlier in *Stagecoach*. Then the stage makes its next stop at Apache Wells. But sharp-eyed location fans are hardly fooled. It is not Monument Valley, just good old Iverson again–a short distance, in fact, from the Garden of the Gods site where Wayne made his first appearance. In fact, only the entrance to the Apache Wells relay station was even at Iverson. The remainder of the lengthy Apache Wells scene used sound stage interiors and exteriors shot, like all the film's interiors, at the old Pickford-Fairbanks United Artists lot at the intersection of Santa Monica Boulevard and Formosa Avenue, which was then in the process of becoming the Samuel Goldwyn Studio and would retain that name until 1980, when Warner Bros. purchased it, renaming it the Warner Hollywood Studio.

The Apache Wells exterior set included some fake Saguaro cactus used to match scenes there with subsequent second unit footage filmed at Mesa. For scenes of a burned-out ferry station, Ford utilized Iverson's Garden of the Gods yet another time. The crew, with Wayne, Andy Devine and George Bancroft in tow, did journey to Kernville, 150 miles northwest of L.A., but only for a brief scene of the stagecoach crossing the Kern River at the ferry site.

After more second unit shots at Monument Valley, oddly interspersed with process shots of the cathedral cliffs of California's Red Rock Canyon (probably filmed during the crew's trip to nearby Kernville), the camera shifts to Indians on a rise above the valley, preparing to attack the coach as its crosses the desert below. Then, the audience is treated to one of the most action-packed chase sequences in western films–but not one shot at Monument Valley. Instead, there is a brief clip of the coach racing through the famous Beale's Cut near Newhall, a few miles north of L.A.. The rest of the chase takes place, however, on the Lucerne Dry Lake near Victorville, California.

John Wayne does actually take part in the chase, shooting at the Indians from the top of the stage and bringing the lead horse to a halt at the end. But the great Yakima Canutt did the most dangerous stunt work for that terrific scene, including his famous fall beneath the horses and coach.

Stagecoach also concludes on a western street set rather than in Monument Valley. Various sources have identified that site as the street set on the Monogram Ranch near Newhall or the Republic western street in North Hollywood. Since a brief scene of the coach picking up Burton Churchill's crooked banker on the outskirts of Tonto early in the picture appears to have been a pick-up shot made on Universal's main western street (with its distinctive large livery stable in view), it is also possible that the Universal set was used for the *Stagecoach* climax. Night filming and the generally tight camera shots make identification difficult. My hunch, though, is that nearly all the final exterior scenes, like all interiors, were shot on the Goldwyn lot–on the same western street set, albeit altered somewhat in appearance, that was used years later

This famous scene from Stagecoach (1939) *was filmed in California, not Monument Valley.*

as "Mineral City" in certain episodes of the Roy Rogers TV series.

However briefly its actual screen time in *Stagecoach*, Monument Valley's splendors clearly had a tremendous impact on audiences and reviewers. "In one superbly expansive gesture," a *New York Times* reviewer wrote, "John Ford has . . . made a motion picture that sings a song of camera. It moves, and how beautifully it moves, across the plains of Arizona, skirting the sky-reaching mesas of Monument Valley, beneath the piled-up cloud banks which every photographer dreams

John Ford has been so closely associated with Monument Valley that this area is even named Ford's Point.

about, and through all the old-fashioned, but never really outdated, periods of prairie travel in the scalp-raising Seventies, when Geronimo's Apaches were on the warpath. Here, in a sentence, is a movie of the grand old school, a genuine rib-thumper and a beautiful sight to see."

Over the next decade, Monument Valley hosted six more movie crews. George Seitz returned for portions of *Kit Carson* (1940), starring Jon Hall. MGM shot some of the Robert Taylor version of *Billy the Kid* (1941) there, although unfortunately that beautiful Technicolor film was plagued with an over-abundance of process shots. John Ford returned for *My Darling Clementine* (1946), *Fort Apache (1948), She Wore a Yellow Ribbon (1949)*, and *The Searchers* (1956). After filming *She Wore a Yellow Ribbon* in the

John Wayne at Monument Valley for She Wore a Yellow Ribbon (1949).

A gripping scene from The Searchers (1956), *considered by many to be the Duke's finest film.*

fall of 1948, however, the director had begun looking for a change of scenery. Someone suggested Moab, Utah, which boasted landscapes in its Professor Valley almost as spectacular as those of Monument Valley, plus a town that could offer more in the way of local support facilities than Harry Goulding was able to provide. During a visit to Moab, the director was introduced to George White, whose cattle ranch stood at the entrance to a series of valleys along the Colorado River–site of Castle Rock, the Priest and Nuns butte, Fisher Towers and other impressive vistas. Observing the area, Ford reportedly exclaimed, "That's the greatest sight I've ever seen!" and decided on the spot to film his next western there. Filming for *Wagon Master* (1950), one of the director's most underrated titles, took place in the late fall of 1949. The next summer, Ford was back in Moab for *Rio Grande* (1950), the last of his John Wayne Cavalry trilogy, with George White's beautiful ranch serving as the site for the fort set prominent in that fine epic's storyline. Wayne returned to Professor Valley for his *The Comancheros* (1961).

Under the leadership of George White and other prominent citizens, Moab established a film commission and began attracting more productions to the area. Soon, its landscape became as familiar to

Entrance to the White Ranch in Professor Valley.

The terrific Roman riding sequence in Rio Grande (1950).

moviegoers as Monument Valley. Productions also began branching out beyond the Colorado River area to other Moab sites. For *Battle at Apache Pass* (1952), featuring Jeff Chandler's reprise of the role of Apache chief Cochise that he had first essayed in Sedona for *Broken Arrow* (1950), veteran western director George Sherman took cast and crew a few miles north to Arches National Monument (later a national park).

Ben Johnson in Professor Valley for Wagon Master (1950).

Arches boasts many spectacular and unusual formations, including Delicate Arch (among numerous other arches), the Balanced Rock, Sheep Rock and the Three Gossips. Over the years, Arches would appear in

The Delicate Arch.

many other western and non-western titles, including William Holden's *Wild Rovers* (1971), the opening scene of Steven Spielberg's *Indiana Jones and the Last Crusade* (1988), the terrific Kurt Russell thriller *Breakdown* (1997), which used many Nevada, Utah, Arizona and California locales, even early episodes in the "Alias Smith and Jones" TV series, which also went south to the nearby Manti-La Sal mountains for forest scenes, as had several other Moab titles.

Indians lie in wait at Arches for The Battle at Apache Pass (1952).

And the Cavalry makes its approach in Professor Valley.

Beginning with *Warlock* (1959), starring Henry Fonda and Richard Widmark, and Clint Walker's *Gold of the Seven Saints* (1961), productions based in Moab sometimes went southwest to Dead Horse Point, which rivals the Grand Canyon for spectacular canyon scenery. And when, years later, the stars of *Thelma and Louise* (1991) took their T-Bird flight into eternity in the climax to that exciting film, they (actually their stunt dummies) went airborne from a rim below the Point, on Potash Trail. The descriptively named

Dead Horse Point.

Goosenecks State Park canyon between Moab and Monument also made infrequent screen appearances (*The Searchers*, 1956), as did Canyonlands National Park (*Birds of Prey*, a 1973 TV movie).

As westerns fell out of fashion in Hollywood, Moab and Monument Valley made fewer big screen appearances. But Kirk Douglas went to Monument Valley for *The Villain* (1979) and the valley's buttes were about the only thing to commend the 1981 Klinton Spilsbury version of the Lone Ranger legend. A number of non-western thrillers, most notably Clint Eastwood's *The Eiger Sanction* (1975), also drew on the valley's magnificent sites. Michael J. Fox included the valley among the many backdrops for his *Back to the Future III* (1990), as did *Forrest Gump* (1993) in his travels.

Moab has also continued to host movie companies, providing sites for *Geronimo: An American Legend* (1993) and *City Slickers II* (1993), among other titles. Over the years, both areas, but especially Moab, have also furnished locales for hundreds of commercials. Who can forget the automobile and other commercials shot high atop Castle Rock? Or the Skoal ad featuring a panoramic shot of Professor Valley and the Colorado River–touched up to eliminate Highway 128, which now runs along the river? Advertisers long ago realized that Moab and Monument Valley furnished unequaled backdrops for pitching their products. Movie fans continue to hope, however, that those two great filming sites will one day resume their prominence in films.

St. George

Kanab was the "Little Hollywood" of southwestern Utah movie locations. But St. George's red cliffs and the white buttes of its Snow Canyon also have their place in film history. Several A-westerns of the golden era lensed at least in part at St. George, including Audie Murphy's *Six Black Horses* (1962), *Bullet for a Badman* (1964) and *Gunpoint* (1966). Republic shot Ray Milland's *A Man Alone* (1955) largely on its back lot. But the studio also used St. George for that title as well as Vaughan Monroe's *Toughest Man in Arizona* (1952), *The Road to Denver* (1955), *The Vanishing American* (1955) and *Santa Fe Passage* (1955).

Bill Witney directed that last title but the *Santa Fe Passage* shoot was not his first visit to St. George. In fact, the studio's action ace first won his directorial spurs there. In January, 1937, Republic producer Larry Wickland took Witney, then a rising film cutter, with him on a location scouting expedition to Utah in search of sites for *The Painted Stallion* (1937), the studio's next chapter play. Wickland ultimately chose St. George and early the next month a crew of seventy traveled by train to Moapa, Nevada, then made the last fifty miles of the trek by cars and buses rented in St. George, where the owner of the town's only hotel served as advance man, helping in the selection of filming sites and the acquisition of extras, livestock, and rolling stock.

According to a February 11 item in the St. George newspaper, the studio hired a large number of local personnel and props, including forty Indians from a nearby reservation, fifteen covered wagons, 35 pack horses and 25 cowboys. The same article reported that the serial's directors were Hollywood veterans Ray Taylor and Alan James. But Taylor's excessive drinking soon produced a change in that lineup, with Taylor sent packing back to L.A. and the baby-faced Bill Witney, at twenty-one, replacing him as principal director.

Two paint horses, with slightly different markings, were also brought in for the shoot and St. George's business leaders did their best to accommodate the movie folks in hopes of attracting other movie makers to the area. The local chamber of commerce, for example, provided the equipment for cutting a passable road into Snow Canyon. Republic also did some filming with locals before the principal actors arrived. Juvenile lead Sammy McKim recalled, for example, that some of his riding long shots were actually filmed with a local boy.

But the use of local livestock and gear posed risks as well. At one point during the filming, McKim was riding with stars Ray Corrigan and Hoot Gibson at the head of a column of covered wagons when the leather rigging on the front wagon broke and the lead horses raced toward him and his pony. Only the "Hooter's" quick action saved McKim from a serious accident.

Even so, the child star would have fond memories of St. George, especially daily trips with his grandfather to a local store for licorice sticks. He also enjoyed working with the serial's other leading players. But he told Gibson at one point that he would like him even more if he didn't "cuss" so much. "Well, hell," the Hooter jovially replied, "I'm not going to stop."

As with most titles shot there, much of the filming for *The Painted Stallion* was done in Snow Canyon and the red cliffs area southwest of town. In addition to using St. George's natural wonders as a backdrop

Ray Corrigan and Julia Thayer in The Painted Stallion (1937).

The Red Cliffs.

for scenes used in the production, the crew also took much additional footage, including shots of the Washington County Courthouse, for its stock footage files or rental to other studios. But not all scenes in *The Painted Stallion* were filmed at St. George. Republic's Mexican and cave sets were also featured, as were the woods near the L.A. River along Republic's northern boundary (seen most extensively in an

Of western stars, Audie Murphy filmed the most titles in St. George.

This action scene is from Audie Murphy's Gunpoint (1966).

Episode 2 rainstorm scene interspersed with St. George footage). Bronson Canyon in the Hollywood Hills, including its largest tunnel entrance and a separate opening that had appeared as the entry to "Murania" in Gene Autry's *Phantom Empire* (1935) serial, was apparently also used. Strangely enough, an Episode 3 chase scene with leads "Crash" Corrigan and Julia (Jean Carman) Thayer (or their stand-ins) riding double on the painted stallion appears to have been shot with a second unit at Kernville and clearly ended with the duo plunging into Lake Sherwood west of L.A. Sammy McKim also remembers Lake Sherwood as the setting for part of the Episode 2 rainstorm scene, with Yakima Canutt doubling McKim when the plot called for him to swim with a horse in the lake. An Episode 7 stagecoach chase was apparently filmed, moreover, in the Agoura area. Limited stock footage included an avalanche scene from *The Three Mesquiteers* (1936), as well as the familiar scenes of Indians crossing the Little Wind River near Lander, Wyo., and the fight between Rex, the Wonder Horse, and a paint, first filmed in the silent days.

Stunt double Babe DeFreest was on screen much more than the female lead. In fact, a local newspaper reported that Julia Thayer had not even traveled to St. George for filming. And while a few of her scenes were clearly shot there (and Sammy McKim remembered her fondly), she is seen primarily in extreme closeups or on Republic's cave set where, according to Bill Witney's wonderful memoir, an encounter with a "pet" mountain lion almost cost Thayer her head as well as her war bonnet, which the cougar mistook for a chicken.

The Painted Stallion may have been Bill Witney's weakest chapter play, far less impressive, albeit more slickly filmed, than Columbia's Bill Elliott starrers *The Great Adventures of Wild Bill Hickok* (1938) and *Overland with Kit Carson* (1939). Without *The Painted Stallion* and Ray Taylor's unquenchable thirst, however, Bill Witney might well have remained in the cutting room, denying front row kids the greatest classics in serial history.

Chapter 8

Arizona, New Mexico and Nevada

Sedona

Like Utah, Arizona, New Mexico and Nevada have also been Hollywood favorites. One of the most spectacular and frequently used Arizona filming locales was Sedona, a two-hour drive northwest of Phoenix and an hour south of Flagstaff. Western novelist Zane Grey set his *Call of the Canyon* in Sedona's Oak Creek Canyon. It was thus fitting that the first movie shot in Sedona was the 1923 film version of Grey's novel, starring Richard Dix.

Two George O'Brien Fox titles based loosely on other Grey epics, *Riders of the Purple Sage* (1931) and *Robber's Roost* (1932), were early sound films featuring Sedona's stunning vistas. And over the years, according to the Sedona Historical Society, at least 76 movies were filmed there, including, in addition to titles mentioned below, *Comanche Territory* (1950), *The Eagle and the Hawk* (1950), *Pony Soldier* (1952), *Apache* (1954), *3:10 to Yuma* (1957), *The Rounders* (1964), *Firecreek* (1968) (although, except for the credits, only scenes done at the North Ranch in L.A.'s Conejo Valley seem to have made it to the final cut), *Kingdom of the Spiders* (1977), even *National Lampoon's Summer Vacation* (1983), as well as initial filming for the short-lived "Harts of the West" TV series (later episodes of which were shot at the Sable Ranch outside Newhall, California), the "Starman" series and countless commercials.

Many of Sedona's red and gray rock formations, surrounded by scattered evergreens, were so distinctive they were given individual names. Bell Rock often towered in the distance of scenes lensed at Sedona, as did Courthouse Rock, a huge rectangular edifice, and the similarly shaped Cathedral Rock. Chimney Rock, a narrow formation jutting up from a hill, can be seen in the background of a scene (filmed at Sedona's western street set doubling as a fort) in Alan Ladd's *Drum Beat* (1954), as can Capitol Butte, another imposing formation.

In appearance, Bell Rock and Chimney Rock clearly resemble their names, as does Coffeepot Rock, which could be seen in the distance at one end of Sedona's western street set. Merry-Go-Round Rock, with

Courthouse Rock and Bell Rock.

George O'Brien's Robbers Roost (1933) *highlighted much of the Sedona landscape, including Bell Rock.*

its huge curving base, was another familiar backdrop in such films as Robert Taylor's *Billy the Kid* (1941) and Richard Widmark's *The Last Wagon* (1956). The cone-shaped formations long ago dubbed Madonna and the Praying Nuns also graced the background of several titles, including Gene Autry's *The Strawberry Roan* (1948) and Dennis Morgan's *Cheyenne* (1947).

Sometimes cameras captured sweeping overhead views of Sedona's wonders. In *Texas Trail* (1937), for example, Hoppy and the boys are seen riding down into the Sedona canyons as they begin their descent into haunting "Ghost Canyon"–actually Blue Canyon on the Hopi Indian Reservation, outside

Coffeepot Rock in 2007, surrounded by "civilization."

Merry-Go-Round Rock in The Last Wagon *(1956).*

Tuba City, many miles to the north. *Strawberry Roan* also included such panoramic shots, as did other titles, such as Randolph Scott's *Coroner Creek* (1948) and *The Gunfighters* (1947), which also made extensive use of the Jauregui Ranch near Newhall.

But perhaps the most scenic Sedona filming site was Red Rock Crossing, with beautiful Oak Creek winding beneath a backdrop of perhaps Sedona's most frequently photographed formation. A smelter set

*The Madonna and Praying Nuns provided a wonderful backdrop for this scene in
Gene Autry's excellent* The Strawberry Roan (1948).

was constructed there for the Ray Milland-Hedy Lamarr starrer *Copper Canyon* (1950). Jimmy Stewart's *Broken Arrow* (1950), Robert Mitchum's *Blood on the Moon* (1948) and Rock Hudson's *Gun Fury* (1953), among other titles, also featured the Crossing.

Film companies utilized sites near Sedona, too. Sterling Hayden's *Flaming Feather* (1951) is apparently the only western to date to use Montezuma's Castle, Indian cliff dwellings south of Sedona, although *Billy Jack* (1971), shot mainly in Prescott, also featured the dwellings.

John Wayne's *Angel and the Badman* (1946) perhaps did the most to attract movie companies to the area. Portions of his *Tall in the Saddle* (1944) were filmed there earlier, but only second-unit shots made the final cut, with the cast's scenes confined largely to the Agoura-Albertson Ranch northwest of L.A. and RKO's Encino western street. *Angel and the Badman*, on the other hand, used Sedona extensively and its crew constructed the Sedona western town site that would see frequent use in later films, including Dick Powell's *Station West* (1948) and Joan Crawford's weird but fascinating *Johnny Guitar* (1954), in which that set was joined cinematically with Republic's North Hollywood western street.

At times, "movie magic" complemented the area's natural settings. To create a cave entrance under a waterfall leading to a hideout in *Johnny Guitar*, for example, the crew reportedly diverted water from an irrigation ditch, allowing it to flow over a tunnel running under Highway 89A. *Johnny Guitar* cast member

Red Rock Crossing hosted this mill set for Copper Canyon (1950).

*The cliff dwellings at Montezuma's Castle, south of Sedona, made
a rare appearance in Sterling Hayden's* Flaming Feather (1952).

Ben Cooper recalled that the Republic crew constructed the unusual hideout cabin used in that title before the cast arrived for three weeks of filming in November, 1953. A tiny area business district appeared, moreover, in *Desert Fury* (1947), the Burt Lancaster-Lizabeth Scott non-western melodrama. A night scene for that title also used a bridge on the road to Tuzigoot.

Republic used Sedona for several titles after *Angel and the Badman*, but often only for second-unit shooting. William Elliott's *The Fabulous Texan* (1949) included cast scenes featuring Sedona sites but most action segments, including the climax, were filmed mainly at the Iverson Ranch at Chatsworth, California. Only second-unit Sedona shots were used in Elliott's *Hellfire* (1949) and in Vaughan Monroe's *Singing Guns* (1950). (As noted earlier, the second of Monroe's two Republic westerns, *Toughest Man in Arizona*, 1952, went to St. George, Utah, rather than Sedona for second-unit shots.)

Sedona location scout Bob Bradshaw doubled Zachary Scott in Shotgun (1959).

The mid-forties saw conversion of a former Civilian Conservation Corps camp into the Sedona Lodge, a facility designed especially for Hollywood crews, who previously had been housed at Flagstaff during Sedona shoots. A sound stage was constructed on the property and the lodge remained the principal host for movie people until torn down for construction of the King's Ransom motel.

At sites used extensively for filming, of course, movie-makers develop ties with local contacts who scout locations, acquire livestock and extras and perform other support functions–the Parry brothers in Kanab, the Gouldings in Monument Valley and George White of Moab, to mention a few.

Sedona was no exception. For much of its filming history, Hollywood's man in Sedona was Bob Bradshaw, who bore a close resemblance to Zachary Scott, whom he doubled in *Shotgun* (1959). A native Ohio, Bradshaw moved to Arizona seeking relief from allergies. In 1945, while working as a carpenter in Prescott, he made a visit to nearby Sedona, fell in love with what he considered "the most beautiful place on Earth" and obtained work as a carpenter on the Sedona Lodge construction project.

Gradually, Bradshaw began working in the area's growing film industry, building sets and doubling for the actors. In 1955, he got his big break. The movie folks discovered that Otto Hallermund, the Sedona location contact at that time, was not only drawing a salary from the studios but also charging them more for rental horses than he was paying local ranchers. Hallermund was out and Bradshaw became the movies' Sedona contact, a position he would hold for the next twenty years.

Ben Cooper had "great memories" of Sedona and the *Johnny Guitar* shoot. He and Ernest Borgnine shared one of the Sedona Lodge's two-bed cabins. "There was a great mess hall there with these gigantic platters. One night, they'd be full of steaks and the next night they'd be full of pork chops. Oh, it was mind-boggling!" At 20, Cooper had already been on Broadway and done literally thousands of radio shows but had always wanted to do westerns. "And here I was in one of the most western-type locations you could ever find . . . getting to play cowboy and they were paying me for it!" To top that off, he rode Blaze, Alan Ladd's sorrel in *Shane*, a horse Cooper rode in five films.

Always anxious to cultivate good relations with the locals, Cooper, Ian McDonald and a couple of other cast members went to a nearby school one evening to crown a beauty queen. Tourists, he also remembered, followed cast and crew everywhere they went during the shoot. Even during the exciting but dangerous action scene with Cooper, Royal Dano, and Borgnine riding below a series of mountainside dynamite blasts, "we had to literally chase the tourists out of there so we wouldn't blast them."

One day, the trio decided to have a bit of fun with a crowd of about 50 tourists. Cooper had been practicing his fast draw for the film and Ernie Borgnine attached some nylon fishing line to the brim of Royal Dano's hat. Cooper and Dano then pretended to get into an argument and Dano, launching into one of his classic whining routines, began to walk away. "Don't walk away from me, Royal!" an apparently angry Cooper shouted. "Dammit, don't you walk away from me!" At that point Cooper fired a blank at Dano, Borgnine yanked the cord, and Dano's hat flew off. "Then, Royal really started whining. He bent over to pick up his hat and I fired another shot. And Ernie flipped Royal's hat again." Poker-faced, Cooper then turned and walked toward the astonished crowd of tourists. "I felt like Moses. They parted like the Red Sea. We never did laugh or break up. We didn't let 'em know it was a joke."

Cooper had his share of real mishaps as well during the shoot. While he was riding Blaze along a sloping sheet of rocky shale, the horse lost his footing and began sliding down toward a sheer, 200-300 foot drop-off. Cooper turned the horse around and anxiously began riding back up the slope, moving as far up on Blaze's neck as possible. Afterwards, one of the wranglers joked, "You're the only one I know who can ride a horse between his ears."

During a bank robbery scene, Cooper's horse also went out from under him, knocking him unconscious for several minutes. But he did the scene and that night the wranglers rewarded the kid with a glass of straight bourbon. On the set, the oft-rumored tension between stars Joan Crawford and Mercedes McCambridge was evident. Watching the rushes of one of McCambridge's "over-the-top" scenes one evening with Cooper, Crawford exclaimed, "Look at that; now I have to go in and work with her tomorrow!"

Cooper had heard all the stories about Crawford but found her "great" to work with. Once Ward Bond realized Cooper could ride a horse, they got along "O.K.," too. Sterling Hayden, Cooper remembers, was "one of the neatest guys in the world. Very funny. . . . Sterling wouldn't let anything bother him." (Hayden dedicated his first book to Cooper's sister.) Scott Brady "just didn't give a damn." And Director Nicholas Ray "couldn't have been more professional and nice."

The final scene shot for the movie was a sound stage closeup of Cooper's booted foot falling out from beneath a tablecloth. That shot was done but the cameraman decided the lighting was not quite right. "And they said, 'O.K., Ben, we're going to do it once more. Just stay there [under the table] and we'll tell you when to move.' And I said, 'O.K.' And I waited. And I waited. And I waited. And finally I thought, 'This is ridiculous,' and stuck my head out. And they'd all left and gone to the [wrap] party!"

Over the years, several other players shared with me their memories of filming at Sedona. While still a teenager, the stunningly beautiful Debra Paget starred with Jimmy Stewart and Jeff Chandler in *Broken Arrow* (1950), shot there in the summer of 1949 when Sedona was "still virgin territory, exquisite."

Paget fondly recalled the 250 White Mountain Chiricahua Apaches brought in to work on the film. "The studio hired them because they all had beautiful long hair and the producer wouldn't have to pay for wigs and extra hairdressers. But when they arrived on buses, all the girls had cut their hair and gotten tonies because they

Jimmy Stewart and a very young Debra Paget in Broken Arrow *(1950).*

were going to be in movies! [laughs]. The hairdressers had to call Max Factor right away for wigs and they were dyeing mops and putting mops on the Indians and putting them way off in the background of scenes until the wigs arrived!"

Behind Sedona Lodge, where the company was housed for the shoot, Paget also remembered, "they put up an outdoor screen and straight benches where we watched the dailies at night. A few of the cast and crew would be there watching in the dark. And all of a sudden, you'd look around and there would be all these Apaches there. They'd come in without making a sound. They'd laugh and joke when they saw themselves on the screen. They were so cute."

Oak Creek proved a real challenge for the young actress and crew. Obliged to wear brown contacts for her role as an Indian maiden, she lost one of the contacts in the creek one day. "And the whole crew was down on their hands and knees in the creek looking for that contact, because I didn't have another pair with me."

Paget had never learned to swim, in fact often had nightmares about drowning. On a rare day off during the shoot, she and her mother went down to Oak Creek to put their feet in the water. While they were hanging onto a raft, some teenage boys (who must have thought they had died and gone to heaven) decided it would be fun to push the young beauty into the water. As she was going under the third time, her frantic mother told the boys her daughter could not swim and one "jumped in and got me out." For *Bird of Paradise* (1951), her next film, *Broken Arrow* director Delmer Daves made certain Paget learned to swim.

On at least one occasion, Paget recalled, "our sets were. . . washed away in terrible electrical storms. We'd be under the makeup tarps and in the tents where we dressed. And that's all we had to protect us from the lightning. They totally washed away the wickiups [Indian huts] along the water."

Superb character actor Morgan Woodward went to Sedona for the filming of opening scenes for *Firecreek*, the 1968 Jimmy Stewart-Henry Fonda starrer, most of which was shot at the North Ranch and elsewhere in the Conejo Valley, northwest of L.A. Riding scenes that ran behind the *Firecreek* credits were shot at a Sedona area airstrip, with the camera truck racing along the runway. But Woodward, Fonda and others also rode through a rough area where a recent fire had left broken and bare Yucca stalks with sharp tips jutting up from the ground. "If any of us had gone down, we would have been impaled. We were all concerned about riding as hard as we did over that very dangerous terrain. But none of us went down, thank God!" What Woodward remembered most about *Firecreek* was its cast. "I have never, ever since worked with a cast like that–all those great character actors. Jack Elam was an ace poker player, great at 'liars' poker.' Jack had a great sense of humor, a great wit. And James Best did a marvelous imitation of Jimmy Stewart." Once while waiting to do a scene in a barn out in the Conejo Valley, Best was doing his Stewart imitation. "And all of a sudden Stewart came up behind Best and we stopped laughing. Best got a funny look on his face and turned around, and there was Stewart!"

Developers are rapidly desecrating Sedona's scenic splendors. A distant shot of the town, then only a tiny village, appears at the end of Marlene Dietrich's *Rancho* Notorious (1952). Now, Sedona has a large business district, many motels and residences. But actors and crew members still have their fond memories. *Johnny Guitar* may or may not be Ben Cooper's favorite film. After all, he had co-starred in *The Rose Tatoo* (1955). But Sedona clearly was his favorite location. "In Sedona, they had a slogan," he remarked several years ago. "'God made the Grand Canyon but lives in Sedona.'"

Tuba City and Blue Canyon

On rare occasions, movie crews ventured north of Sedona and Flagstaff to Navajo and Hopi Indian land in the Tuba City area. Richard Dix's silent classic *The Vanishing American* (1925) was shot there. So, too, were the few exterior scenes in Jane Russell's *The Outlaw* (1943). Dick Jones, who had a small role in *The Outlaw*, recalled the experience several years ago. "Howard Hughes picked that location, I guess, because of his eccentricities. There was nothing there [then] but an Indian trading post. And he built a couple of Spanish adobe houses, and then he kept the whole crew and all the actors in walled tents. Wood floors, a wall on the side about three foot and canvas on the top. Everybody had his own tent. We stayed there, God, I think I was there thirteen weeks. And if you blinked your eye [in the movie], you didn't see me."

Universal filmed the wild-horse yarn *Stormy* (1935), with Noah Beery, Jr., in Blue Canyon out from Tuba City. Scenes from that title and others of horses stampeding through area canyons with steep cliffs also appeared as stock footage in countless later films. But undoubtedly the locale made its most scenic

Blue Canyon's white cliffs.

appearance in Hopalong Cassidy's *Texas Trail* (1937), another wild horse story. Early ranch scenes in that title were shot on the Fox Ranch in the pines between Sedona and Flagstaff. When Hoppy and company leave the ranch for mysterious "Ghost Canyon," they are first pictured riding down into Sedona. The starkly beautiful desert canyon floor they reached, however, was clearly not Sedona.

I searched for "Ghost Canyon" for years without success. Then, Grace Bradley Boyd, who was honeymooning with Hoppy during the filming of *Texas Trail* and naturally had vivid memories of the experience, told me that the scenes were shot at Tuba City. Later,

Hoppy's sidekicks in Blue Canyon for Texas Trail *(1937).*

Henry Donovan, property manager on the Hoppy films, recalled that some of the title was filmed in a wash just outside of town. Scenes featuring cathedral-like cliffs similar to those at Red Rock Canyon, California, where some of *Texas Trail* was also shot, were filmed, he added, in Blue Canyon–part of the film's "Ghost Canyon."

The Hopi Indians provided horses as well as a location guide for the shoot. At one point, Henry

Blue Canyon's red cliffs appeared in Noah Beery, Jr.'s Stormy *(1935).*

Donovan remembered, "the guide began warning us that a storm was coming and that we had better get the hell out of there! There wasn't a cloud in the sky and we didn't think it could possibly rain." But they reluctantly heeded the warnings, pulling equipment, cast and crew out of the canyon. And well they did. Soon, a huge storm flooded the canyon. In fact, in some scenes obviously filmed shortly after the rain had subsided, the cast and horse herd can be seen riding by a large pool of water on the canyon floor!

When I began attempting to access the canyon several years after my conversation with Henry Donovan, I soon developed vicarious feelings of deja vu myself. A storm over the area prevented my first descent into the canyon. On my second attempt, I made it down into the canyon, but soon had to leave or else be trapped by an approaching storm. Finally, on a third attempt, I was successful. A visit to Blue Canyon is well worth the effort. But be careful!

Directions: To reach Blue Canyon, take Highway 264 southeast from Tuba City about thirty miles to Bureau of Indian Affairs 7, a dirt road on the left, between Mile Marker 355 and 356. Take BIA 7 about fifteen miles to the canyon. 4W vehicles with high clearances only.

Prescott

The typical B-western and serial was filmed in California, most in fact within a few miles of Los Angeles. But production crews occasionally ventured out of state to unusual locales, hopeful of giving their budget oaters a more expensive look and fans a break from the all-too-familiar California filming sites.

One of the most scenic such settings was Prescott, Yavapai County, in the hill country of northwest Arizona. Local legend has it that Cecil B. DeMille considered filming *The Squaw Man* (1914) there, but moved on to L.A. when a blinding blizzard greeted his arrival in Prescott. In 1912, however, Romaine

Fielding did fifteen silents in Prescott for the Lubin Co. The next year, Selig Polyscope opened a satellite studio at 712 Western Ave. and began work on a series of shorts directed by silent star William Duncan at Selig's Diamond S. Ranch east of town. Duncan starred in several of those titles (e.g., *Range Law*, 1913, *Sallie's Sure Shot*, 1913), with future cowboy super-star Tom Mix in a supporting role.

Soon, though, Mix became the star (and Myrtle Stedman his frequent leading lady) while also reportedly taking part in the steer riding and bull-dogging competition (that some say was fixed) during Prescott's 1913 Frontier Days celebration at the local fairgrounds. Titles in the series of over fifty one-reelers included *Law and the Outlaw* (1913), *Made a Coward* (1913) and, fittingly, *Sheriff of Yavapai County* (1913). They were shot primarily in the Diamond Valley area and its Slaughterhouse Gulch, a dry wash east of Prescott.

The ranch house Mix and his family occupied, much modified in appearance, served years later as the clubhouse for the Yavapai Hills subdivision. A "hanging tree" often seen in the Mix flicks also stood in the area. Local opinion varies on whether the star owned or simply rented the property. One source indicates that Mix and his family lived on Selig's Diamond S. spread.

In mid-1915, the Selig operations moved to Las Vegas, New Mexico, but Mix returned to Prescott several years for filming. April, 1922, items in the local newspaper noted, for example, the star's return to town for yet another oater (working title, *Gun Fanner*). Filming on that epic was slated for the rodeo grounds and other local sites, with area citizens available for crowd scenes. Mix had last visited the area, according to the newspaper account, two years earlier for an entry that featured a huge explosion outside town.

Nor would Tom Mix be the only western star to ride the Prescott range. In 1939, Ben Judell, independent film distributor and producer of several exploitation quickies (e.g., *Rebellious Daughters*, 1938), formed Producers Distributing Corporation (a.k.a. Producers Pictures Corporation) with ambitious production plans, including a Tim McCoy series and "The Sagebrush Family," a western version of Fox's popular Hardy family series.

Perhaps at the suggestion of PDC contract director Robert Tansey, whom the Prescott newspaper would later dub the community's "Ambassador to Hollywood," Judell also decided to establish a studio in Prescott. By late November, PDC had completed initial construction of a western street in a clearing overlooking Watson Lake and situated in the Granite Dells five miles northeast of town, a picturesque collection of rock formations amid scattered pines, reminiscent of Lone Pine's Alabama Hills. In early December, the company filmed *The Sagebrush Family Trails West*, first in a planned series of eight titles starring 13-year-old junior rodeo champion Bobby Clark. The film also featured, as the sheriff and titular action lead, Archie Hall (1909-1978)–father of Arch Hall, Jr., who became infamous in the 1960s for such films as *Eegah* and *the Choppers*, many of which his father helped write/produce–as well as Earle Hodgins, essaying yet another of his medicine show barker roles.

Later that month, Tim McCoy arrived for work on *Texas Renegades* (working title *Renegade Riders*). Noting that the area was just as convenient to Los Angeles as his Wyoming ranch, McCoy told a reporter that he intended to make Prescott his motion picture headquarters. Even before any filming started, the studio and local chamber of commerce were also making plans for a "Bobby Clark Day" to celebrate the opening of the Prescott facilities. In a November 27 letter to Arizona governor R. T. Jones, PDC public director Eddy Graneman invited the governor to serve as official host for the event.

But the PDC chapter in Prescott's film history was soon to have an abrupt and unhappy ending. Sidelined with a severe bronchial infection, Governor Jones informed the chamber of commerce that he would be unable to attend the celebration, sending an emissary instead. By that point, though, the governor's health was the least of PDC's worries. The Clark and McCoy titles were released in mid-January 1940. But

The Prescott western street.

The town set in the Granite Dells overlooked Watson Lake,
which also appeared in films.

"Bobby Clark Day" was postponed indefinitely, the "Sagebrush Family" series (mercifully) bit the dust and PDC, facing severe financial difficulties, including a $90,000 lien held by the Pathe film lab, was forced to reorganize. Ambitious PDC became, first, Sig Neufeld Productions, then humble Producers Releasing Corporation–the runt, it has been said, of the B-western litter. The PRC folks made fast-moving and cheap little oaters–emphasis on cheap. No exotic locales for them!

Prescott's filming days, however, were not over. Actress Dorothy Fay was a Prescott native. Her father, Dr. Harry T. Southworth, was one of Arizona's most prominent physicians , often treating western actors and production crew members, including Tom Mix, when they were injured or became ill during filming in Prescott. Dr. Southworth died while Dorothy was in high school but her brother remained a Prescott resident and after going into pictures, Dorothy did her part to encourage film-making there and elsewhere in Arizona. Monogram's *Rollin' Westward* (1939), pairing Fay with future husband Tex Ritter, had its

A production shot from a Tex Ritter title being filmed in the Granite Dells. Note Tex, his stunt double and their matching white steeds in the lower right of the picture.

"world premiere" in Prescott and Phoenix, with personal appearances by the stars in each city. The duo also appeared in *Rainbow over the Range* (1940) and *Rollin' Home to Texas* (1940), both shot in Prescott. Then, on June 14, 1941, Tex and Dorothy married in an elaborate ceremony at Prescott's First Congregational Church.

But Tex was not the only star in Monogram's western stable. In early March of that year, acting Prescott

The "Rough Riders" at Prescott.

Mayor E. A. McCabe journeyed to L.A. to finalize plans for further Monogram productions in Prescott. By that point, the city had taken over the western street PDC had built in the impressive Granite Dells on a hill overlooking scenic Watson Lake, a few miles northeast of town. In early May, Monogram production chief Scott Dunlap and veteran cowboy star Buck Jones arrived in Prescott to announce plans for production there of the first entry in what was to become one of the best-loved oater series, "The Rough Riders," co-starring Buck, Tim McCoy and veteran western sidekick Raymond Hatton.

At a banquet feting the Hollywood visitors at the Hassayampa Hotel, Dunlap told local leaders that Robert Tansey had "been shouting Prescott in my ear for a year, but I waved him away." Finally, the Monogram head was persuaded to make a trip to Prescott. "I came, I saw," Dunlap told his audience, "and we will make the first Buck Jones picture here starting June 1."

Calling Prescott the "Cowboy Capital of the World," Mayor McCabe and other dignitaries presented Jones, Dunlap and Tansey ten-gallon hats. The next day, the trio toured local filming sites as Dunlap revealed plans to enlarge the Granite Dells western set, adding five buildings, lengthening the street and perhaps adding a cross street. Before they left for Hollywood, Tansey also told a reporter he would be returning to Prescott later that month for filming of an entry in Tom Keene's Monogram series.

Shooting on Keene's *Wanderers of the West* (1941), co-starring child actor Sugar Dawn as well as Betty Miles, recent winner of the top cowgirl title at the Saugus Rodeo, started in Prescott on May 19. Keene's *Dynamite Canyon* (1941) also made effective use of Prescott sites, especially Watson Lake, which had appeared, too, in Tex's *Rainbow over the Range*.

Keene's remaining Monogram starrers stayed close to the studio's home range, utilizing primarily Monogram Ranch, Walker Ranch, Jauregui Ranch and other Newhall locations north of L.A. On June 10, 1941, however, Buck Jones, Scott Dunlap and their wives arrived in Prescott to begin filming *Arizona Bound*, the first title in the Rough Riders series. A production crew of 50 was to arrive the next day, with filming to start June 12 under Dunlap's personal direction. Shooting began at Prescott's Burnt Ranch (the title, interestingly, of one of the first films shot in the area, a Romaine Fielding silent from 1912) then moved to the Granite Dells street set, on which Monogram had recently spent $3,000 in improvements. Running inserts were shot along the Granite Dells road. Other scenes featured plains areas near the street set and along what is now Highway 89-alternate northeast of Prescott. One impressive shot in *Arizona Bound* pictured a closeup of Buck Jones on Silver, posed before a chimney rock formation situated northeast of town.

When shooting ended a week later, Raymond Hatton told a reporter that he had "never seen a more beautiful location or a friendlier city than Prescott." The Prescott *Evening Courier* indicated that Monogram would resume production on July 7 with two more Tom Keene titles, followed by the second entry in the Rough Riders series. And Scott Dunlap once again praised Prescott's potential as a permanent filming location.

Alas, it was not to be. The remaining seven titles in the Rough Riders series were shot mainly in the Newhall area, and *Dynamite Canyon* was the only other Keene entry filmed at Prescott. In later years, big budget films occasionally featured Prescott locales. The visually stunning Gene Tierney-Cornel Wilde melodrama *Leave Her to Heaven* (1945) was shot at nearby Sedona and other exotic spots but also utilized a rural swimming pool off Granite Dells road that was bordered by large boulders at one end. The ramshackle pool and pavilion were still there when I visited in 1999.

During my visit, several locals tried to convince me that the western street set had been located in a clearing beyond the swimming pool. But photographs available in the Prescott library indicated that it overlooked Watson Lake, although the lake was never visible in scenes using the street set.

Parts of later films also used Prescott, including Steve McQueen's *Junior Bonner* (1972), *Wanda Nevada* (1979), *Billy Jack* (1971), *Bless the Beasts and Children* (1971), *Creepshow 2* (1987), the 1994 version of *The Getaway* with Alex Baldwin, and establishing scenes for the Lloyd and Beau Bridges TV series "Harts of the West" (1993)–although, as noted elsewhere, most exteriors for that series were actually shot at the Sable Ranch and Rancho Maria outside Newhall, not in Arizona.

For western movie fans, however, Prescott had its film heyday when Tom Mix, Tex Ritter, the Rough Riders, Tim McCoy and Tom Keene rode the Prescott range.

Yuma

Mention Yuma, Arizona, and most film fans think immediately of the wild west and such oaters as *3:10 to Yuma* and *Fort Yuma*. In fact, comparatively few westerns were actually filmed in the area. Yuma does have a long history as a filming site, however, and titles shot there include a couple of classic B-westerns as well as one of John Wayne's Mascot cliffhangers.

According to local historian Frank Love, the first film shot in the area was *Bandit Joe and the Lovely Heroine's Rescue*, starring future Mack Sennet comedian Ben Turpin and produced by Essanay Film Co. (then headquartered in Chicago) during the winter of 1909. By 1914, a third title was in production there. But the first major film lensed at Yuma was the Ronald Colman version of *Beau Geste* (1926), followed the same year by Valentino's *Son of the Sheik* and in 1929 by *The Desert Song* with John Boles as well as the William Powell/Richard Arlen rendering of *Four Feathers*.

In 1930, a town set was built on the banks of the Colorado River near Yuma for Wayne's *The Big Trail*, with the Colorado substituting for the Mississippi River at the beginning of the settlers' trek west. By 1990, Yuma had played host to more than forty titles, including the 1939 Gary Cooper and 1966 Guy Stockwell versions of *Beau Geste*, Tyrone Power's *Suez* (1938), Bogart's *Sahara* (1943), James Mason's *The Desert Fox* (1951), Jimmy Stewart's *Flight of the Phoenix* (1966), desert scenes for the superb political thriller *Seven Days in May* (1964) (in which ace stuntman Bill Catching, a later Yuma resident, had a small role), the *Return of the Jedi* (1982) entry in the "Star Wars" series, Sylvester Stallone's *Rambo III* (1988), a couple of the Hope-Crosby "Road" pictures, Jerry Lewis' first solo outing, *Sad Sack* (1957) and such A-westerns as Alan Ladd's *The Badlanders* (1958) and *Last of the Comanches* (1952) with Lloyd Bridges and Broderick Crawford.

For fans of the Saturday matinee, though, the Yuma area is best remembered as the setting for three of our favorites: Tom Mix's *The Rider of Death Valley* (1932), which was filmed in the Yuma area rather than Death Valley; Wayne's *The Three Musketeers* (1932) serial; and Gene Autry's exceptional *Red River Valley* (1936).

According to local news articles, Mix and a company of 59 arrived in March of 1932 for two weeks' filming coordinated by the Yuma Motion Picture Cooperative Association, while a Republic crew of about 25 began a week's shooting January 20, 1936, on an unnamed title that must have been *Red River Valley*. The two features and Wayne chapter play were shot in part at the area's most frequently used locale–Buttercup Valley in California's Imperial Sand Dunes, a few miles northwest of Yuma and the Arizona border. When a plotline required sand dunes, a movie company might venture up to the dunes area south of Lone Pine, a couple hundred miles north of L.A., or sometimes to another spot. But when massive dune scenes were featured in a title, they were most often shot in the Imperial Dunes, or "sand hills," as locals called them.

Filming for *The Three Musketeers* and *Red River Valley* also included another familiar Yuma landmark, the old territorial prison. More than 3,000 inmates were confined in Yuma's prison from its opening in 1876 until 1909, when the last convicts were transferred to a new facility at Florence. The local high school then occupied its buildings from 1910 to 1914–with the school's athletic teams called, appropriately enough, "The Criminals" during that period. During the Depression it became a shelter for the homeless. But the prison, including its impressive main gate, also played a variety of roles in *The Three Musketeers* and its cell row and other facilities were put to excellent use in *Red River Valley*. The latter title also featured Yuma's Laguna Dam, on the spillway to which Gene and heavy George Chesboro staged an exciting and dangerous fight sequence. The small train that figured prominently in the *Red River Valley* plot line was used "in real life" to haul ore from area mines. The engine to one like it (or perhaps the same engine, modified in appearance over the years) is now on display on the lawn of a Yuma museum. A scene for Mix's *The Rider of Death Valley* was shot on the Ballance Ranch near Somerton, southwest of Yuma, which unfortunately has been swallowed up by one of the huge and lush farming operations made possible in more recent years by the harnessing of the Colorado River. Scenes from the Mix title were also shot at Black Butte and Telegraph Pass, east of Yuma.

Yuma residents generally welcomed the movie companies and the money they brought to the region. Some have fond memories of their contacts with the players. One recalled, for example, that Jimmy Stewart dropped by Murray's, a local diner, most evenings after shooting for *Flight of the Phoenix*, as friendly and relaxed over a cup of coffee as in his screen roles. But occasionally relations between town and movie folk grew strained. For example, when Carolco productions sought $15 per night motel rooms for the crew filming *Rambo III* (1988) during Yuma's peak winter tourist season, the locals balked, although Carolco predicted the project would pump more than $1 million into the local economy.

The area continues to play host to movies and commercial shoots. But Yuma, like so many other film sites, had its cinematic high in the golden era.

The Yuma prison cellblock.

Yuma's then new Laguna Dam appeared in an exciting scene for Gene Autry's Red River Valley (1936).

Old Tucson and Mescal

One of the better known western filming sites has also long been a major Arizona tourist attraction. Old Tucson had its origins in the decision of Columbia Pictures executives to shoot *Arizona* (1940), the epic Jean Arthur-William Holden starrer recounting the state's pioneering days, where it actually occurred rather than at familiar California locales. On a 320-acre stand of Saguaro cactus in a valley fifteen miles west of Tucson, with Golden Gate Peak, the area's most distinctive landmark, looming in the background, the studio constructed a full-scale replica of the town as it had looked in 1859–a walled, adobe settlement roughly the size of a modern city block. Working on

The Arizona (1940) *set, with Golden Gate Peak in the background.*

property leased from Pima County, local technicians and carpenters took just forty days to erect a set of more than fifty buildings, at a cost variously estimated to be between $150,000 and $250,000.

Director Wesley Ruggles began construction of Old Tucson in July of 1939. The September outbreak of war in Europe temporarily halted the project and budget-conscious Columbia's concerns about spiraling costs caused further delays in production. In March 1940, however, the cast and crew returned to Old Tucson. By late summer, Arizona filming had been completed. And on November 11, 1940, Arizona hosted a premiere at Tucson's State Theater, followed by a week-long celebration.

For the next six years, Old Tucson lay largely dormant, its sets becoming seriously deteriorated. Scenes for *The Bells of St. Mary's* (1945), starring Bing Crosby and Ingrid Bergman, were reportedly shot there. Beginning in 1946, Tucson's Junior Chamber of Commerce leased Old Tucson from the county on a dollar-a-year basis. Hampered by an almost non-existent budget, the Jaycees were able to make only minor improvements to the sets, including construction of a new jail and installation of underground wiring and a sewage system.

Even so, several features were shot at the facility during the Jaycee period. Fittingly, Gene Autry, who was beginning his long post-war association with Columbia Pictures, was first, using Old Tucson, plus much stock footage from *Arizona*, for his *The Last Round-up* (1947). Other area sites had parts as well. A nearby Civilian Conservation Corps boys camp, now occupied by the excellent Desert Museum, appeared, for example, as heavy Ralph Morgan's ranch. During the 1950s, Old Tucson also hosted Jimmy Stewart's

Winchester 73 (1950), Ronald Reagan's *The Last Outpost* (1940), *The Lone Ranger and the Lost City of Gold* (1957), and *Rio Bravo* (1958), the first of four John Wayne titles to be shot at Old Tucson.

In July 1959, Old Tucson came under new management when Midwesterner Robert Shelton formed the Old Tucson Development Company, obtained a lease from the county and began restoration of the sets. Shelton also made an additional decision that was to assure a bright future for the facility: In 1960, he opened the Old Tucson Studios as a family fun park as well as a movie location. Providing versatility for both tourists and movie-makers, he augmented the original adobe buildings with a Midwestern street (called "Kansas Street") of two-story commercial establishments, including a hotel, bank and mercantile. In 1970,

The former CCC camp that served as villain Ralph Morgan's ranch in The Last Round-up (1947) *is now home to the Desert Museum. Note Golden Gate Peak in the distance.*

Old Tucson also purchased MGM's back-lot steam engine, "Reno," originally built in 1872 for Nevada's Virginia & Truckee line. But Reno was not the only addition to the Old Tucson landscape appealing to film companies. In 1968, Shelton added a 13,000 square foot, air-conditioned sound stage, disguised as a large stable, to the facilities. The same year, Old Tucson purchased Mescal, a location ranch near Benson, 40 miles southeast of the main sets, that had been built for Lee Marvin's *Monte Walsh* (1970), providing an

The Mescal set.

additional street set and other structures for film crews attracted to Tucson. Beginning in 1970, with the purchase of part of MGM's wardrobe collection, Old Tucson also acquired a huge wardrobe inventory. In 1966, Shelton had also acquired many props used in John Wayne's *The Alamo* (1960), including, reportedly, all the cannon, saddles and wagons that appeared in that epic.

Drawn in part by Shelton's improvements, the movie studios made reasonably frequent use of Old Tucson's facilities during the 1960s and early 1970s. Sam Peckinpah directed *The Deadly Companions*

Old Tucson also hosted Randolph Scott.

And Audie Murphy, too, seen here in The Guns of Fort Petticoat (1957).

(1962) there. Robert Mitchum's *Young Billy Young* (1968) was the first title to use the sound stage Shelton had installed. Mescal appeared in *Dirty Dingus Magee* (1970), with Frank Sinatra, Paul Newman's *The Life and Times of Judge Roy Bean* (1972), *Tombstone* (1993) and *The Quick and the Dead* (1994), among other titles. Audie Murphy, who had originally gone to Old Tucson for *The Guns of Fort Petticoat* (1957), returned with Buster Crabbe for *The Arizona Raiders* (1964).

Crews shooting on the facilities also often constructed additional standing sets, further enhancing Old Tucson's cinematic appeal. John Wayne's production crews, for example, built a saloon, bank and doctor's office for *Rio Bravo* (1959), a railroad depot for *McLintock* (1963), various sets in the adobe section for *El Dorado* (1966), and a cantina, artificial creek, jail and ranch set for *Rio Lobo* (1970).

Television productions, including "Bonanza" and "Gunsmoke," also made occasional visits to Old Tucson. The "High Chaparral" series even made the site its permanent home during its 1966-71 TV run. With its main ranch house and stables set against the impressive backdrop of Golden Gate Peak, that series had an authentic look its video competitors, with their penchant for sound stage "exteriors," clearly lacked.

The "High Chaparral" set.

Eventually, Bob Shelton gave up his lease and in 1986, DRD Ventures II, a Tucson firm, took control of Old Tucson's operations. But the site's ability to attract feature, television, and commercial advertising productions never ceased. Clint Eastwood had filmed *Joe Kidd* (1971), including its explosive railroad climax, there and returned for portions of *The Outlaw Josey Wales* (1976). Old Tucson and Mescal also hosted *Posse* (1975) and *The Villain* (1979) with Kirk Douglas, and even became the sites for a number of comedies, including Burt Reynolds' *Cannonball Run II* (1984) and *Three Amigos* (1986), starring Chevy Chase, Steve Martin and Martin Short. For the latter title, portions of the existing sets were modified to resemble 1919 Mexico and an entire mission set was also erected.

Television series and made-for-TV movies continued using the facilities as well. In fact, Old Tucson was the production base for the "Young Riders" series during its two-season run (1989-91). In the early nineties, the site also hosted such major features as *Tombstone* (1993), *The Quick and the Dead* and TNT's retelling of *Geronimo* (1993).

On April 24, 1995, a major fire destroyed approximately 40 percent of Old Tucson, including the sound stage, Kansas Street and the train depot. But filming reportedly resumed in June for the TV series "Legend" in the original adobe section and other sets that survived the fire, as well as at Mescal. In January 1997, the rebuilt park–by far the site's major money-maker–reopened to the public. It continues to thrive as the third most popular tourist attraction in Arizona, as well as an occasional filming site. Mescal has also been opened to the public. But both sites remain vulnerable to the elements and human error. A 2007 storm, for example, caused the collapse of one of Mescal's buildings.

For location fans, Old Tucson's Disneyland atmosphere can be a bit traumatic. In fact, before driving into the valley where the facility is located, visitors may wish to stop along Gates Pass high above the valley and observe Old Tucson and its spectacular surrounding scenery from a distance. That sight should bring to mind fond memories of *Arizona*, Gene Autry's *The Last Round-up* and other favorite films. Touring the current Old Tucson probably will not have that effect.

Directions: To reach Old Tucson from town, take Speedway west through Gates Pass. Turn left at Kinney Road. Old Tucson is at 201 South Kinney Road. After years of being closed to the public, Old Tucson Studios began offering tours of Mescal. To reach Mescal from Tucson, take I-10 east toward Benson to Mescal Road. Go north on Mescal Road several miles and turn left where the pavement ends. Go west a half mile to the town entrance.

Other Tucson Area Locations

South of Tucson toward Nogales and the Mexican border are other western movie sites. Situated along Highway 83 about 18 miles south of Interstate 10, the huge Empire Ranch and its 22-room adobe and wood frame main house played host to many films, as did neighboring ranches in the Sonoita, Elgin, Patagonia and San Rafael Valley areas. A "Spanish Bit" ranch set was constructed in the Empire Ranch area for *Duel in the Sun* (1946), which also included filming in Tucson's Starr Pass as well as, of course, other locations. At Patagonia, Sonoita Creek, with its overhanging trees, furnished a

Sonoita Creek.

beautiful setting for scenes in such films as *Last Train from Gun Hill* (1959). Cattle drive and other scenes for John Wayne's great *Red River* (1948) were set primarily in the Elgin area and on the Empire Ranch, which also hosted the cattle roundup scenes for *Duel in the Sun*. Elgin played Contention City in the Glenn

Empire Ranch main house.

Ford version of *3:10 to Yuma* (1957) and its train depot appeared in the musical *Oklahoma* (1955). The depot, like much of the little community, is long gone. But a cistern seen in *3:10 to Yuma* was still there in 2007.

Apacheland

Phoenix frequently played host to western movie and TV productions. A studio at suburban Cudia City, where most of the Russell Hayden-produced series "26 Men" was filmed, succumbed to urban sprawl years ago. But the area's other principal filming site, Apacheland, survived for many years.

In 1955, several local businessmen went to Spencer D. Stewart, chairman of the board of Phoenix's Home Savings & Loan. They wanted financing for construction of a movie studio, complete with western street and other sets, near Apache Junction in the Superstition Mountains, 35 miles east of the city. The board turned them down flat but Stewart thought the project was a terrific idea and agreed to personally guarantee the loan.

He probably should have listened to his board. By 1959, Apacheland's original owners had defaulted on their note and Stewart had himself a movie studio. Originally constructed for episodes of "Death Valley Days," the site, according to its current owner, also hosted episodes of "Wyatt Earp," "Have Gun, Will Travel," "Gunsmoke" and other television series, as well as portions of several features, including portions of Jason Robard's *The Ballad of Cable Hogue* (1970) and Elvis Presley's *Charro* (1969). When demand for the site as a filming location declined in the early seventies, Apacheland became an amusement park featuring public appearances by such stars of TV oaters as Peter Brown of "Lawman," Robert Fuller of "Laramie" and Doug McClure of "The Virginian."

The Apacheland street in the 1990s.

In 1977, Stewart's daughter Sue Birmingham bought the property from her father, continuing to rent it to film crews for features and commercials. The amusement park closed in 1984 and afterwards the area was seen primarily in commercials, which had begun lensing there as early as 1958 and included the famous Volkswagen spot featuring a minister in front of the Apacheland church set, as well as commercials for Toyota, Dodge trucks, the GM Montana, Jeep, Colt 45 malt liquor, even an ad for a Turkish TV set.

Features have occasionally lensed there in recent years, too. "Blind Justice," an HBO feature starring Armand Assante, was filmed at Apacheland, as were exteriors for Kenny Rogers' "The Gambler–The Adventure Continues." The site has also played host to several soft-porn videos, including a 1995 "Playboy" entry in which the "stars" cavorted on the town gallows and in its barn, among other sets, as well as "Arizona Babes," one untitled video and "Minor Leaguers," an interactive CD-Rom.

HBO's use of Apacheland for "Blind Justice" brought an added bonus. In exchange for a special rental price, the pay-TV giant agreed to clear away the brush in the area surrounding the sets, reinforce the buildings, and generally spruce up the town.

But the site had its share of fires. In 1969, a blaze caused by a discarded cigarette set the town ablaze, destroying all the sets but its barn, church and the original structures on the property--a stone house and stone corral built by William Augustus ("Tex") Barkley, the original settler and a friend of Teddy Roosevelt's, who according to local lore helped Barkley build his homestead.. The sets were rebuilt on the same foundations with essentially the same designs, albeit with some modifications.

When first built, Apacheland included a soundstage but a tornado blew off its top years ago and it gradually deteriorated. In the early days, Apacheland's soundstage and sets saw considerable activity. Production crews lodged at the Superstition Ho inn in nearby Apache Junction, where the owners' young sons took turns short-sheeting the beds of "Death Valley Days" hosts Ronald Reagan and Robert Taylor, as

The Apacheland barn.

well as other celebrities.

Sue Birmingham had pleasant memories of those years. Elvis, she recalled, was a "nice guy"; John Wayne and his buddies "drank a lot!" In recent years, the Birminghams attempted a variety of ventures to make the site a financial success. In 1996, they opened a large restaurant and bar with facilities for catered affairs. On occasion, too, major corporations rented Apacheland to shoot day-long comic western videos featuring their top salesmen and executives. A Scottsdale businessman even proposed to turn the site into a movie-theme tourist attraction, with rabid western fans paying several hundred dollars apiece to star in a 25-minute video horse opera.

Then, on February 14, 2004, disaster struck. A fire believed caused by an electrical malfunction destroyed 14 of the 21 buildings on the site. With no plans to rebuild Sue Birmingham and her husband sold the property to a developer. At this writing, some effort was continuing to rebuild the facility at another location. But Apacheland's glory days are long gone. For an visit to the site, take U.S. 60 (the Superstition Freeway) east from Phoenix to Apache Junction, take a right there onto Kings Ranch Road. Apacheland is at 4369 S. Kings Ranch Road.

Canyon de Chelly

Ironically, one of the most spectacular Arizona filming sites was so difficult for movie crews, with their heavy trucks and equipment, to access that it rarely appeared in films. Canyon de Chelly National Monument, located near Chinle in northeastern Arizona, on the Navajo reservation, encompasses three major

Cliff dwellings in Canyon de Chelly.

canyons–de Chelly, del Muerto and Monument–and covers 83,840 acres comprised largely of steep winding canyons with sheer walls rising nearly a thousand feet from the canyon floor.

Human occupation of the canyons dates back about 2,000 years. The cliff-dwelling Pueblo or Anasazi Indians lived there nearly a thousand years before vanishing in the mid-13th century. The Navajo later migrated to the area, which is now located entirely within the Navajo Nation. The ruins of the cave dwellings dot the sandstone canyon walls and Navajo residents live along the canyon floor.

Of the various Pueblo ruins, the most impressive are the White House ruins, so named because of the white coloring of those cliffs. The reddish, phallic-like Spider Rock, which rises 800 feet from the canyon floor, is the most distinctive of many canyon rock formations.

Colorado Territory (1949), starring Joel McCrea and Virginia Mayo, includes second unit and process shots featuring de Chelly's cliffs. But those scenes were mixed with principal photography completed at Gallup, New Mexico, southeast of Canyon de Chelly.

Major scenes for Gregory Peck's *MacKenna's Gold* (1969) were filmed, however, in the canyon, although scenes of the cliff walls collapsing in that title's climax were obviously a product of "movie magic." As a film, *MacKenna's Gold* is mediocre at best. But it was a wonderful western travelogue. The vulture soaring behind the credits began its journey at Bryce Canyon, north of Kanab. The film also included rare shots of the Glen Canyon area east of Kanab, among other locations. But the Canyon de Chelly sequences, in which Spider Rock played a prominent role, were visually the most impressive in an otherwise disappointing picture.

Spider Rock, in MacKenna's Gold (1969).

Gallup

New Mexico has been a favorite film-making site since the beginning of motion pictures. In fact, the Thomas Edison company shot a fifty-second documentary, *Indian Day School*, there in 1898. D. W. Griffith filmed *A Pueblo Legend*, starring Mary Pickford, at the Isleta Pueblo in 1912. Romaine Fielding shot many featurettes in the teens at Silver City and Las Vegas, New Mexico, for the Lubin Company. And beginning in 1914, Selig and its star/director Tom Mix reportedly produced up to thirty western shorts at Las Vegas.

Gallup, along I-40 and old Route 66 in the western part of the state, arguably provided the most scenic New Mexico filming sites and certainly the most familiar locales to fans of the western's golden age. In 1880, railroad paymaster David L. Gallup established a headquarters in the area along the construction site for the southern transcontinental railway route. Railroad workers began "going to Gallup" to get their pay and in 1881 a town sprang up there.

The Great Divide (1915), starring House Peters, Sr., was probably the first title shot at Gallup and Richard Dix's *Redskin* (1929), shot at Gallup and the Acoma pueblo as well as on the Navajo Reservation, was another early area title. Director King Vidor utilized Gallup, including its Kit Carson Cave (so-called because the great Indian fighter and his men camped near there during the 1863-64 campaign against the Navajos), for MGM's 1930 version of *Billy the Kid*, starring future B-western great Johnny Mack Brown. Vidor returned for Paramount to direct *The Texas Rangers* (1936) with Fred MacMurray, Jack Oakie and Lloyd Nolan.

In December of 1937, the El Rancho Hotel–built according to hotel literature by R.E. "Griff" Griffith, brother of the great silent director–opened in Gallup, quickly becoming the headquarters for movie crews and stars shooting in the area. Among others, the El Rancho played host to the company for Wallace Beery's comedy western *The Bad Man* (1941); *Sundown* (1941) with Gene Tierney; *Streets of Laredo* (1949), the William Holden-William Bendix-McDonald Carey remake of *The Texas Rangers*; Lew Ayers' *New Mexico* (1950), and Dennis Morgan's *Raton Pass* (1951).

Located in Indian country amid Navajo, Hopi and other reservations, Gallup could provide a large supply of Indians for Cavalry flicks. But the area's scenery was its strongest attraction for movie-makers. The most familiar of several area filming sites is now Red Rock State Park, off I-40 a few miles east of Gallup. Red Rock features a long expanse of relatively smooth rock walls resembling at points modeling clay in texture. Visible through a gap in those cliffs is another filming landmark, Church Rock, an edifice of gray-white stone so-called because of its likeness to a large cathedral. A few miles east of the park are even more impressive red cliffs than those in the park. The vicinity also includes a box canyon featuring Cleopatra's Needle, yet another impressive formation.

Johnny Mack Brown at Kit Carson Cave.

Church Rock.

Several films put the area to particularly effective use. An excellent pan of the park's main wall of cliffs runs behind the credits to Alan Ladd's *Red Mountain* (1951) and the box canyon with Cleopatra's Needle provided backdrops for an exciting stagecoach-Indian chase near the beginning of Errol Flynn's *Rocky Mountain* (1950) as well as its well-staged climax. The cliffs, canyon and other settings made appearances as well in Ben Johnson's *Fort Defiance* (1950), Joel McCrea's

The Red Rock formations.

Fort Massacre (1957), Troy Donahue's *A Distant Trumpet* (1963) and Burt Lancaster's *Hallelujah Trail* (1965). Perhaps the park formations' most visually stunning appearance lensed for a romantic interlude in William Holden's *Escape from Fort Bravo* (1953), which also made extensive use of Death Valley settings.

Nor were the area's film roles limited solely to Cavalry and western features. It also provided the setting for Billy Wilder's personal favorite of his titles, *Ace in the Hole* (retitled *The Big Carnival*, 1950). The Tracy-Hepburn dust-bowl epic *Sea of Grass* (1947) used Gallup as well, as did the musical *The Desert Song* (1943) and *Sudan* (1945).

Cleopatra's Needle appeared in Rocky Mountain (1950).

North of the park's red cliffs a mile or so are some gray-white cliffs that include cone-shaped rock formations. They and similar formations at Lupton, Arizona, west of Gallup, also appeared in features. The Lupton rocks had a role, for example, in Raoul Walsh's *Pursued* (1947) and especially in *Red Mountain*. *Rocky Mountain* also made use of the cone-shaped formations.

Pyramid Rock, another prominent Gallup edifice, appeared in the background of this scene from Billy the Kid.

Other locales in the Gallup vicinity were occasional stars, too. Canyon De Chelly's cinema role has already been noted. Inscription Rock at the El Morro National Monument, along Hwy 53 southeast of Gallup, forms part of the plot line in Joel McCrea's *Four Faces West* (1948). The huge Shiprock, 90 miles north of Gallup, also appeared in a few films, including *The Hallelujah Trail*.

Features filmed partially at Gallup, of course, regularly made use of L.A. area sites also.

Inscription Rock.

Corriganville's Ft. Apache set made appearances in *Streets of Laredo* and *Escape from Fort Bravo*, while the Monogram town set at Newhall saw service in *Streets of Laredo* and *Fort Defiance* and the Iverson Ranch's town appeared in *Red Mountain*. But a Gallup area fort set originally constructed for Gregory Peck's *Only the Valiant* (1951) made appearances as well, as did an area town set of uncertain origin and location.

Several years ago, child actor and "Range Rider"/"Buffalo Bill, Jr." TV star Dick Jones shared with me his memories of working on *Rocky Mountain*. Jones appeared in a number of films shot in Utah and Arizona, including *The Great Adventures of Wild Bill Hickok* (1938) at Kanab, Howard Hughes' *The Outlaw*

Dick Jones (lower right) considers Rocky Mountain (1950) *his favorite movie of the many in which he appeared.*

(1943) at Tuba City, Arizona, and Gene Autry's first color feature *The Strawberry Roan* (1948) at Sedona. But *Rocky Mountain* would be his only Gallup film visit and it remained his personal favorite of all his titles.

In those days, Jones recalls, "you could walk from one end of Gallup to the other in five or six minutes." Cast and crew stayed at the El Rancho, the crew in cabins along the rear and the cast in the main lodge. The director insisted Jones stay with the little dog that had a prominent role in the film. Allowing a one-time exception to its "No Dogs" policy, the hotel agreed, lodging Jones and the dog in a large suite at the end of one wing of the hotel.

Jones has fond memories of Errol Flynn, whom he described as a true journeyman actor. But the star and his co-star/future wife Patrice Wymore, he said, "fought like cats and dogs" throughout the shoot. Flynn had brought one of his many lady friends with him to Gallup and invited Jones and "Buzz" Henry, another former child actor in the cast, to join them for supper one evening.

About an hour after they were to meet in the hotel lobby, Flynn's girlfriend appeared alone. The star, it seemed, had fallen asleep in the bath tub, so she pulled the plug, leaving Flynn to sleep it off.

Fans envision nights on a location shoot as a continuing round of booze, poker games, partying and other diversions. But Jones had a different memory of his *Rocky Mountain* experience. "We were too damn tired. We'd finish working after the sun would go down and we'd have to bus back into town. By the time we washed all that red sand off ourselves and had dinner, we were flaked out in the sack."

The *Rocky Mountain* shoot gave Jones a chance, though, to get "revenge" against Yakima Canutt. In Wayne's *Westward Ho* (1935), the great stuntman was an outlaw who kidnapped Jones, playing the Duke's younger brother, from a wagon train. But the *Rocky Mountain* script called for Jones to "shoot" his former nemesis.

Canutt was not only in the cast but coordinated the film's terrific action scenes as well. At one point, Jones recalled, the stuntman had rigged a stagecoach to overturn at a particular spot. But the cinematographer placed one of the three cameras for the scene at the same place, ignoring Canutt's warning to reposition the camera. "When Yak pulled the trip on the stagecoach, it dumped right on top of that $35,000 camera. Just busted it up in little pieces."

One of Jones' own memorable gags for the film involved his dropping off the side of his saddle and shooting an Indian from under the neck of his horse. When he began filming for the "Range Rider" TV series in October after the Gallup shoot ended in August, his director insisted he repeat that stunt for the series prologue. Jones reluctantly obliged but later remembered that "it was a lot wilder down there in Gallup. The camera car was wide open. And when the Indian bumped my horse, I just fell over on my side. If the horse had gone down, that would have been the end of Dick." Fortunately for all his fans, the gag played out to perfection and provided an exciting beginning for his series entries as well.

Rocky Mountain, Jones also recalled, was Slim Pickens' first film. "He was having a difficult time getting his dialogue down and how to deliver it so the camera could pick it up. Buzz Henry and I gave Slim a real bad time."

Gallup has continued to be used, albeit sparingly, in more recent years. *Superman* (1978) apparently included some shooting there, as did the black comedy *Enid Is Sleeping* (1990) and the thriller *Dark Blood* (1993). But the thirties through the mid-sixties were the high point for Gallup as a western film capital.

The Santa Fe Ranches

If Gallup was the favorite New Mexico filming site during filmdom's golden age, the Santa Fe area has dominated the state's cinema industry during the modest revival of western movies that began in the mid-1980s. Santa Fe's role in films had actually begun three decades earlier, however, when portions of Jimmy Stewart's *The Man from Laramie* (1955) were shot outside Santa Fe on the huge Bonanza Creek Ranch, then known as the Jarrett Ranch.

According to local lore, Louie Clifford, a former chauffeur to silent star Mary Pickford, was operating a taxi company in nearby Albuquerque when he brought Santa Fe to Hollywood's attention. But the Stewart title was only the beginning. Bonanza Creek's rolling green pastures fed by an artesian spring, ponds surrounded by ancient Cottonwoods and 14,000 acres of range land furnished ideal settings for western films. In 1957, director Delmer Daves made *Cowboy* (1958), starring Glenn Ford and Jack Lemmon, there. The 1,200 cattle brought up from Mexico for that shoot stampeded at one point, tearing down a mile and a half of railroad fencing before scattering, some far into the mountains northeast of Santa Fe. Overall, however, the venture was a success for both Bonanza Creek's Glenn Hughes and the movie companies, who hoped that exotic new locales for their outdoor titles would slow the mass exodus of audiences from theaters to TV sets.

Nor was Bonanza Creek to be the only Santa Fe spread attracting movie makers. It was to be a few more years before western blockbusters would find their way to the area. But in 1984, director Lawrence Kasdan and his brother Mark flew over in a helicopter while scouting locations, liked what they saw and built a western street and other sets on the Cook Ranch at Galiesteo (1985),

The "Lonesome Dove" house on the Bonanza Creek Ranch.

starring Kevin Kline, Kevin Costner and Danny Glover. When shooting was completed, ranch owner Bill Cook planned to burn the sets down, but yielded to pleas from the state film commission that they be preserved as a means of attracting further productions to Santa Fe.

For "Lonesome Dove" (1989), the much-acclaimed TV mini-series starring Robert Duvall, the *Silverado* sets were revamped for service as towns in four different states, with camera angles for each capturing a different sort of terrain, and the nearby Galiesteo River useful for filming as well. The Cook Ranch was even larger than Bonanza Creek–20,000 acres in all–and an elaborate but unobtrusive network of roads facilitated the film companies' access to remote parts of the spread.

Glenn Hughes' Bonanza Creek Ranch also continued to attract film and TV companies. A town set built there for *The Legend of the Lone Ranger* (1981) had been dismantled after that shoot. But in 1989, a European producer approached Hughes about building a large town set for "Lucky Luke," a television series with Terence Hill, a star of Italian westerns. A two-story Victorian house built on the ranch for *Silverado* and later used in *Lonesome Dove* became a mercantile in Daisy Town, the western street constructed for "Lucky Luke." A large ranch set situated next to a pond was also built for the series.

The main house of a third Santa Fe location ranch actually appeared in a TV series. "Empire," which starred Richard Egan, Terry Moore and Ryan O'Neal, aired in 1962-63 and was filmed on the J.W. Eaves Ranch. Several years later, Eaves, who had bought the spread in 1957, agreed to lease it for a year to Columbia Pictures for filming part of *Where Angels Go, Trouble Follows* (1968), starring Rosalind Russell and Robert Taylor.

The next year, the multi-talented dancer-singer-director Gene Kelly approached Eaves about filming portions of the comedy western *The Cheyenne Social Club* (1970), starring Jimmy Stewart and Henry Fonda, on the ranch. With Kelly's production company splitting the costs equally with Eaves, a town set was constructed there over a five-month period, including the time needed to erect power lines and build roads to the set. John Wayne used the title for *Chisum* (1970) and other titles followed over the years, including Kevin Costner's *Wyatt Earp* (1994). Eaves died in 2001, at age 85. But in its third annual Best of the West competition in 2004, *True West* magazine declared the Eaves town the best western movie set (even though its readers, not surprisingly, chose the Brackettville, Texas, replica of the Alamo examined elsewhere in this volume and seen in the John Wayne epic as well as other accounts of the Alamo saga).

The Eaves Ranch in 2007.

The Cook and Bonanza Creek ranches have also remained active. In September 1998, a scripted explosion went awry, causing major damage to the Cook Ranch's western street during filming of *Wild Wild West* (1999), the Will Smith-Kevin Kline feature version of the old television series. "Three buildings were rigged to explode and the stunt went off without a hitch," a publicist for Warner Brothers, the producer, told a reporter. But a gust of wind spread the blaze from the explosion to adjacent buildings. Fortunately, the ranch's contract with the studio called for Warner Brothers to rebuild the set and there were no injuries to stunt people, crew members, animals or members of the fire department.

In the summer of 2007, Bonanza Creek briefly became embroiled in unfavorable media coverage of "Kid Nation," a CBS reality show detailing the exploits of forty children who create a kids-only society in a New Mexico ghost town, with Bonanza Creek in the ghost town role. One parent complained of exhausting working conditions and threats to the children's health and safety. Several, it was charged, required medical attention after drinking bleach from an unmarked soda bottle; another burned her face with hot grease while cooking. But Glenn Hughes' widow, Imogene, told reporters that she had never heard of any problems on the set and most of the children and their parents had nothing but praise for the experience. In terms of recent productions, moreover, Bonanza Creek appears to be the most active of the Santa Fe movie spreads, so active, in fact, that new sets have been built close to the highway bordering the ranch.

Fashion designer Tom Ford recently purchased the Cook spread for a reported $23 million. But at this writing filming has not been halted on the Ford Ranch, now called the Cerro Pelon Ranch, either. In 2005, for example, Steven Spielberg filmed portions of the TNT mini-series "Into the West" there, with train specialist Jim Clark laying 2,000 feet of track and bringing in rolling stock for the shoot and the rebuilt town site substituting for several towns in the series. *3:10 to Yuma* (2007), the Russell Crowe remake of the Glenn Ford classic, was also filmed in part at the Ford and Bonanza Creek spreads.

Most of the exteriors for *3:10 to Yuma* were shot, however, at another Santa Fe area site–Ghost Ranch in nearby Abiquiu. Its name derived from tales of ghosts and lynchings that dot its history, Ghost Ranch comprises 21,000 acres that were originally part of a Spanish land grant. In 1955, then-owner Arthur Peck donated the property to the Presbyterian Church. In the years since, the ranch has grown into a nationally

Ghost Ranch.

known study and conference center. In 1990, a division of the ranch's operations was also established in Santa Fe.

Watched over by staff archeologists to assure that no permanent damage is done to the ranch's scenic wonders, movie crews regularly film on the spread, with titles shot there including not only *3:10 to Yuma*, but also *The Missing* (2003), *Wyatt Earp* (1994), *Silverado* (1985), even *City Slickers* (1991). In fact, Jack Palance's cabin from the latter title is located near the ranch entrance. With its skull ranch logo and magnificent buttes, Ghost Ranch is a perfect site for western filming.

Nevada

Many western actors no doubt made regular visits to the Las Vegas and Reno gaming tables. But relatively few films were shot in Nevada during the movies' golden age. Those that were generally used the Valley of Fire and Red Rock Canyon outside Las Vegas, the Moapa Valley area northeast of Vegas toward St. George, and sites in and near Carson City and Lake Tahoe.

During the silent era, *The Covered Wagon* (1923), *The Iron Horse* (1924) and Jack Holt's *Born to the West* (1926) were among titles shot in Nevada, as well as other locales. Just months before his official teaming with Stan Laurel, Oliver Hardy also made a very menacing and convincing villain (complete with eye patch) in *No Man's Law* (1927), a tale of two miners lusting after the same beautiful damsel that was filmed largely in the Moapa Valley.

After World War II, Republic Pictures chose Las Vegas sites for two of its three big-budget Roy Rogers titles shot beyond the California home range–*Heldorado* (1946) and *Bells of San Angelo* (1947). (The third title was *Home in Oklahoma*, 1946, examined elsewhere in this book.) Capitalizing on Las Vegas' thirteenth annual "Helldorado" celebration, *Heldorado* included scenes shot during the event's parade and rodeo,

Roy Rogers and Andy Devine in Nevada's Red Rock Canyon for Bells of San Angelo (1947).

outside the Last Frontier Hotel and at Boulder Dam in the mountains souheast of town. But most exteriors were filmed at the Iverson Ranch outside Chatsworth and at the Chatsworth depot in California's San Fernando Valley.

Republic had originally planned to shoot *Bells of San Angelo* at Lone Pine, California, in the late fall of 1946. But weather conditions there forced a shift to Las Vegas, where the shoot for *Heldorado* the previous May had taken only five days. Unfortunately, the Las Vegas weather and complications involving use of Republic's Trucolor process (Black horses became green in Trucolor prints!) extended what was intended as a seven-ten day Vegas shoot to forty-five days. In fact, in late December, cast and crew went back to L. A. for Christmas and back lot shooting, then returned to Nevada in January to complete location filming.

Bells of San Angelo clearly benefitted, however, from location shooting. Whatever the limitations of the Trucolor process, the Valley of Fire and Red Rock Canyon made truly impressive appearances, as did the beautiful scenery on the Red Rock Canyon Bar Nothing Ranch of Chester Lauck of "Lum and Abner" fame–a spread that was later to be owned by German actress Vera Krupp (who gave the property its current name, Spring Mountain Ranch) and later, briefly, by Howard Hughes. Mine scenes for the title were shot

Roy Rogers gets his man (stuntman David Sharpe) in the Valley of Fire.

at Nelson, in the mountains above Las Vegas.

Over the years, production crews occasionally returned to the Las Vegas area for western filming. Burt Lancaster's *The Professionals* (1966), for example, utilized the Valley of Fire as well as the Box Canyon area outside Indio, in California's Coachella Valley, examined in another chapter. Jason Robard, Jr.'s *The Ballad of Cable Hogue* (1970) was filmed, moreover, at the Valley of Fire and at Apacheland, outside Phoenix.

Other Nevada sites made appearances in films as well. The ghost town of Rhyolite, a few miles west of Beatty, Nevada, near the entrance to Death Valley, played a prominent role in Buck Jones' *Desert Vengeance* (1931). In fact, although Rhyolite played the ghost town of "Skyfields" in that fine film, its real name is clearly seen in a closeup of the entrance to a bank. *Ride Him, Cowboy* (1932), one of the

Remains of the Nelson mine reportedly used in Bells of San Angelo.

entries in the brief John Wayne B-western series released through Warner Bros., included scenes of the Rhyolite train depot. But that title was a remake of, and included stock footage from, the Ken Maynard silent *Unknown Cavalier* (1926) and it is difficult to discern whether any of the Rhyolite scenes in the Wayne title were original.

Rhyolite remains.

Several researchers include *Rough Riders Roundup* (1939) among Rhyolite titles. But that Roy Rogers title includes only one quick stock shot of a ghost town and while it could have been Rhyolite, it resembles more a Republic studio miniature than an actual site.

At least one episode in Rod Cameron's "State Trooper" (1957-1959) TV series was filmed in Rhyolite. Oddly enough, however, even though a Rhyolite house built of 50,000 beer and liquor bottles figured prominently in the series episode entitled "Boulder Joe's Bottle House," the exterior to that Rhyolite landmark did not appear in the episode.

Overall, "State Trooper" provided a feast for location fans. Filming took place not only in Rhyolite and the Lake Tahoe-Carson City area, where the series was set, but in the Valley of Fire (Episode 49, "Perilous Picnic") and at other Nevada and California sites as well.

The Carson City-Lake Tahoe area also hosted other productions. The Nevada State Railroad Museum in Carson City has an impressive collection of locomotives and railroad cars, including several used in films.

The museum's records indicate that five titles included railroad scenes shot in the area: Bob Baker's *Courage of the West* (1937), Dan Dailey's *Chicken Every Sunday* (1949), Don Barry's *Train to Tombstone* (1950) and *Roar of the Iron Horse* (1951), the Columbia serial starring Jock Mahoney, plus *Thundering Rails* (1950), a 20-minute documentary produced by Universal studio for the Association of American Railroads, to celebrate the golden age of American railroading.

Jock Mahoney and Virginia Herrick in Carson Valley for Roar of the Iron Horse *(1950).*

The Barry and Mahoney titles suffered, of course, from the tight budgets that regularly afflicted B-westerns and serials. During Indian attacks on the train in the Barry title, for example, the process shots of the Indians racing alongside the train windows were often out of proportion, with the attackers at times assuming giant sizes. During exciting railroad chases in the Carson Valley for *Roar of the Iron Horse*, moreover, contemporary houses could be seen in the distance despite the film's frontier setting!

Carson City also had the distinction of hosting John Wayne's last film, *The Shootist* (1976), with the city's historic district, including its Krebs-Peterson House (mixed in with shots of a house on Warner Bros.' Burbank studio Midwestern Street), playing a prominent role and outdoor scenes shot in the nearby Washoe Lake area, now a state park. Although various sources list other locations for Randolph Scott's *Santa Fe* (1950), rail scenes for that title may have used track around historic Virginia City, a few miles from Carson City.

For fans of western TV shows, however, the Carson City-Lake Tahoe area would be most closely associated with the "Bonanza" series and its "Ponderosa Ranch," mythical mega-spread bordered on the south by Lake Tahoe. Some filming for that series was done in the area. Interestingly, though, it was not until the third season that the opening credits were shot in the area's Bourne's Meadow, with Lake Tahoe in the background. The opening for Season 1 combined shots made in the Conejo Valley near Thousand Oaks with others made at L. A.'s Elysian Park, while Season 2 opening credits were shot against a Big Bear Lake backdrop.

Carson City's Krebs-Peterson house appeared in The Shootist (1976).

The series soon became so identified with Lake Tahoe, however, that a local contractor associated with the production persuaded NBC and the show's producers and stars to build a replica of the Ponderosa Ranch (the original for which was on a studio sound stage in

The "Ponderosa Ranch" tourist attraction at Lake Tahoe.

Hollywood) near the Lake Tahoe shore as a tourist attraction. The Incline Village amusement park opened in July 1967 and members of the "Bonanza" cast made appearances there through 1971-72, the show's thirteenth season. Footage of the house and grounds, filmed in 1968, was used for establishing shots for several later episodes in the series. At one point, the site was reported to be attracting a quarter million tourists annually. In 2007, however, it was closed to the public, with no plans for reopening.

Chapter 9

Wyoming and Montana

At the end of each entry in Monogram's short-lived but excellent "Rough Riders" series, stars Buck Jones, Colonel Tim McCoy and Raymond Hatton bade their fans farewell, riding off in different directions to their home spreads. A great scene! But when Colonel Tim told audiences that he was "heading for Wyoming," he was not simply following a script–McCoy actually owned a Wyoming ranch!

The colonel also starred in several films made in his adopted state, including two titles that contained what would become, via repeated use as stock footage, one of the most familiar sequences in western film history–the scene of mounted Indians leaving their village and riding across a shallow river against the backdrop of a massive cliff.

That impressive scene was filmed along the Little Wind River on the Shoshone Indian reservation near Fort Washakie, north of Lander. Apparently, it first appeared in McCoy's *War Paint* (a.k.a. *Rider of the Plains*, 1926), a silent MGM production, then was used, or reshot, for his *End of the Trail* (1932), released by Columbia. From that point until the end of the golden era, the scene showed up regularly in A and B productions, especially Columbia titles.

One of the most familiar scenes in western moviedom.

Locating the huge cliff, which the Indians call Prayer Mountain and now overlooks a reservoir formed from the shallow Little Wind River, will be easy for location fans. It is so large that it will be immediately spotted by anyone driving south into the valley north of Lander where the Shoshone reservation headquarters is located. Visitors will lose sight of the cliff as they descend into the valley and directions from reservation

Prayer Mountain, on the Wind River Reservation near Lander, Wyoming.

personnel will be needed to locate the reservoir, which is a rather lengthy ride over rough terrain. The view, however, will be well worth the effort!

The Shoshone reservation, of course, was not the only Wyoming filming site movie-makers visited; nor was Tim McCoy the only star of titles shot there. According to Walt Farmer, who produced two excellent CD-ROM books on film-making in Wyoming, *Wyoming Roundup*, a 1904 documentary, was the first film produced in the state. Other silent titles soon followed, including *Charge of the Light Brigade* (1912), *Man from Bitter Root* (1916), *The Fighting Shepherdess* (1920), *Cowboy and the Lady* (1922) and *The Thundering Herd* (1924).

Not surprisingly, film crews seeking Wyoming filming sites often chose Jackson Hole. For obvious reasons, French Canadian trappers long ago named the spectacular peaks near Jackson "Les Trois Tetons," or "The Three Breasts"–the Grand Teton, Middle Teton and South Teton. Mountain men also dubbed any high valley surrounded by mountains a "hole"–hence the area's name, "Jackson Hole."

Jackson and its magnificent peaks offered film companies the state's most visually stunning cinematic locales. John Wayne's *The Big Trail* (1930) was one of the earlier sound titles making effective use of the Tetons. *Son of Lassie* (1945), the first color movie shot in Wyoming, utilized Jenny Lake and other Jackson

John Wayne and the Tetons in The Big Trail *(1930).*

Wayne and Marguerite Churchill at Jackson Hole's Jenny Lake.

Hole sites as well.

Jackson also played host to one of the most unusual B-westerns ever released. *Down the Wyoming Trail* (1939), one of the many Tex Ritter features producer Ed Finney made for Grand National and Monogram, told the story of Tex's battle with rustler Charlie King (naturally), who stampeded an elk herd across a valley to clear a path in the snow for his stolen cattle. The snow scenes were shot northeast of Jackson on the

National Elk Refuge, which had been created in 1912 to promote the survival of the herd.

A combination of daunting weather conditions and limited production facilities gave the film a cheap look, despite its wonderful locale. Cameraman Marcel Picard's photography is often jumpy, the camera speed erratic. As Tex croons to heroine Mary Brodel at the end of the show, the elk herd footage running on a process screen behind them ends and restarts at least once, with the abrupt break in continuity annoyingly obvious. The producer deserves credit, however, for shooting a low-budget title, with an unusual plot, at such a lengthy distance from Hollywood. Besides, *Down the Wyoming Trail* is entitled to some notice as surely the only western in which the hero donned a Santa Claus outfit!

But it was George Stevens' *Shane* (1953), one of the most outstanding westerns of all time, that best displayed the visual splendor of the Tetons and Jackson Hole. Like *High Noon* (1952) and *Stagecoach* (1939), *Shane* bore many of the characteristics of a B-western. And its storyline and actors alone would have assured it

The Starrett homestead in Shane (1953).

Alan Ladd and his children during the making of Shane (1953).

top ranking, whatever its filming locales. Even so, George Stevens' decision to film amid the grandeur of the Tetons, in whatever weather nature chose to provide, and to construct an entire town set and homesteads on the wind-swept prairie land north of Jackson, made *Shane* truly special.

While *Shane* was being filmed, Howard Hawks produced another outdoor picture in the Jackson Hole area. *The Big Sky* (1952), based, like *Shane*, on the writings of novelist A.B. Guthrie, Jr., starred Kirk Douglas and Dewey Martin. It told the story of fur traders who went up the Missouri River by keel boat in the 1820s to obtain furs from peaceful Blackfoot Indians and were obstructed at every turn by a rival and ruthless band of traders. For the production, RKO set up an elaborate camp of tent cottages outside Moran, 30 miles north of Jackson and the *Shane* production site. Wyoming's Snake River impersonated the Missouri River in the picture and filming also took place at Jackson Lake.

At a cost of $28,000 each, RKO had constructed two replicas of the historic keel boat "Mandan" for the picture. Experienced river men, garbed in the costumes of Missouri River boatmen, were brought over from Idaho, adding authenticity to the production. After the picture was completed, RKO donated one of the Mandan replicas to the Montana Historical Society in Helena, which in 1954 loaned it to Paramount for its production at Moran of *Far Horizons* (1955), the

The Mandan.

Fred MacMurray-Charlton Heston retelling of the Lewis and Clark expedition.

In later years, film companies returned to the Tetons often for outdoor titles. Glenn Ford's *Jubal* (1956) utilized the Triangle X Guest Ranch and other Tetons sites, as did *Spencer's Mountain* (1963), the fine Maureen O'Hara-Henry Fonda starrer that became the basis for "The Waltons" TV series.

From the beginning, however, film companies had used a wide variety of Wyoming locales. Jack Holt's *The Thundering Herd* utilized the Buffalo ranch in the Yellowstone park near Cody. *The Pony Express* (1925), with Wallace Beery, was shot on a ranch near Cheyenne. Ken Maynard's *Cheyenne* (1928) utilized downtown Cheyenne and its "Frontier Days" rodeo. According to Walt Farmer, Maynard's *The Red Raiders* (1927) may also have been filmed near Cheyenne, as was the fine little Budd Boetticher-directed film, *Bronco Buster* (1952). *Yellowstone* (1936), with Andy Devine, utilized that historic site. And in later years, the magnificent Devil's Tower, which in 1906 President Theodore Roosevelt had designated the first national monument following enactment of the Antiquities Act, hosted the spaceship landing in *Close Encounters of the Third Kind* (1977).

Wyoming's sister state also played host to western and other outdoor films. Yakima Canutt noted in his terrific autobiography that his silent feature *The Devil Horse* (1926) was filmed in Montana. "We set up a complete camp on the shores of the Little Big Horn River, not far from the Custer Battlefield," he recalled. "We built a log fort for [an] Indian battle scene and at times used as many as four or five hundred Indians."

The infamous "Rex, the Wonder Horse," played the title role. Rex, Yak remembered, "was a big, beautiful well-trained black, but every so often he would get mad and try to kill anyone near him. After Rex killed his keeper he was sold to Hal Roach," producer of *The Devil Horse*. Anyone who has seen the film, stock footage from which later appeared in countless titles, knows that in *The Devil Horse*, Yak almost suffered the same fate as Rex's late keeper!

John Wayne's *The Big Trail* (1930) also reportedly utilized Montana as well as Wyoming, Utah, Arizona, California and Oregon sites. While most exteriors for Joel McCrea's *Buffalo Bill* (1944) were filmed in Paria Canyon outside Kanab, Utah, the buffalo hunt scenes for that visually stunning Technicolor epic were shot on M. H. Tschisgi's huge Antler Ranch, utilizing bison from the Crow Indian reservation near Billings.

By law and tradition, the Crow were allowed to kill a number of buffalo each year as part of the tribe's annual Sun Dance rituals. According to the account of an Antler Ranch co-owner that appeared in a 1967 issue of the *Billings Gazette*, the *Buffalo Bill*

From a newspaper clipping, the filming of the buffalo hunt for Buffalo Bill (1944).

production crew, taking full advantage of the situation, filmed the shoot with actors firing blanks while sharpshooters with high-powered rifles did the actual killing from the sidelines and a Humane Society representative stood by to assure that wounded buffalo (there were two) were promptly and mercifully put down. The result was a gripping (and, for animal lovers, traumatic) depiction of the massive buffalo slaughter that, like the nation's treatment of native Americans, formed one of the darker elements in the history of westward expansion.

Film companies did not begin going to Montana on anything approaching a regular basis, however, until 1950. In January of that year, an Helena movie palace hosted the world premiere of *Montana*, starring Errol Flynn and Alexis Smith. That title was filmed closer to Hollywood. But in August, Nat Holt Productions arrived in Billings with 23 actors, 20 stunt riders, over a score of technicians and a fleet of motor vans crammed with costumes and props (including a reported 18,000 rounds of ammunition) to begin shooting *Warpath* (1951), a cavalry picture starring Edmond O'Brien, Forrest Tucker and James Millican as General George Armstrong Custer. Sporting false fronts and the addition of porches and chimneys, facilities at Billings' Midland Empire Fairgrounds became Fort Abraham Lincoln, the North Dakota fort that served as home to the Seventh Cavalry in 1876, the year of Custer's disastrous defeat at Little Big Horn, part of the *Warpath* storyline. Other exteriors used the nearby Little Big Horn area itself, giving the film added authenticity, and use of the fairgrounds auditorium for interior shooting enabled the crew to complete filming on location–a fact local officials regularly boasted to reporters.

Like any other motion picture, of course, *Warpath* was not entirely authentic–Crow Indians, for example, portrayed their one-time enemies, the Sioux. There were also the usual mishaps that plague location shoots. An actor portraying the chief of a wagon train suffered several chest contusions and a possible fractured rib at the hands of his Indian "captors." And when the crew sprayed a pond beside the Yellowstone River with creosote to keep down mosquitoes during filming of a battle scene, they soon noticed several sizable trout flopping on the pond's surface,

Billings' Midland Empire Fairgrounds served as Fort Abraham Lincoln in Warpath *(1951).*

The exciting Indian-Cavalry battle along the Yellowstone River for Warpath.

gasping for breath, before being netted for a quick transfer to the river. But producer Nat Holt was

Edmond O'Brien, fighting the Indians in Billings, Montana.

inducted into the Crow tribe, the production provided a nice short-term boost to the economy and at least one local reporter predicted that audiences "getting a bit tired of seeing all the western epics filmed in Monument Valley" would welcome a film shot in Montana on the actual sites of the events depicted in *Warpath*'s plot.

Although neither a western nor Cavalry picture, *The Thing* (1951), which did have future "Gunsmoke" star James Arness in the title role, was almost filmed in Montana. In late 1950, an RKO crew arrived in Cut Bank and built a set for the polar scientific base in which most of the story was to take place. But the weather was decidedly uncooperative. The best the crew got was five inches of snow in early February; high winds quickly swept away what snow did fall and at other times the weather was simply too cold for snow. Finally, after limited shooting in Lewistown and a trip to North Dakota in a vain search for a more suitable double for the North Pole, Director Christian Nyby gave up, ordering the company back to California for completion of *The Thing* on a less realistic, but more accommodating, sound stage and at RKO's Encino ranch.

In July of that year, a 20th Century-Fox cast and crew did arrive in Missoula to film one of the more exciting outdoor titles shot in Montana. *Red Skies of Montana* depicted the exploits of smoke jumpers for the U.S. Forest Service, who were regularly dispatched on planes of the Johnson Flying Service from Missoula's Hale field and Region 1's smoke-jumping headquarters (where the remains of the original facilities, prominently displayed in the movie, were still standing at the local airport several years ago) for dramatic parachute jumps into fire areas across the Pacific northwest and as far away as New Mexico.

Shooting had originally started in the summer of 1950. But a motorcycle accident sidelined Victor Mature, one of the original stars, for six months and John Lund, the other principal star of the title, was the victim of a severe hornet attack that left him out of commission for several days. As a result of those mishaps, filming was abandoned for the year. When the shoot resumed the following July, Richard Widmark and Jeffrey Hunter had replaced Mature and Lund as the picture's stars.

As technical adviser to assure an authentic depiction of the smoke jumpers' exploits, Fox also acquired the services of Fred I. Stillings, supervisor of an Idaho national forest and former head of Montana's smoke-jumping operations, to oversee the filming, as well as final editing and sound mixing in Hollywood. In a further nod to accuracy, Fox had trees cut in Montana and shipped to California for scenes filmed at the studio.

During a Kiwanis Club meeting at Missoula's Fremont Hotel, a Fox publicist told the audience that the budget for the film would probably exceed $3 million, while principal speaker Alfred E. Spaulding, current chief of Region 1's operations, discussed the history of aerial and ground fire-fighting in Montana.

Although real forest fires were and are a regular occurrence in Montana, $114,000 of Fox's budget was used to create an artificial, five-acre fire for fire sequences in the film. But scenes for one of the largest fires depicted in the film were shot at the studio.

In addition to the smoke jumper headquarters at Hale Field, location shooting took place at Hayes Creek, Pattee Canyon, in the Nine Mile area (training ground for smoke jumpers), and at Missoula's local federal court building. In the gymnasium at Fort Missoula, the production crew also constructed duplicate sets, which allowed filming to continue indoors when rain prevented outdoor shooting.

Local residents appearing in *Red Skies of Montana* included not only the smoke jumpers themselves, but extras used in a local dance sequence and a crowd scene on the steps of the federal courthouse steps following a hearing in the building on a tragic forest fire that was part of the plot line. In fact, journalists who rushed Richard Widmark on the court steps were actual Missoula reporters rather than actors.

Fox also agreed with Fred Stillings' suggestion that Jack Hughes of the Johnson Flying Service, rather than a Hollywood stunt pilot, be hired to helm a low-flying airplane for close-range shots of the Moose Creek mountains. Stillings later overheard the director saying that Hughes had accomplished in two hours what would have taken any movie flying specialist two days to accomplish.

When Fox held a Missoula premiere in January 1952, Widmark, Hunter, and the film's female lead were unable to attend. Instead, William Lundigan, former radio singer and Fox contractee Bob Graham and actress Helene Stanley stood in for the stars. But the absences hardly dampened the festivities, which included a parade complete with bulldozers, smoke jumpers, even truck loads of logs, and two Johnson Flying Service planes (a Ford tri-motor and a helicopter) passing back and forth over the throng.

Soon, it may have appeared to locals that Missoula was rivaling Hollywood as a site for movie premieres. In January 1955, another title shot in Montana had its world premiere in the Montana city. *Timberjack* (1955) was yet another effort in the continuing but futile campaign of Republic Pictures Corporation head Herbert J. Yates to make a star of his wife, former Czechoslovakian ice skater Vera Hruba Ralston. The historical epic told the story of the struggle between Sterling Hayden and David Brian for domination of area logging operations. With Yates along to keep a watchful eye on Miss Ralston, a cast and

Sterling Hayden in Missoula for Timberjack *(1955).*

crew that included 15 staff members and 80 actors had arrived Labor Day weekend the previous September to begin the shoot. While a crowd of spectators watched, the company devoted the first day of filming to a logging train sequence at Camp 10 of the Anaconda Copper Mining Co.'s lumber department on the Clearwater River, 55 miles north of Missoula. Other filming locales included St. Mary's Lake, site for the climactic gun fight between Hayden and Brian, and, outside Missoula, McNamara's Landing on the Blackfoot River. Lumber camp scenes were shot at the Hubbard reservoir forty miles west of Polson.

Although plagued by the limitations of the Trucolor process that budget-conscious Republic favored, as well as the studio's preference for sound stage "exteriors," the process screen and extensive use of second units and doubles for the stars in location filming, *Timberjack* gave relatively extensive play to the Glacier National Park and the area's other natural splendors. Readers of local

Republic boss Herbert J. Yates, cast members and studio western star Rex Allen at the Timberjack *premiere.*

newspapers also got an inside look at "movie magic." One item noted, for example, that a cabin used prominently in the film was actually only a false front braced on the back side. A piece of charcoal placed on a platform in the chimney made smoke rise and gave the cabin the appearance of being inhabited. "Stonework" on the cabin looked real but was only pressed fiberboard, cut off in slabs and stuck to the cabin's facade.

In early January, the company returned to Montana for the *Timberjack* world premiere, flying to Butte, then proceeding by motorcade to Missoula. Sterling Hayden failed to make an appearance and illness prevented Hoagy Carmichael, who had a prominent role in the film and apparently once lived in Missoula, from attending the festivities. But Brian, Ralston and Yates were in attendance, as was Brian's wife Adrian Booth, a favorite of Republic action fans, and two other cast members, the popular Chill Wills and Hollywood veteran Adolph Menjou. The festivities consisted of a two-day series of events highlighted by a massive street parade, a Chamber of Commerce banquet at which Yates gave the principal address and the premiere. Ever mindful of the bottom line, the studio head also managed to host a luncheon for Montana theater exhibitors.

Brought from Hollywood to emcee the events was Republic western singing star Rex Allen, whose musical numbers for the crowd included "Lazy River," a Hoagy Carmichael hit that would become one of Allen's signature songs as well. Chill Wills, referring to the group's late arrival at the Butte airport, joked that Wilbur Wright must have piloted their plane!

In the same period, Montana also hosted other productions. *Cattle Queen of Montana* (1954), starring Barbara Stanwyck and Ronald Reagan, made scenic use of the Glacier area, as did *Dangerous Mission* (1954), an underrated film noir starring Victor Mature and Piper Laurie.

Over the years since, Montana has continued to be an occasional filming site. Portions of the Dustin Hoffman starrer *Little Big Man* (1970) not only utilized the Custer battlefield area but also drew on the historic Montana ghost towns of Virginia City and Nevada City. In preparation for the shoot, pavement of the Montana highway running through town was liberally sprinkled with gravel and traffic was detoured. The towns were also literally "spruced up," with pine branches used to hide utility poles and entire trees transplanted to conceal modern construction.

Son of the Morning Star (1991), a creditable TV movie retelling the Custer epic was filmed around Billings. Other more recent productions utilizing Montana sites include *A River Runs Through It* (1991), *The Horse Whisperer* (1997) and *Don't Come Knocking* (2004). In fact, shortly after our son married a wonderful Montana girl at a pavilion in the mountains outside Bozeman, I learned that it had been a filming site for *The Horse Whisperer*.

Perhaps because of its growing popularity as a tourist site, and Canada's growing attraction for film-makers, Wyoming has played host to fewer film companies in recent years. But Charlton Heston and Brian Keith did go to Jackson for portions of *The Mountain Men* (1980) and Clint Eastwood for *Any Which Way You Can* (1980). And the company for *Starship Troopers* (1997) went to Casper for filming. The later films hardly compare, however, with the titles shot in Montana and Wyoming during Hollywood's golden era.

Chapter 10

Texas, Oklahoma and Colorado

When I was a boy growing up in Alabama, a relative from Texas came east for a visit. My younger brother Steve was skeptical. "He can't be from Texas," the youngster whispered to our father. "He's not even wearing a cowboy hat or boots!" To Front Row kids, the Lone Star State was indeed the "land of the cowboys." And while relatively few titles were shot there during filmdom's golden age, Texas hosted its share of western production crews.

According to Carlo Gaberscek's meticulous compilation of western movie locations, filming in Texas began in the early silent era with *Cyclone Pete's Matrimony* (1910), followed the next year by *The Fall of the Alamo* (1911), the latter starring Francis Ford. Other silent titles with Texas footage included Jack Holt's *North of '36* (1924) and *Border Patrol* (1928), with Harry Carey, Sr.

Gene Autry's *The Big Show* (1936) was probably the first Hollywood sound production to utilize a Texas location. Much of that title was filmed on Republic studio's North Hollywood lot and at the Iverson ranch outside Chatsworth, California. But *The Big Show* also included scenes shot at Dallas' Texas Centennial Exposition, celebrating the 100th anniversary of the state's independence from Mexico.

Created at a cost of $25 million, including construction of 50 buildings, the exposition had as its highlight, and a prominent part of the movie's storyline, the Cavalcade of Texas, a pageant honoring four centuries of Texas history. The exposition lasted from early June to late November 1936. Republic began filming there in mid-September, with the crew returning to the studio at the end of the month to complete production.

1938 saw the release of an extremely low-budget independent feature recounting the Alamo epic, which was filmed entirely at Mission San Jose in San Antonio. Variously entitled *The Fall of the Alamo* and *The Alamo: Shrine of Texas Liberty*, that feature, which may have been released as early as 1935, had no dialogue; instead, its soundtrack consisted entirely of narration and organ music. According to one source, "many extras" were recruited for the picture at the local unemployment office! More respectable Texas productions of that period were two Paramount titles–Randolph Scott's *The Texans* (1938), shot in part at Indianola and Laredo, and *Geronimo* (1939), filmed partly at Fort Bliss.

Another decade passed before filming resumed in Texas and the initial product was hardly cause for celebration. *Rio Grande* (1949), filmed partly in Juanita, could never be confused with the Wayne classic of the same title (although that may have been its producer's intention). Instead, it was one of those incredibly bad independents former Republic Pictures star Sunset Carson was reduced to making after ample quantities of booze and wild living brought his career at that studio to an abrupt halt.

The next year, however, several Amarillo area ranches hosted production of an interesting little Eagle Lion release that garnered some favorable critical review. *The Sundowners* (1950), a tale of feuding ranchers that pitted brother against brother, starred Robert Preston, Robert Sterling and John Barrymore, Jr., son of the great actor and father of Drew Barrymore. But that superb character player Jack Elam was the cast member most critical to assuring that *The Sundowners* made it to the screen. In exchange for his first sizable

Robert Sterling, Robert Preston and John Drew Barrymore in Texas for The Sundowners *(1950).*

movie role, Elam, at that time a film industry bookkeeper-accountant, helped raise financing for the shoot! Amarillo's cattle ranchers must have been of enormous help as well. When the film appeared, its opening credits carried the following unusual prologue: "All of this picture was made near Amarillo and Canyon, Texas, on the ranches of these cattlemen: Newton Harrell, John Currie, Hugh Currie, Frank Miller; and in the Palo Duro Canyon with the help of more Texas people than can be named on this screen." A reproduction of each rancher's brand appeared under his name.

Giant

The same year, Eagle Lion also released *High Lonesome* (1950), another Texas title starring young Barrymore and filmed partly at Marfa, Texas. But *High Lonesome* was not to be Marfa's main claim to

James Dean in perhaps the most famous still from Giant (1956).

cinema fame. In the summer of 1955, a production company of nearly 250 arrived in the town of 3,600 to begin shooting exteriors for *Giant* (1956), director George Stevens' magnificent film version of the Edna Ferber novel about the epic clash of old (cattle ranching) and new (oil) wealth in the Lone Star State.

Soon, the crew, headquartered in Marfa's Hotel Paisano, was at work on the Evans Ranch outside town, constructing (in front of the spread's actual main house) the facade for Reata, the large Victorian mansion (reportedly modeled after one in Decatur, Texas) occupied by Bick and Leslie Benedict (Rock Hudson and Elizabeth Taylor) in the film. Nearby, miniature oil derricks–representing the rise of Jett Rink (brilliantly played by the ill-fated James Dean) from rags to riches–also sprang up on Marfa's dusty plains. The two-month *Giant* shoot was Marfa's day in the sun. Locals found work as extras, drivers and caterers. One occasionally drove Chill Wills and other cast members down to Ojinaga, Mexico, for a night south of the border. The local high school band was recruited for a key scene in the movie. Area teenagers were wild about James Dean, Hollywood's latest heart-throb. One night, a high school majorette and her friends invited Dean to a party. On arriving, he quickly realized that he was the only male there! "He was very polite," one of the girls remembered years later, "but acted shy and uncomfortable. He left after a short time."

During the shoot, Dean often went out in the evening with a young Marfa man, reportedly to shoot jackrabbit. Most other cast members mingled easily with the townspeople and sightseers, too. George Stevens had decided to film on an open set and hundreds of onlookers rushed up seeking autographs from the cast between takes. To escape the intense heat that sometimes rose to 115 degrees during the day, Elizabeth Taylor usually retreated to her air conditioned trailer when not needed on the set. But other cast members readily obliged their fans.

Former child star Jane Withers, playing boisterous Benedict neighbor Vashti Snythe, was particularly popular with locals. But former Republic cowboy star Monte Hale, who had a small part as Bale Cinch, another friend of the Benedicts, was probably the local favorite. Contrary to studio publicity, Monte was a native of Oklahoma, not Texas. But he spent much of his early life in the Lone Star State. And when Chill Wills and a couple of dozen other performers traveled through the state on a World War II tour selling war bonds, Monte got a chance to accompany western movie sidekick Lee "Lasses" White on the guitar for a couple of weeks. That and the recommendation of Texas theater owner Phil Isley, father of actress Jennifer Jones, led to a screen test at Republic, where studio boss Herbert J. Yates offered him a contract. Years later, when Wills interviewed George Stevens for the part of Uncle Brawly in *Giant*, Hale went along, snagging a role in the film when the director was impressed with his genuine Texas drawl and, apparently, with the way he plopped his hat on his head with one hand when leaving a room. After dinner most evenings at the Hotel Paisano, the affable Monte entertained, to the delight of cast, crew and townspeople.

Alamo Village

If *Giant* was one of the finest films ever made in Texas, *The Alamo* (1960) was nothing less than a near life-long obsession with its producer-director-star. John Wayne saw the Texas freedom fighters and their valiant 1836 stand against the forces of Mexican general Santa Anna as the very essence of the American pioneering spirit and thirst for liberty and independence from tyranny. He had long dreamed of making an epic to end all epics about the Alamo story. When he approached Herbert Yates with the project, the Republic studio boss was initially receptive. But when Yates realized that the Duke had in mind a big-budget film shot at a distant location, the tight-fisted studio chief quickly changed his mind. Undeterred, Wayne ultimately pieced together financing from wealthy Texans and other sources, including United Artists, which agreed to put up a portion of the money and release the film–if Wayne agreed not only to produce and direct, but especially to star in his epic.

Ironically, given his growing image as a super-patriot, Wayne at first planned to shoot his film south of the border, where wages and other production costs would be considerably lower than in the states. Initially, he chose a settlement on the Pacific side of Panama, which he and John Ford apparently had discovered during a voyage down the coast. Later, he decided on a site in Sonora, Mexico. But when word of his plans leaked out, Texans were outraged. The Sons and Daughters of the Republic of Texas, official custodians of the actual Alamo in downtown San Antonio, vowed to boycott the film. Wealthy notables informed the Duke that any production not shot in Texas would be an insult to every native Texan. Reluctantly, Wayne agreed to find a Texas location.

Perhaps in an act of spite against the Duke's plans for a film about the Alamo story, Herbert Yates had produced his own version, *The Last Command*, starring Sterling Hayden and Richard Carlson, in 1956. Wayne later dismissed that effort as "a quickie." Stuntman Chuck Roberson, who worked on both the Republic film and Wayne's project, called it a "half-assed, grade-B version of the battle," although many consider the battle scenes in the Republic title–directed without credit by studio action ace Bill Witney–superior to those in Wayne's production.

Whatever Wayne's feelings about *The Last Command*, however, he chose the same Texas location for his film that Herbert Yates had selected for his production. In 1950, Brackettville, a town of about 2,000 inhabitants located 120 miles due west of San Antonio, was reeling from the effects of a severe drought and the Army's 1946 closing of Fort Clark, an old U.S. Cavalry installation. In a bold venture, its new mayor,

The Alamo (1960).

James T. "Happy" Shahan, launched a campaign to rejuvenate the town's economy by luring movie companies to the area, and especially to his 18,000-acre ranch, seven miles outside town.

During a ten-day trip to Los Angeles, Shahan attracted the interest of Paramount, which decided to film Charleton Heston's *Arrowhead* (1953) at Brackettville. Republic followed with *The Last Command*. And in 1959, Texas oilman Glenn H. McCarthy–reportedly the model for the "Jett Rink" character in *Giant*–produced the low-budget *Five Bold Women*, with Jeff Morrow, on the Shahan spread.

Those titles relied only on Fort Clark and limited, temporary sets. But in 1957, John Wayne had begun constructing massive sets for *The Alamo* at Brackettville. In return for using "Happy" Shahan's ranch, the Duke agreed to allow Shahan to be general contractor on the project, build permanent sets with interiors, and retain ownership of all sets after the filming was completed. When Wayne first met Chato Hernandez, the Mexican with a third-grade education whom Shahan had selected to supervise construction, he was skeptical at best. "Mr. Hernandez," he asked, "do you think you can build the Alamo?" "Senor Wayne," Hernandez shot back in broken English, "can you make a movie?" Laughing uproariously, the Duke turned to Shahan. "That's good enough for me!"

Under Hernandez's direction, several dozen Mexican workers made 12 million adobe brick used to create a virtual replica of San Antonio as it looked in 1836–more than 200,000 square feet of permanent buildings suitable for both interior and exterior filming. Six deep wells were also sunk to guarantee a daily supply of 12,000 gallons of fresh water. Fourteen miles of blacktop were laid between Brackettville and the set. Twelve miles of water and sewer lines were constructed, as well as 500 acres of livestock corrals. Construction of a large landing strip allowed quick access to and from the set, as well as daily flights to San Antonio for film developing.

The daily production costs on location were huge. To provide lodging for the entire permanent cast and crew of 342, Wayne had the facilities at Fort Clark entirely refurbished. Sixteen hundred horses were leased. Costumes were made for more than 6,000 extras. The 45 workers the caterer kept full-time on the set served 190,000 meals during the shoot.

Although the Duke provided plenty of food and reasonably comfortable housing for his cast and crew, the conditions under which they worked were hardly ideal. When filming first began in early September 1959, afternoon temperatures hovered near a hundred degrees. The humidity was oppressive, with Wayne and other cast members often requiring changes of costume while shooting a scene. Character actor Hank Worden, a veteran member of the Wayne stock company, later said, too, that "there were something like thousands of rattlesnakes every square mile." Scorpions, skunks and other pests were equally plentiful.

Wayne's biggest annoyance, however, seemed to be the frequent presence on the set of his mentor John Ford, ever ready with unsolicited advice for the novice director, while the Duke was equally determined that *The Alamo* was to be *his* film alone, whatever its merits. Finally, cameraman William Clothier offered a solution. Ford was kept busy with Wayne's son Michael shooting second unit footage, most of which never made it into the film's final cut.

Location work was completed in late December and *The Alamo* opened to mixed reviews the following October with a San Antonio premiere. But Brackettville's days as a filming site were not over. Under his agreement with Wayne, "Happy" Shahan retained ownership of the sets. Augmenting his "Alamo Village" with a "Front Street" and other traditional western sets to maximize filming possibilities, Shahan would continue to attract feature, television, music video and commercial producers for years. James Stewart showed up first, for John Ford's *Two Rode Together* (1961) and later for *Bandolero* (1968). Not surprisingly, several television versions of the Alamo story were also shot in Brackettville, including the James Arness-Alec Baldwin starrer *The Alamo: Thirteen Days to Glory* (1986), which used stock footage from the terrific battle scenes Bill Witney had helmed for Republic's *The Last Command*, filmed there 30 years earlier. (For the most recent Alamo retelling, Billy Bob Thornton's 2004 television version, battle scenes were filmed at Dripping Springs, Texas, rather than at Alamo Village.) With the additional sets Shahan had constructed, Brackettville was also suitable for most western films, such as *Bad Girls* (1993) and "Lonesome Dove" (1989). And when former cowboy star Sunset Carson hosted his "Six Gun Heroes" series on educational television in the 1980s, screening B-westerns for old and new fans alike, he was pictured riding through Alamo Village at the beginning of each episode.

Shahan also turned Alamo Village into one of the Lone Star State's major tourist attractions, open daily except five days during Christmas. He died in 1996 and, in 2004, his widow put the sets up for sale. But we all hope to be able to continue to visit this great movie location and "Remember the Alamo!" for many years to come.

Brackettville Alamo set in recent years.

The familiar church set at Brackettville.

Brackettville's Midwestern village set.

Oklahoma

If Texas hosted relatively few western productions during filmdom's golden years, the Lone Star state's northern neighbor Oklahoma played an even more limited role in the history of western movies. Except for a few silent titles, including *In the Days of the Thundering Herd* (1924), only three theatrical productions were shot in Oklahoma. As noted elsewhere in this volume, Republic filmed train scenes for *Rock Island Trail* (1950), starring Forrest Tucker, at McAllister, Oklahoma, where the studio was given permission to use an abandoned stretch of Rock Island track, as well as trains and equipment loaned the producers by the Baltimore and Ohio railroad and the Railroad and Locomotive Historical Society, Inc.

But another Republic title shot in Oklahoma was clearly closer to the hearts of Front Row kids. For the outstanding *Home in Oklahoma* (1946), the second Roy Rogers title directed by Bill Witney, cast and crew traveled to an area of Oklahoma cattle ranches near Davis, known as Hereford Heaven. Some of the film's exteriors were done on the Republic lot and along the L.A. river bed on the studio's northern boundary. But many exteriors were shot at Bill and Alice Likens' Flying L Ranch at Sulphur, Oklahoma, with some scenes also filmed at the nearby ranch of Oklahoma governor Roy J. Turner, a breeder of prize-winning Hereford cattle. The pastures, livestock, houses and barns of those fine spreads gave *Home in Oklahoma* an authentic look rarely achieved in programmer westerns.

So, too, did use of the area's impressive Turner Falls for scenes in which murderous duo Carol Hughes and George Meeker pursue young Lanny Rees, the lawful heir to the huge ranch they are seeking to steal. The appearance in the film of a local oddity, an unusual streetcar-like train with combined engine and

Roy Rogers, Dale Evans and "Gabby" Hayes with ranch owner Alice Likens.

passenger sections, for a scene of Dale Evans arriving at the local depot, further enhanced the title's special appeal, as did a climactic fight aboard a train speeding through the Oklahoma countryside.

Local folks also got into the act for the films' final shootout and other scenes. And if some of their horses, unlike trained movie livestock, immediately began bucking when the shooting started, so much the better; after all, that is probably what would have happened in "real life."

Turner Falls.

Governor Turner was as movie-struck as the others. "Hereford Heaven," for which the governor had written the lyrics and music,

Carol Hughes, pictured here with Gabby and Roy on the Likens ranch,
made a terrific villainess in Home in Oklahoma.

was one of the songs featured in the movie. And the recently renamed Flying L Ranch Quartet, a singing group Turner was then promoting, performed that number in the film.   One local recalled years later an unpleasant encounter with what he claimed had been a drunken, cursing Roy Rogers following a premiere of *Home in Oklahoma* at a local civic auditorium. But according to one area native, "Everybody in town thought [Roy and Dale] were great." One lad napping in a rocker on the front porch of a country store awoke to find a smiling, friendly Roy standing over him. Another claimed that a fan cut off part of Trigger's tail, obliging the studio to fly in a fall for its equestrian star.

Clearly, Roy and Dale had enjoyed their visit to the area. When they married on December 31, 1947, the ceremony was performed at the Flying L Ranch. Bill Likens gave Dale away and Governor Turner was among nearly fifty guests who braved a blizzard to be present. In a nod to frontier authenticity, the Oklahoma City minister who performed the ceremony rode to the ranch on horseback, arriving two hours late as a result of the rough weather conditions. Obliged by the storm to delay their honeymoon, Roy took Dale to nearby Nebo for a coon hunt on their wedding night!

The following summer, Walter Wanger Productions came to the area to film exteriors for *Tulsa* (1949) on Governor Turner's ranch. An oil-drilling saga starring Susan Hayward and Robert Preston, the cast included Oklahoma horseman Rowland Jack in a featured role. When a gusher erupted in the film, a local pinto, painted to resemble a buckskin and trained to buck on cue, did his bit for the camera. The action highlight of the film was an exciting oil field fire. But those watching the shoot could hardly have been impressed; after all, the blazing "oil derricks," one local recalled years later, were only about three feet tall! The visiting stars, however, were clearly a hit, especially Susan Hayward, who, one native remembered, was "absolutely gorgeous," and graciously agreed to ride in a Hereford Heaven parade.

Colorado

Colorado's scenic wonders, especially the San Juan Forest around Durango, attracted far more motion picture productions than Texas and Oklahoma combined. In fact, the Durango area was to become such an appealing filming location that it became known as the "Hollywood of the Rockies." When Darryl F. Zanuck and his family vacationed at a Durango dude ranch in the 1940s, ranch owner Bob Venuti made certain that the 20th Century-Fox boss became fully acquainted with Durango's spectacular scenery and wonderful potential as a filming site for outdoor titles. Zanuck needed little convincing. In the summer of 1948, he chose the area for *Sand*, a wild-horse yarn based on the Will James novel, with filming done on the Pagosa Springs ranch of J. R. Stevens and at the R. E. Hutchinson ranch outside Durango.

Sand producer Robert Bassler, an avid fan of narrow gauge railroads, was intrigued not only with Durango's wonderful landscape, but especially with the little narrow-gauge line running from Durango to Silverton, through the area's most spectacular scenery. The Durango-Silverton line, which had its inaugural

The Durango-Silverton train in the 1990s.

run in 1882, had been built to haul silver and gold ore from the San Juan Mountains. In 1967, it would be designated a national historic landmark and in 1981, it became a popular tourist attraction. Long before that, though, it was to have a featured role in many films.

Mary Loos and Richard Sale, a husband-wife scenarist duo, were also avid model railroad enthusiasts. To inaugurate film use of the Durango-Silverton line, they came up with a script for *A Ticket to Tomahawk*

(1950), a musical comedy about westward rail expansion. "We did a lot of research and looked at all of the narrow gauge trains," Loos recalled for a Durango newspaper reporter many years later. "But the incredible Animas Canyon [between Durango and Silverton] was the deciding factor to make the movie here. I'm glad because you get a beautiful look at a beautiful place that wouldn't be known without the train."

Principal filming for *A Ticket to Tomahawk* was done in Animas Canyon north of Rockwood. Locales in Durango and Silverton were also used. For example, a climactic Indian attack was shot at Durango's Reservoir Hill, now the site of a local college.

For one fight scene in Animas Canyon, Rory Calhoun's stunt dummy was hurled from a train to the rapids below. Soon, someone reported seeing a body at the bottom of the gorge. Forest rangers took two days packing down to the site, only to discover the movie prop.

As usual, though, soon-to-be star Marilyn Monroe, playing a bit part as a chorus girl in the film created the greatest local interest. One day, the film folks and a Durango softball team played a game to raise money for the local hospital. "Marilyn," Mary Loos later recalled, "rigged it so her blue jeans slipped and fell to her ankles while [she was] running to first base," revealing her black lace underpants!

When a stunt man on the shoot was injured, the assistant director offered $50 for a horse fall to any of the Navajos brought in for the picture. There were no takers. "We are Navajos," they insisted. "We don't fall off horses." Only when told that they were playing Apaches in the movie did they readily fall from their steeds on cue.

MGM's location preparations for Clark Gable's *Across the Wide Missouri* (1951), the next production based in Durango, were the most extensive in that studio's history to that point. A tent city for cast and crew, a wilderness fortress and two Indian villages were constructed. For one of the Indian settlements, built on the east side of Molas Lake, 1800 aspen poles, 22-26 feet long, were necessary. Near the area's Haviland Dam, which had to be camouflaged from the camera's view, a thousand aspen logs were used in building the fortress, which included a guard tower, cabin set and two huge gates.

Clark Gable was then married to the actress Sylvia Sidney. Unlike most of the cast, the couple stayed at a nearby dude ranch rather than the tent city during the filming. But conditions were too primitive for the urbane Sidney's taste. Gable had to grow a thick beard for early scenes in the film. "You have no idea how that beard scratches," his wife told a reporter. "I hope this is his last cowboy and Indian picture."

In the summer of 1951, a year after filming had first begun, *Across the Wide Missouri* premiered at a Durango theater. But when scenes for Gable's *Lone Star* (1952) were shot at Durango, he and his co-stars remained in Hollywood, shooting on the MGM lot, while a second unit filmed at Cortez, Colorado, on the Pine River east of Durango and at a 1360-acre Durango ranch. For the filming, a life-line was stretched across the Pine River, and with good reason. During an action scene, stuntman Chuck Roberson took an unscripted spill from his horse and was swept several hundred feet down the rushing, rock-lined river before being pulled to shore. For a posse chase near Bayfield, Glenn Skewes, a local liaison with film crews, put out a call for over a hundred extras. "Those who come," he announced, "should be dressed in old cowboy hats, be ready for a morning of hard riding and bring their own lunches. Those who have guns and holsters should wear them but leave live ammunition at home."

The Durango-Silverton line was put to its most impressive use in another 1952 release, Paramount's *Denver & Rio Grande*, a story of competing railroad lines starring Edmond O'Brien and Sterling Hayden. Highlight of the film was the actual head-on collision of two trains along a stretch of track in Animas Canyon where a resort would later be located. To capture the action, seven Technicolor cameras were positioned at the crash site. According to a contemporary newspaper account, the scene required almost 30 hours of preparation. At director Byron Haskin's signal, the two engines and several boxcars loaded with 150 sticks of dynamite and 50 pounds of black powder, began to back slowly apart along the 500-yard clearing in which the crash was staged, then halted. Exactly five minutes later, the trains moved forward. Then, the engineer and fireman on each locomotive shoved the throttles wide open and leaped to safety. Gaining speed rapidly, the engines raced toward a point of collision forever after to be known as "Scrap Iron Junction."

The thrilling crash in Denver & Rio Grande (1952).

According to the newspaper account, "the crash jarred the ground for several hundred yards as the roar of exploding dynamite and steam rebounded from the hiss. Pieces of wood and steel shot high in the air above the smoke, sliced like shrapnel through the tops of the trees and thudded like heavy hail over the entire clearing. One big piece of metal sailed over the heads of the cameramen and splashed in the Animas River. Another dropped within 15 feet of [a] watching group of railroad officials and their families more than 400 yards away."

When the steam and smoke died down after several minutes, the two little engines could be seen still standing on the rails. Haskin yelled "cut" and producer Nat Holt walked out to inspect the wreckage, a broad grin on his face, while cast members and others chatted excitedly.

"Only a few men walked slowly away, their faces sad and a little pale," reported the paper. "They were [the] president of the D & R G and others who helped build and were now executives of the railroad. Although the valiant little engines were to be scrapped anyway, and the steel will aid the country's defense effort, some of the heart of each railroad man present yesterday rode the tiny trains on their last run." But what a terrific scene!

For train scenes in Marlon Brando's *Viva Zapata* (1952), another Darryl Zanuck production, the Emma Sweeney, the locomotive featured in *A Ticket to Tomahawk*, was brought back into service. On this occasion, however, filming was set on a spur line running south through Wildcat Canyon at Porter, west of Durango, rather than along the Durango-Silverton route.

The next Durango title, MGM's *The Naked Spur* (1953), starring Jimmy Stewart, Robert Ryan and Janet

Leigh, had no rail scenes but did include exciting action above and in the raging Animas River. That production also marked the San Juan basin's official designation as the "Hollywood of the Rockies." By that point, the area had appeared in fourteen films and a celebration was in order. During the shoot, a six-limousine motorcade met visiting dignitaries, including Governor Dan Thornton, at the Durango airport for a drive to the filming site. There they were greeted by Jimmy Stewart–as Durango's honorary mayor–and other cast and crew members. Following lunch and an afternoon watching the movie-makers, they were guests for cocktails and dinner at Bob Venuti's El Rancho Encantado. To conclude the festivities, Governor Thornton, Miss Leigh and Jimmy Stewart unveiled a monument honoring the area's role in motion pictures at Durango's Fissbinder Park.

In September 1955, Republic Pictures veteran Joe Kane directed Barbara Stanwyck and Scott Brady in *The Maverick Queen* (1956), based loosely on the exploits of Butch Cassidy, the Sundance Kid (Brady) and their notorious "Hole in the Wall" gang. The Durango-Silverton railroad was among the stars. But filming was also done at a deserted ranch near Silverton and on the town's streets.

Two years later, Jimmy Stewart was back in town for *Night Passage* (1957), which also starred western

Elaine Stewart and Jimmy Stewart in Silverton for Night Passage (1957).

movie great Audie Murphy as the Utica Kid, Stewart's outlaw brother. This exciting story of a gang of train robbers made excellent use of the Durango-Silverton line as well as Molas Lake, Red Mountain, Silverton and two mines (the Shenandoah-Dives and Mayflower) north of Silverton.

To give the line a closer connection with the Silverton business district, the track there was extended a block and a second depot constructed. Stewart made his first appearance at the Shenandoah-Dives mine site, riding up on his horse to accept a cup of coffee from that grand character

This Silverton building, pictured in the 1990s, appeared in Night Passage.

actress Olive Carey, wife of Harry, Sr., and mother of Harry, Jr. The final shootout in the picture took place at the Mayflower mine. But the most thrilling scenes, not surprisingly, were set along the Durango-Silverton line.

As usual, the visiting stars, including luscious Elaine Stewart, attracted considerable local attention. Miss Stewart was arrested when she created a traffic jam while posing for cheese cake photos on the rocks of the Animas River in Durango and ignored a police officer's warning to stop. But a gallant local judge quickly came to the damsel's rescue, dismissing all charges. "Anytime we can add an Elaine Stewart to the scenic wonders of Colorado," declared the judge, "I'm all for it. Hereafter, let it be known that we'll appoint a special police detail to direct traffic while the beauty poses to her heart's content."

The serious accident that stuntman Bob Morgan suffered several years later, during filming of rail scenes for *How the West Was Won* (1962), occurred at Globe, Arizona, east of Phoenix. But that blockbuster production went to Durango for winter railroad scenes. When the Cinerama lenses used for the filming proved too wide for the narrow canyons through which the Durango-Silverton line ran, the movie-makers built their own track, but leased Denver & Rio Grande equipment. A December 1961 newspaper article reported that snow plows were clearing space for filming and that "MGM crews are making progress on construction of the mock up train." But a studio spokesperson insisted that extras hired for the shoot must sport at least a two-day growth of beard for their scenes. At one point, it became necessary to blow snow onto the roofs of buildings when nature declined to accommodate the camera. But MGM was happy with the rail scenes shot there for the movie, which, while a disappointment in many ways, won an Oscar nomination for cinematography.

Toward the end of the decade, 20th Century-Fox shot scenes for the Paul Newman-Robert Redford hit *Butch Cassidy and the Sundance Kid* (1969) in the Durango area. That wonderful sequence in which Butch and Sundance, unable to persuade an unbelievably loyal railroad employee to open the express car he was guarding, dynamite the car–accidentally blowing up the entire train–was shot at Florida Mesa, southeast of Durango. The special effects crew had constructed a car of balsa wood and the explosion was not expected to be very strong. In fact, fans had been placed along the track to assure that money from the car was appropriately scattered in the explosion's wake. But the blast proved so powerful that crew members had to gather up pieces of the car and throw them back into camera range in order to finish the shot. An hilarious, if partially unscripted, scene!

In another well-remembered sequence, the pair (actually, of course, their stunt doubles) prepare to jump from a high bluff near Baker's Bridge to the river far below when Sundance informs Butch that he had never learned to swim. "Hell," Cassidy replies, "the fall's gonna kill ya." That harrowing jump, incidentally,

The production crew got a much more potent explosion than they expected for this scene in Butch Cassidy and the Sundance Kid.

ended for our heroes (or their stunt doubles) with a plunge into a Malibu Creek pool at the Fox Ranch outside L. A., not in the Animas River.

Durango's natural splendors also enhanced *Support Your Local Gunfighter* (1971), the comedy western starring James Garner and the third Durango picture in which perennial scene stealer Jack Elam appeared (the previous two being *A Ticket to Tomahawk* and *Night Passage*). "In the final scene," Elam later related, "we had this great shot of the train in the Animas Canyon. I'm standing on the end of the train, and they're shooting the scene from a helicopter overhead. . . . Now you have to understand that I'm scared witless of heights. I'm practically unconscious before we start the scene, so they have me chained to the train. This didn't help me much, until [director Burt] Kennedy had himself chained to me, but out of camera range." At the end of the scene, Elam delivered that famous last line, "and me, I go off to become a big star in Italian Westerns."

Movie companies have continued to come to Durango for films, of course, including Billy Crystal's *City Slickers* (1991) and even Chevy Chase's *National Lampoon's Vacation* (1983).

Other Colorado sites also became movie stars, or at least featured players. Producer Hal Wallis apparently considered shooting Fort Smith scenes for John Wayne's *True Grit* in Arkansas. But ultimately, the county courthouse at Ouray, Colorado, stood in for hanging judge Issac Parker's Fort Smith courtroom and the town of Ridgway was the setting for most of the Fort Smith scenes in that fine movie. The hanging sequence was shot, for example, in the main city park. Fans may remember the "Chambers Grocery" sign on the wall of a building adjoining a vacant lot that is visible in the background of an early scene. The sign is still there but is now an interior wall of the True Grit (naturally) restaurant, which has taken over the vacant lot and is filled with Wayne memorabilia.

Other *True Grit* scenes were also filmed in the Ridgway area. The final shootout ("Fill your hands, you son of a bitch!") took place, for example, in a beautiful meadow near the top of Owl Creek Pass, at the base of the majestic Courthouse mountain and its huge chimney rock . Until recently, at least, the barns, though

This Ridgway park appeared in True Grit (1969).

not the homestead, were still standing on Last Dollar Road, where the Duke and his steed jumped the fence at the fadeout. The old fire department building in Ridgway, also seen in the film, is still there, too. Other Colorado sites graced *True Grit* as well, including Wilson Peaks in the San Juan National Forest.

During the *True Grit* filming, other cast members were flown in each day from Grand Junction. But the Duke chose to stay at a motel in Ouray, near Ridgway. The son of a local police deputy assigned as Wayne's bodyguard recalled the star years later as a "regular guy." "His favorite spot was The Outlaw–back then it was more of a bar, with pool tables–he loved to play pool with the locals. . . . He played five dollars a ball, and his favorite game was eight-ball. Sometimes he would peel off his hat and take off his wig. And he would put back good, sizeable amounts of bourbon." Each day, the actor invited the youth and another child of the boy's choice to have lunch with him.

So did the local fire department.

The Canon City area, a hundred miles southwest of Denver, also had a part in Colorado's cinema history. It is best known, of course, as the setting for *Canon City* (1948), the exciting prison-break movie starring Scott Brady, much of which was filmed in the Colorado State Prison there. Director Bill Witney also took his cast and crew to Canon City for his fine *The Outcast* (1954), starring John Derek, Joan Evans

John Wayne and Kim Darby at the farm on Last Dollar Road.

Villain Robert Duvall on Courthouse Mountain for the final shootout.

and Jim Davis, where he utilized Mountain Meadow Ranch in Wet Mountain Valley and an Arkansas River site at nearby Florence.

One of the earliest features made in Colorado was also shot in the area and at Glenwood Springs, 150 miles west of Denver. In July 1926, the great Tom Mix arrived by train in Glenwood Springs with a cast and crew of 55 and 22 horses. For the next three weeks, the troupe shot scenes for *The Great K & A Train Robbery* (1926), considered by many to be the star's greatest film. Each day, crowds of spectators gathered to watch Mix perform his own stunts, rappelling down the walls of Glenwood Canyon for one scene, galloping Tony the length of Shoshone Dam for another. But the star and his company traveled to Canon City for the most memorable sequences–exciting scenes on a train racing along the winding Arkansas River through the steep, narrow, breathtakingly beautiful Royal Gorge.

About eight miles west of Canon City on Highway 50, visitors will find Buckskin Joe, a Colorado version of Old Tucson that, like the famed Arizona site, doubles as a tourist attraction and filming location.

Buckskin Joe.

The original Buckskin Joe, a gold rush boomtown named for a settler with a penchant for buckskin attire, was established in 1859. When the mines played out, most of the populace moved on, leaving a decaying ghost town in their wake. In the late 1950s, however, Buckskin Joe was recreated at its current site. Buildings from the original town were dismantled and reassembled at the new location. In an effort to maintain the atmosphere of an Old West mining town, no vehicles were allowed on the streets and residents donned period costumes. As an additional attraction for tourists, the town was constructed next to Royal Gorge, with a small gauge train transporting visitors to the canyon's edge to view the gorge and the Royal Gorge bridge.

Within a few years of the town's 1958 opening, it also had become a backdrop for film shoots. The Lee Marvin-Jane Fonda comedy western *Cat Ballou* (1965) was perhaps the first but the area also hosted scenes from Wayne's *The Cowboys* (1972), the Goldie Hawn-George Segal starrer *The Duchess and the Dirtwater Fox* (1975) and *The Sacketts* (1979), among other features and TV movies.

The list of westerns shot in Colorado goes on and on. For snow scenes in *The Searchers* (1956) and *Cheyenne Autumn* (1964), John Ford chose Gunnison. Robert Taylor's underrated *Saddle the Wind* (1958), with John Cassavetes as the ultimate, over-the-edge, gun-crazy kid brother, was made outside Canon City, as was Burt Lancaster's *Vengeance Valley* (1951). Taylor's *Devil's Doorway* (1950) utilized Aspen and Grand Junction sites. Indeed, not just Durango but the entire state deserves the title, "Hollywood of the Rockies."

Chapter 11

Trains, Planes
and other Things

A tour of western and serial filming locations would not be complete without separate attention to a number of special settings that have enhanced many an action movie title.

Movie Railroads

Railroad sequences furnished some of the most thrilling scenes in westerns and serials of the golden age. Various companies in and out of California provided rental locomotives, rolling stock and other rail equipment to production units. A number of the major studios even acquired their own movie trains. But the equipment and depots of the Southern Pacific RR and other working lines appeared most often in low budget oaters and cliffhangers.

Of depots, the Chatsworth station at the end of Southern Pacific's Burbank-Chatsworth stretch was clearly the most popular with film makers. Republic's *Mysterious Dr. Satan* (1940) serial probably made most effective use of the

The Chatsworth depot appeared in more titles than any other railway station.

Chatsworth facility for exciting fights on its loading platform. But the station, which succumbed to suburban sprawl in the 1970s, also made a brief appearance as the "Atsworth" depot in the first chapter of Columbia's *Superman* (1948) chapterplay, as well as in scores of other serials and westerns, including Roy Rogers' *Heldorado* (1946) and *Three Outlaws* (1956), with Neville Brand.

The nearby railroad cut and tunnel (running beneath Santa Susanna Pass Road) adjacent to the Iverson Movie Ranch, northwest of Chatsworth, were not only familiar sites in B-westerns and serials, but major productions as well. The exciting opening to James Cagney's *White Heat* (1949) was set in that area, for example.

The Chatsworth railroad tunnel beneath the Santa Susanna Pass Road.

Stretches of track in the San Fernando Valley southeast of Chatsworth were well used also. In an exciting chapter ending for *Batman and Robin* (1949), the Caped Crusader leaps from his convertible to a racing train for a fist-fest climaxing with our hero appearing to crash, via rear projection, into the top of the tunnel outside Chatsworth.

Depots in the Lone Pine area also appeared in films. The Lone Pine station itself made an appearance in Gene Autry's *Boots and Saddles* (1937), complete with its

The Lone Pine depot.

correct name above the loading platform. That depot also had roles in two "Annie Oakley" episodes ("Annie and the Brass Collar" and "Cinder Trail"). But producers more often utilized the depot at nearby Keeler, which appeared, for example, in Gene's *The Blazing Sun* (1950), as well as Hoppy's *Sinister Journey* (1948).

The Keeler depot appeared more often in Lone Pine titles than the Lone Pine station itself.

Gene Autry made his most impressive movie railroad appearance, however, when he, rather than his stunt double, executed a smooth transfer from Champion to a locomotive for *Gaucho Serenade* (1940), in a scene shot partly in the San Fernando Valley and in part on a stretch of track between Fillmore and Saugus, northwest of L. A., which appeared often in films. The Saugus depot appeared in a number of westerns but played its most memorable role in the low-budget political thriller *Suddenly* (1955), with Frank Sinatra perfectly cast as a deranged would-be presidential assassin.

The Saugus depot as been on display in Newhall's William S. Hart park for years.

Among B-western and serial directors, Republic's Bill Witney made most regular and effective use of railroad sequences. The exciting train scenes for his *Zorro Rides Again* (1937) were shot on track running along San Fernando Road, near where Highway

14 and I-5 now intersect a few miles north of L.A. In fact, the highway overpass (or a descendant) seen in the background of one actionful chapter ending is still standing, just as it was when Zorro stunt double Yakima Canutt, his boot wedged in the track, faced (almost) certain death beneath a speeding train.

In one of the most exciting Witney-directed railroad cliffhanger sequences, Yakima Canutt raced a tank alongside a speeding train, then transferred to a railroad car for a fierce fight with heavies. For that scene in *Dick Tracy's G-Men* (1939), Witney chose a stretch of track near Acton, between Saugus and Palmdale.

Perhaps Witney's most picturesque railroad scenes were shot, however, for two of Roy Rogers' post-war Trucolor titles, *Night Time in Nevada* (1948) and *Sunset in the West* (1950). Utilized for those sequences was a stretch of track along what is now Highway 26, between Fillmore and Saugus, as well as cattle loading pens along the track, probably owned by the area's huge Newhall Ranch and Cattle Co. Much of that track has now been removed and the original two-lane road replaced with a more modern, and later four-lane, highway. But some of the eucalyptus trees seen along the railroad bed in those Rogers titles and, of course, the surrounding hills are still there.

As noted elsewhere in this book, the climactic railroad chase for one of Roy's Witney-directed black and white features, *Home in Oklahoma* (1946), like most of that fine title, was shot near Davis, Oklahoma, where Roy and Dale Evans were married. But *Home in Oklahoma* also featured another, very unusual piece of railroad equipment—a gasoline-electric railroad car with combined engine/mail car, followed by a passenger car, on which Dale rode into town. The particular car used for the scene was an M. 155, which made regular runs through Oklahoma 1936-47.

Other budget titles, including John Wayne's *Hurricane Express* (1932) and several other Mascot serials, also used equipment and track rented from working lines. Scenes for Tex Ritter's *Utah Trail* (1938) were filmed, for example, on a stretch of track running by Corriganville, with the slanting peaks of that movie ranch clearly visible in the background of scenes.

For their railroad sequences, however, the major studios relied primarily on studio-owned trains and equipment as well as rental companies that specialized in such props. Budget production crews sometimes also rented their equipment from such rental companies as well. The most famous of the rental lines was the Sierra Railway, located in central California's Tuolumne County near Yosemite, examined elsewhere in this book.

Another famous rental line, examined in the chapter covering Colorado film-making, operated in southwestern Colorado and northern New Mexico. A narrow-gauge road originally built in the 1880s, the Denver & Rio Grande Western RR first made movie appearances in *The Texas Rangers* (1936) and *Colorado Territory* (1949) but had its initial starring role in the Dan Dailey musical *Ticket to Tomahawk* (1950), which was also the first title to use the line's 45-mile, fabulously beautiful Silverton branch, now a famous tourist attraction. In later years, such western titles as *Run for Cover* (1954), *Three Young Texans* (1954) and *Maverick Queen* (1956) were filmed in the area. Edmond O'Brien's *Denver & Rio Grande* (1952) featured the actual head-on collision on the line of two locomotives in what must have been one of the most thrilling rail scenes in film history. The Jimmy Stewart-Audie Murphy title *Night Passage*, shot there in the fall of 1956, was the last title filmed on the line for a 12-year period. Then a TV pilot was shot there, followed by action scenes for *Butch Cassidy and the Sundance Kid* (1969), as well as occasional titles since that time.

When the Rio Grande sought to abandon another branch of the line in 1967, Colorado and New Mexico purchased 64 miles of track between Chama, New Mexico, and Antonito, Colorado, creating the Cumbres & Toltec Scenic Railroad. Robert Mitchum's *The Good Guys and the Bad Guys* (1969) and Gregory Peck's

Shootout (1971) were among the first titles shot on the new line, which also hosted Dean Martin's *Showdown* (1973) and Gene Hackman's *Bite the Bullet* (1974).

Yet another rental facility was made possible in 1927, when the Baltimore & Ohio RR moved its entire

The Chama depot in 2007.

collection of antique power and rolling stock to Baltimore for exhibition at the B & O Railroad Museum, during that line's centennial celebration. One of its trains was sent to Chico, California, for Joel McCrea's *Wells Fargo* (1937), the first use of a B & O train in films. In 1949, the B & O's Thatcher Perkins, named for the line's master mechanic, journeyed to Oklahoma, to be featured as one of the trains in Republic's Trucolor

A production crew filming in the mountains on the Cumbres & Toltec line.

Rock Island Trail (1950), starring Forrest Tucker. In 1955, two B & O trains also saw service for scenes in Walt Disney's *The Great Locomotive Chase*, shot at Clayton, Georgia, on the Tallulah Falls line.

In the desert east of Phoenix, a 28-mile short line connecting the Magna Copper Co.'s mine at Superior with a branch of the Southern Pacific was regularly featured in action flicks. First used on a regular run (and thus without fee) for an episode of the "26 Men" TV series, the Magna Arizona Railroad, along with parts of studio-owned trains, saw spectacular play in *How the West Was Won* (1962). The line later appeared in *Cheyenne Autumn* (1963) and *Blood on the Arrow* (1964), although *Cheyenne Autumn* also included scenes filmed on the Warner Bros. back lot in Burbank.

The Life and Times of Judge Roy Bean (1971) may have been the last Magna RR title to feature steam locomotives, but scenes using diesel engines have been shot on the line since that time and Magna locomotives have also seen duty in other locales. One appeared, for example, in scenes for *The Long Riders* (1979) shot in Texas.

The Natonal Railway of Mexico, which included both standard and narrow-gauge locomotives and maintained one standard gauge in Durango specifically for film use, became a regular in John Wayne's stock company of players. The earliest known U.S. titles to feature the Mexican line were the Duke's *Sons of Katie Elder* (1965) and *The Wild Bunch* (1968), shot in the desert near Durango. But Wayne's *Rio Lobo* (1970), *Big Jake* (1971), *The Train Robbers* (1972) and *Cahill, U.S. Marshal* (1973) also used the National Railway, as did Burt Lancaster's *Cattle Annie and Little Britches* (1979) and Lee Marvin's *Great Scout and Cathouse Thursday* (1976).

The major movie studios, of course, also purchased their own trains for use in their features and rental to other companies. The studios bought most of their locomotives, rolling stock and other equipment from Nevada's Virginia & Truckee RR, a short line originally used for ore shipments from that state's Comstock Lode. In the 1930s, Hollywood discovered five 1870-era Virginia & Truckee locomotives in the company's Carson City engine house and dozens of wooden freight and passenger cars in its yard. Between 1937 and 1947, movie companies bought four locomotives and more than two dozen cars from the Virginia & Truckee. Paramount was first, purchasing V & T's No. 22 for use in Randolph Scott's *High, Wide and Handsome* (1937), then a number of other cars for an initial appearance in Joel McCrea's *Wells Fargo* (1937), plus No. 18 and more rolling stock for his *Union Pacific* (1939). No. 22 also appeared in Hoppy's *Showdown* (1940) in a scene filmed at the Chatsworth depot.

Other studios, especially MGM, frequently leased Paramount's equipment but in 1945, MGM bought its own locomotive, V & T No. 11. Southern Pacific's Burbank-Chatsworth branch ran through the middle of RKO's Encino ranch in the San Fernando Valley until the mid-1940s. When the branch was relocated, 2,000 feet of old track were left in place on the ranch, forming a dead-end spur off the branch and giving RKO its own ready-made "railroad," which first appeared with V & T's No. 18, leased from Paramount, in Randolph Scott's *Badman's Territory* (1946). In 1947, RKO

*The RKO depot set at the studio's Encino ranch,
in* Badman's Territory.

leased V & T's No. 25 from the railroad, intending to feature it in John Wayne's *Tycoon* (1947). While that locomotive ultimately did not appear in the Wayne title, RKO bought No. 25 later that year for $5,000. That same year, Paramount and MGM also returned to V & T for more equipment, including a wrecking crane used by Paramount in Alan Ladd's *Whispering Smith* (1948).

Several studios purchased equipment from other lines as well. In late 1939, Warner Bros. acquired from the Hobart Estate Co., for use in *Torrid Zone* (1940), its "Eureka" 3-foot gauge locomotive, originally built in 1875 for Nevada's Eureka & Palisade RR. When Warner Bros.'s Burbank lot was later down-sized, the studio's railroad equipment was moved to its Calabasas ranch property, but returned to the studio in the late 1950s, where it was placed on a 200-foot stretch of track at the south end of WB's famed Laramie Street, which, as noted in another chapter, the studio had constructed primarily for its TV oaters.

In 1941, Universal purchased its Nevada Co. Narrow Gauge No. 5, a 3-foot gauge originally built in 1875 to transport timber from Lake Tahoe to Virginia City, for use in *The Spoilers* (1942), starring John Wayne and Randolph Scott. No. 5 also appeared in Jimmy Stewart's *Winchester 73* (1950) and John Payne's *Rails into Laramie* (1954), which also featured the V & T's No. 18 and No. 22, leased from Paramount.

At least five films were shot in Nevada, moreover, on the V & T RR itself, including Jock Mahoney's *Roar of the Iron Horse* (1951) chapter play. 20th Century-Fox's train, the Dardanelle & Russellville RR's No. 8, was a fifty-year veteran on various Midwestern lines. No. 8 made its first screen appearance in Tyrone Power's *Jesse James* (1939), on lease from the company. In 1945, Fox purchased No. 8 for its musical *Centennial Summer* and within a short time the studio's back lot railroad included two depots, an engine house, several hundred feet of track and more than a dozen wooden and steel cars. In the late 1950s, Fox moved its railroad equipment to its Malibu Canyon ranch northwest of L.A. By that point, however, the studio preferred to shoot most rail scenes on location.

The V & T RR's No. 27, which appeared in Roar of the Iron Horse (1951), *now rests in the railroad museum at Carson City, Nevada.*

Studios with trains also did a brisk rental business with other studios. Paramount, for example, leased Republic its No. 18 for use in Roy Rogers' *Nevada City* (1941) for rail scenes shot in Soledad Canyon near Newhall, one of which was later used in the opening to Republic's "Stories of the Century" TV series. No. 18 also appeared for Republic in Duke's *Dakota* (1945) and Jim Davis' *Last Stagecoach West* (1957). The Pacific Coast Chapter Railway Locomotive & Historical Society's No. 21 (a former V & T engine) saw service in Forrest Tucker's *Rock Island Trail* (1950), which, as noted earlier, featured a train rented from the B & O RR. Republic used RKO's No. 25 in William Elliott's *The Last Bandit* (1949), which also featured the Lang and Ravenna depots in Soledad Canyon northeast of Newhall. Randolph Scott's Warner Bros. title *Carson City* (1952) featured Paramount's No. 22 and Universal's *Rails into Laramie* (1954), shot in part on a spur midway between Lone Pine and Mojave, featured both No. 18 and No. 22.

328

The Ravenna depot appeared in Bill Elliott's The Last Bandit ((1949).

Eventually, the studio-owned railroads fell victim to the collapse of the studio system. When Desilu Productions purchased RKO in the 1950s, that studio's rail equipment was put in storage for years and ultimately became the property of the state of Nevada, where some of its locomotives are now on display at the railroad museum in Carson City. In 1970, all of MGM's equipment was auctioned, with its No. 11 sold to the Old Tucson location/tourist attraction and the studio's equipment also winding up there after a side-trip to CBS Studio Center, the old Republic lot, for use in Jim Garner's comedy *Support Your Local Gunfighter* (1971).

The Lang station appeared in the same title.

Paramount's No. 22 made her last run for a TV episode of "Wild Wild West." Then, in 1971 the studio began selling off its railroad equipment.

But railroad scenes have hardly disappeared from movie/TV plotlines, videos or commercials. Short Line Enterprises bought some of Paramount's equipment and the Fox railroad collection. Headquartered in Fillmore, Short Line operated excursion trains between Fillmore and Santa Paula and also contracted for film and TV work, such as the "Adventures of Briscoe County, Jr." series.

James Clark, a former Chrysler Corp. factory-sponsored drag racer and antique car restorer, became one of the leading railway specialists in the modern film industry. Clark first developed his expertise as a provider of railroad services for the movies while working in the late 1970s with a Carson City company restoring antique engines and cars and as owner of the Nevada Film Agency, a firm providing location and related services to film units working in Nevada. In 1985, he returned to California, opening the Newhall Ranch Movie Train Co. on an abandoned stretch of track in the Santa Clarita Valley. Over a four and a half year period, the Newhall facility worked on 74 features, TV series and commercials, including the Charles Bronson actioner *Assassination* (1986), Robert Mitchum's ABC mini-series "War and Remembrance" (1987), *Throw Momma from the Train* (1987) and *Lost Boys* (1986), as well as episodes of "MacGyver," "Kung Fu, the Next Generation" and "Unsolved Mysteries."

In 1990, Clark began a five-year stint with Short Line Enterprises in Fillmore, adding another 100 titles to his resume, including Steven Seagal's *Under Seige II* (1994) (shot in the Colorado Rockies), *Money Train* (1995), *City Slickers II* (1993), *Chaplin* (1991), *Of Mice and Men* (1991) and episodes of "Dr. Quinn, Medicine Woman" (for which he constructed the railroad set and worked on 22 episodes) and "Briscoe County, Jr."–in which one exciting transfer from Briscoe County's trusty steed "Comet" required repeated retakes when the riderless horse, after each transfer, easily outran the locomotive, appearing to grin at engineer Clark as the horse left the "speeding" train in the dust.

In 1995, Clark left Short Line to form the Santa Clarita Railway Co. and was soon enjoying a brisk business in that enterprise. During a 53-week stint on the feature version of *Wild Wild West* (1999), starring Will Smith, for example, he took three locomotives, ten cars and a crew of seven to New Mexico for filming at the King Ranch and on Santa Fe's famed Cook movie ranch (also used in *Silverado*, 1985, among other titles), laid two miles of track in California, New Mexico and Arizona, filmed on Idaho's scenic Camas Prairie RR (also used in *Breakheart Pass*, 1975) and did some work at Disney's Golden Oak Ranch near Newhall.

Later, he moved to Arizona and opened the Tombstone Mercantile Company, stocked with western antiques and collectibles. But Clark also continued to provide railway thrills for moviegoers and TV fans, working, for example, on the six-part series, "Into the West," which Steven Spielberg produced for TNT–and thus helping to maintain the tradition of exciting railroad scenes so prominent in our great films.

Movie Dams

Roy Rogers' *Heldorado* briefly showcased Nevada's Boulder Dam, in the mountains above Las Vegas. But some of the most exciting B-western and serial scenes featured California dam sites.

Action shots for Roy's *The Far Frontier* (1949) and *Bells of Coronado* (1950) were filmed at Littlerock Dam near Palmdale, about an hour's drive north of L.A. Completed in 1924 to provide water for the area's pear orchards, the 170-foot-tall multi-arch structure is located only a few miles from the San Andreas fault and has been a perennial concern of state bureaucrats–so much so, in fact, that it has at times been drained of water. Littlerock's familiar arched side and impressive downstream view remained on my last visit exactly as they appeared in the Rogers films.

The Littlerock Dam's most familiar side.

The Littlerock Dam's less familiar side also appeared in Bells of Coronado (1950).

Overlooking the San Fernando Valley in the hills northeast of L.A. is the Pacoima Dam at the southwest end of the Pacoima Canyon. Completed in 1929, 372 feet high and 640 feet wide, Pacoima was the setting for an exciting chapter ending in *Zorro Rides Again* (1937), as well as action shots for the 1936 Jack Perrin cheapie *Desert Justice* and a 1934 William Berke featurette *Wild Waters* with stuntmeister Dave Sharpe and the dog Flash. When I visited the dam in the 1990s, the steep climb to its top was via an enclosed tram rather than the open flatcar seen in the *Zorro* chapter ending. It is still a harrowing experience, believe me. Also, a visit required payment of a $50 fee and jumping through several bureaucratic hoops. But what a treat to find and visit!

The St. Francis Dam, across the San Francisquito Creek near Saugus, about forty miles north of L.A., was the setting for Ken Maynard's *$50,000 Rewar*d, filmed during the dam's construction and released in 1925. The St. Francis collapsed two years after its completion in March of 1928, leaving 400 dead and millions of dollars in agricultural losses. The dam's designer William Mulholland, chief engineer for the L.A. water and power department, had also designed the Mulholland or Hollywood Dam, completed in 1924 in the hills east of L.A.'s Hollywood Freeway. The Hollywood Dam has appeared in such A-features as *Earthquake* (1974) and may also have been the site for some serial scenes, although that is doubtful.

Pacoima Dam.

Dam scenes for *Dick Tracy's G-Men* (1941) were filmed at the Morris Dam in the San Gabriel Mountains near L.A. Constructed in the early 1930s and located along

Morris Dam.

Highway 39 about fifteen miles northeast of Pasadena, the Morris facility is 245 feet deep and 750 feet wide at its crest. It was also used in *Dick Tracy Returns* (1938) and *King of the Texas Rangers* (1941), although the exploding dam spillway sequence featured in those serial greats was stock footage from a Lydecker brothers miniature first created at Republic for Ralph Byrd's *Born to be Wild* (1938).

Morris Dam spillway.

Other dam appearances have been examined elsewhere in this volume. A partially fake cliff next to the Lake Sherwood dam near Thousand Oaks was used for thrilling spills and dives in many films and an exciting sequence for *Adventures of Captain Marvel* (1941) actually took place on the curving top of that dam. As also noted elsewhere, the dam, water wheel and mill house at little Cedar Lake above Big Bear were the setting for exciting scenes in many

The wonderful Lydecker brothers Morris Dam miniature.

films. But that site was put to best use in *Trail of Robin Hood* (1950). Roy Roger's chasing Cliff Young across the dam and to his death in a fall from the Cedar Lake water wheel furnished a thrilling climax for our hero's last color series film.

The dam at the end of Big Bear Lake itself still looks as it did in the filming days, when it played host to a particularly exciting cliffhanger in Episode 9 of *King of the Royal Mounted* (1940), with stuntman Dave Sharpe doubling Mountie Allan Lane in a water fight with a heavy, ending with Sharpe/Lane apparently

Big Bear Dam.

The Big Bear dam spillway hosted an exciting chapter ending in the Republic serial great King of the Royal Mounted *(1940).*

falling to certain death through the dam spillway–only to be saved at the beginning of the next chapter by a rope thrown "in the nick of time."

The Lake Hemet dam across from the Garner Ranch near Palm Springs was also used in films and Yuma's Laguna Dam appeared in Autry's *Red River Valley* (1936).

As noted elsewhere in this book, other dams also had parts in the movies. The Tinemaha Dam, located 33 miles north of Lone Pine on the highway to Bishop, was used, for example, in Roy Rogers' first starrer, *Under Western Stars* (1938).

Airfields

Westerns and serials sometimes included scenes filmed at airfields in the Los Angeles area. One of the most popular was the L. A. Metropolitan Airport at Van Nuys in the San Fernando Valley. Opened in 1928, the Van Nuys facility originally consisted of 80 acres amid scattered trees and farmlands. Soon, it included six hangers and an art-deco control tower with such Tinseltown luminaries as Howard Hughes, Hoot Gibson, Wallace Beery and Gene Autry reportedly flying their own planes there.

In 1939, Metropolitan Airport played host to a number of major films, including *Lost Horizon* (1937), *Men with Wings* (1938), *Storm over the Andes* (1935) and Laurel and Hardy's *Flying Deuces* (1939). During World War II, the Army purchased 163 acres adjacent to the airport for a military airfield and the airport made its most notable screen appearance in *Casablanca* (1942). A hanger seen in that fine Bogart film is no longer part of the now huge Van Nuys airport but at this writing could still be seen on Waterman Drive near Woodley Avenue on the edge of the airport property.

Metropolitan Airport's art-deco control tower, in Junior G-Men *(1940).*

Metropolitan Airport also appeared in several serials. Its art-deco tower and two of its hangars were featured in Chapter 9 of *Junior G-Men* (1940), while its runway and a hangar, which in 1941 was situated on the north edge of the airport, made less distinctive appearances in *Tailspin Tommy* (1934), *Tailspin Tommy in the Great Air Mystery* (1935), *Flying G-Men* (1939), *Junior G-Men of the Air* (1942) and *Hop Harrigan* (1946), among other chapter plays.

Another San Fernando Valley airport made an appearance in at least one serial. The Glendale Airport (not to be confused with the still thriving Burbank-Glendale-Pasadena Airport, into which movie fans often fly) was featured in *Sky Raiders* (1941), with signs for its Grand Central Air Terminal and the Trimm

The old Glendale airport in the 1990s.

Aircraft Corp. (also located there in the filming days) clearly visible in various scenes. When friends and I visited it several years ago, the Glendale Airport terminal, which also appeared (complete with incongruous palm tree) as the London airport in a "Sherlock Holmes" entry and in the opening scenes of *Hollywood Hotel* (1937), was still standing at 1310 Air Way, near the San Fernando Road exit to the Pasadena Freeway (Freeway 134).

Griffith Observatory

Another Los Angeles landmark appeared in one of the most famous western serials, as well as other chapter plays and features. The generosity of controversial mining tycoon and land speculator Griffith J. Griffith gave moviedom two favorite filming sites: the 3,015-acre L. A. park and observatory that bear his name. A penniless Welsh immigrant who amassed a fortune in the golden state, Griffith donated the parkland to L. A. in 1896. In 1912, he offered the city $100,000 to build an observatory on the property and another $50,000 the next year to erect a Greek theater.

By that point, Griffith had also served a year in San Quentin for shooting out his wife's eye during a drunken argument. Under those circumstances, city fathers would accept no gift from the convicted felon. After his death, however, a trust the philanthropist had established turned his dream into a reality. Griffith had envisioned an observatory and theater high atop Mount Hollywood but an area on the slope of the mountain proved to be a more financially feasible site. Construction began in December 1933 and was completed seventeen months later at a cost of over $655,000. The facility was a huge concrete structure topped by three copper-covered domes, the largest and most familiar a hundred feet across and the smaller two thirty feet wide.

The observatory's 25-cent planetarium shows became an immediate hit but, from the beginning, it also attracted many movie crews. The 1955 James Dean-Natalie Wood hit, *Rebel Without a Cause*, made the most extensive use of the site, including the front of the observatory building, its theater and a forty-foot-high monument to major astronomers. More recent movies shot there included the 1987 *Dragnet* spoof, *The Terminator* (1984), the serial-influenced *Rocketeer* (1990) and the 1999 version of *The House on Haunted Hill*. The facility also hosted such TV series as "Superman" and "Wonder Woman," as well as a number of earlier features, including Charleton Heston's *Dark City* (1950) and *War of the Colossal Beast* (1958).

Griffith Observatory.

The very first title to utilize the site, however, was Gene Autry's futuristic Mascot western serial *The Phantom Empire* (1935), filmed the year construction was completed. With the observatory playing the underground city of Murania, Gene did battle with the baddies on various exterior walkways and steps and against the backdrop of the facility's copper roof and art-deco wall. A good shot of the observatory's largest dome appears repeatedly in Republic's *The Purple Monster Strikes* (1945) serial. But only two brief scenes were actually filmed there–an Episode 1 shot of stars Dennis Moore and Linda Stirling seeking to gain entry to scientist James Craven's observatory from a walkway around the largest dome, while heavy Roy ("Purple Monster") Barcroft does the first of his endlessly repeated body exchanges with the hapless Craven, plus a quick scene in Episode 2 of the leads getting in their coupe, apparently in the observatory driveway.

One might have expected Universal's *Flash Gordon* and *Buck Rogers* serials to give the observatory prominent display as well. As a matter of fact, newspaper articles on the observatory's history claim it served as Emperor Ming's lair on the planet Mongo. But those Buster Crabbe chapterplays made *very* limited use of the site; indeed, a quick shot of the largest dome as backdrop for the title card to Episode 1 of *Flash Gordon Conquers the Universe* (1940) may have been the observatory's only appearance in filmdom's most famous sci-fi serials.

Jungleland

Although never a western movie location, to my knowledge, a Thousand Oaks business that was both a tourist attraction and the world's largest provider of jungle animals for movie shoots provided animals for western titles and actually appeared in jungle serials and features. First called Goebel's African Lions and at one point known as the World Jungle Compound, Jungleland was the brainchild of Louis Goebel. Born in 1896 in Buffalo, New York, Goebel was the son of a meat slaughtering and packing house operator who became a skilled meat cutter at an early age. But in 1919, he decided, over his parents' objections, to seek a new life in sunny California. The next year, he got a job as caretaker for the zoo animals at Universal Pictures in North Hollywood, living in a cottage on the grounds.

When Universal head Carl Laemmele decided to dispose of the studio's menagerie in 1926, Goebel bought six of their big cats with plans to rent them to movie companies. After a number of false starts, he purchased five lots in the then new community of Thousand Oaks , along the old Ventura Highway northwest of L. A., for the incredibly low price of ten dollars per lot. There, with a loan from his mother, he built his animal compound as well as a large building that could be used for community events.

Louis Goebel (left) at his compound.

Not all area residents were happy with their noisy new neighbors. But when Kathy Parks, the daughter of a local couple, marched over to the compound, her brown eyes flashing, to complain that the roar of the lions was disturbing the family milk cow, the handsome Goebel also acquired a wife, later joking that it was "cheaper to marry her" than risk a lawsuit. Married in 1928, they remained a devoted couple until Goebel's death in 1981.

Situated beneath a canopy of large oak trees, the compound would eventually house a diverse collection of exotic animals, including not only lions and elephants, but also pumas, tigers, panthers, monkeys, camels, kanagaroos, snakes, deer, bears, baboons, water buffalo, hippos, zebras, wolves and birds. In 1929, Goebel opened the compound to the public. To attract crowds, he advertised in local directories and school annuals. A 15-minute promotional record was also sold to visitors for $1.50. But the main attractions, of course, were the movie animals. When Johnny Weissmuller's *Tarzan, the Ape Man* was filmed at nearby Lake Sherwood in 1931, Goebel provided the animals, as he did for a number of other entries in that series. Compound animals also appeared in such major productions as *Samson and Delilah* (1949), *The Robe* (1953), *The Egyptians* (1954), *Demetrius and the Gladiators* (1954) and *The Lion and the Horse* (1952), as well as *Bedtime for Bonzo* (1951) and *Bonzo Goes to College* (1952).

B-titles in which the compound starred included *Valley of the Headhunters* (1953) and other entries in Weissmuller's *Jungle Jim* series. Serial appearances included not only Republic's *Jungle Girl* (1941), filmed largely at Lake Sherwood, but also Columbia's *The Monster and the Ape* (1945), Ralph Byrd's *The Vigilante* (1947) serial about the exploits of a movie cowboy, Don Mcguire's *Congo Bill* (1948) and Buster Crabbe's *King of the Congo* (1952). For *Jungle Girl*, director Bill Witney even convinced star Frances Gifford to ride Bunny, one of the compound's elephants, although Helen Thurston and other stuntpeople handled most of her action scenes.

The compound's snarling satin-black panther, Midnight, not only menaced many heroines in serials and features but in 1963, Midnight or a descendant, actually escaped from its cage, terrorizing the countryside. "Wild Panther On Loose Near Thousand Oaks," a Los Angeles *Herald Examiner* headline exclaimed. Hounds brought in by actor/singer Stuart Hamblin ultimately discovered Midnight under a building at the compound but the frightened cat had to be put down.

Some Jungleland animals became movie stars of sorts. Jackie and other compound lions played Leo, the MGM logo lion, for example, and Goebel's chimp Jiggs appeared as Cheeta in several Tarzan entries. Other animals achieved fame outside the movie industry. One Goebel lion became Gilmore, an oil company mascot.

Naturally, Goebel's animals were frequently taken from the compound to studios or exterior locations for filming; for example, two elephants who appeared as prehistoric mastodons in *One Million B. C.* (1940). But some shooting did take place in a huge pen and a large water tank, among other compound sites. The facility also sometimes doubled as a zoo. Several amusement rides made it suitable for carnival scenes as well and in 1947, a small circus was erected at the site for the first Conejo Days celebration. Officially named Circus Days in 1949, then Stagecoach Days and Pioneer Days in 1950 and 1952, respectively, the event was official dubbed Conejo Valley Days in 1957 and included, over the years, rodeo and carnival rides, among other attraction. In fact, Ralph Byrd's *The Vigilante* probably drew on celebration facilities and Goebel's compound for its carnival/zoo and rodeo scenes.

The facility also attracted some of the most famous wild animal trainers in the business, most notably Melvin Koontz, who worked at the compound from 1946 until his retirement in 1964, and Mabel Stark, billed as the "Most Famous Woman Animal Trainer in the World." In Episode 1 of *Congo Bill* (1948), Mel Koontz played a bit part as a novice whom Congo Bill (played by Don McGuire) is supposedly teaching to train lions. Koontz also worked lions for the exciting night club scenes in *Mighty Joe Young* (1949).

Louis Goebel did not remain with the compound through its entire history. In 1946, he sold the property to Trader Horne, a Saint Louis animal importer, and Billy Richards, who at one time was owner-manager of the Selig Zoo in Los Angeles. Renaming the facility the World Jungle Compound, the new owners specialized in providing animals and facilities for movie productions. But in 1955, they sold to movie executives James Ruman and Sid Rogel, who renamed the site Jungleland, got options to increase its size from its original twenty acres to 178 acres, and planned to build a tramway that would circle the facility and carry visitors to an area south of the newly completed Ventura Freeway, which was to be called Safari Land and would feature animals in natural habitats.

Within five years, that venture failed and the property reverted to Louis Goebel, who entered into an agreement with descendants of a German family of zoo operators to open The New Jungleland. When that partnership failed, Goebel again attempted to run the facility on his own. The compound's animals continued to make appearances in movies, including *Dr. Doolittle* (1967). By that point, however, Disneyland and Knotts Berry Farm had become stiff competition for Jungleland as a tourist attraction.

A serious and highly publicized accident on the property was no help either. The compound had survived a 1940 fire in which a number of animals were destroyed as well as a variety of mishaps, including Goebel's mauling by a lion during filming of a Buster Crabbe feature at the facility. But in 1966, a lion seriously injured Jayne Mansfield's young son, Zoltan, during the actress' visit to Jungleland for a photo shoot. The actress was killed in an automobile accident the next year but her estate sued Jungleland for $1.6 million.

Faced with the lawsuit and other setbacks, Jungleland filed for bankruptcy in 1968. The next year, 1800 birds and animals as well as many fixtures were sold at auction–a sad event for Louis Goebel, who had devoted most of his life to Jungleland. He persuaded local officials to have the property rezoned for commercial development and the colorful Jungleland sign, visible for years to freeway motorists, was soon all that was left of Goebel's dream. The property is now home to Thousand Oaks' civic arts center.

L. A. County Arboretum

Typically, studio black lots included a "jungle" section for those titles. But the L. A. County Arboretum and Botanic Garden in Arcadia, near Pasadena, also provided a perfect setting for such scenes. Long part of the estate of California tycoon Elias Jackson "Lucky" Baldwin, the property was purchased by the state and county in 1947 for creation of the arboretum. But the lush, jungle-like foliage on the estate obviously preceded the state's acquisition, because the area began appearing in Tarzan and other titles as early as the mid-1930s. Later, portions of the Jungle Jim series were shot there. According to some reports, Johnny Sheffield's Bomba series also used the arboretum, although most "jungle" scenes in those films, according to Sheffield, used the tiny jungle set created for the series on one of Monogram's two tiny studio sound stages.

Interestingly, no serials apparently utilized the arboretum. But it did appear briefly in Gene Autry's *Roundup Time in Texas* (1936), although most of the "Africa" scenes for that title used the jungle section on Republic's back lot and the L. A. river bed on the studio's northern perimeter.

Over the years, the arboretum has continued to make regular film and video appearances. Queen Anne's Cottage, an historic structure on the property, and a backlot replica were regulars on the "Fantasy Island" TV series. Earlier, the cottage's exterior was seen repeatedly in the Republic serial, *Federal Agents vs.*

The Los Angeles County Arboretum.

Underworld, Inc. (1949). And a replica of a portion of the White House was constructed at the arboretum for the 1993 Kevin Kline comedy *Dave*.

Racetracks

An L. A. landmark adjacent to the arboretum has also appeared in many films. In the early days, "Lucky" Baldwin built a racetrack on his Rancho Santa Anita. It closed. But in 1934, a group of investers headed by producer Hal Roach opened the Santa Anita Park, which was to become the most famous of California's thoroughbred racetracks, on the same site.

Will Rogers' *In Old Kentucky, Charlie Chan at the Race Track* (1936) and the Marx Brothers classic *A Day at the Races* (1937) were among early titles reportedly shot there. But westerns and other titles with a horse-racing plot line typically drew, at most, on Santa Anita newsreel footage mixed with principal photography filmed elsewhere. Shirley Temple's *The Story of Seabiscuit* (1949) utilized, for example, newsreel footage from various racetracks, including color footage of the Santa Anita Handicap.

When westerns with a modern-day plot line included original racetrack footage, those scenes were usually shot at the smaller Devonshire Downs in the San Fernando Valley community of Northridge. That racetrack, the site for which is now part of the Northridge campus of California State University, was very likely the location for the climactic race in Roy Rogers' *My Pal Trigger*, although "training" for the race took place on the exercise tracks of the Kentucky Park Farm (now Ventura Farms) and another Hidden Valley ranch, near Thousand Oaks.

Automobile Chase Roads

Mention western and serial chases and most fans think immediately of Mulholland Drive, the dangerously winding road that runs across the top of the hills separating Hollywood from the San Fernando Valley, then continues west toward the coast. Through various stages of development, Mulholland appeared in countless features and serials from the silent days on. But the highway and surrounding area were put to most effective use in "flying" sequences for Republic's *Adventures of Captain Marvel* (1941) and *King of the Rocket Men* (1949). The sight of Captain Marvel (actually his stunt dummy suspended on wires) racing along Mulholland after a moving van carrying heavies and heroine Louise Currie was truly exhilarating, as was Marvel stunt double David Sharpe's race across the top of the van and daring leap into its cab. The Rocket Man stunt dummy's race down a mountainside into the camera (and bed of another truck of heavies) also furnished one of the more stunning visual images of all serialdom.

But Mulholland was hardly the only setting for car chases. In his memoirs, Clayton (Lone Ranger) Moore recalled filming along Topanga Canyon Road and Malibu Canyon Road in Woodland Hills and the Calabasas–Agoura areas. He no doubt had in mind, among other scenes, the exciting car chase climaxing Episode 1 of Republic's *The Crimson Ghost* (1946), filmed on a portion of the Topanga road a few miles south of Ventura Boulevard. That stretch of highway was also used in the studio's *The Purple Monster Srikes* (1945) for, among other sequences, the spectacular Episode 3 cliffhanger featuring a car-truck collision and explosion. The collision-explosion, of course, took place in miniature (with the studio's special effects whizzes slightly off in their timing for perhaps the only time in Republic's history) but the establishing chase was filmed along Topanga. Columbia's *Holt of the Secret Service* (1941), starring the venerable Jack Holt, used the same stretch of road, which looked at this writing much as it did in the serial era.

The portion of the Santa Susanna Pass Road running past the Iverson location ranch outside Chatsworth, at the northwest end of the San Fernando Valley, also appeared in several later serials, including Columbia's *Superman* (1948) and *Batman and Robin* (1949), and Republic's *The Invisible Monster* (1940). Embarrassingly, Iverson's trails were sometimes obliged to play suburban streets–complete with street signs at "intersections" on the dusty roads!

Devonshire and other Chatsworth area roads were featured in a number of serial titles, including Republic's *Federal Agents vs. Underworld, Inc.* (1949), *Radar Patrol vs. Spy King* (1950) and *the Crimson Ghost*. In such scenes, sharp-eyed front-row kids could occasionally spot Stony Point, a prominent Chatsworth formation with a chimney rock at one end, seen in the background of much Iverson Ranch

Holt of the Secret Service (1941) *gets his man along the winding Topanga Canyon Road.*
Note the outlines of the road in the background of this scene.

filming.

Among serial makers, Columbia was most likely to venture north of L. A. to the Palmdale-Lancaster area for desert chase scenes through stands of Joshua trees (*Hop Harrigan*, 1946, *Bruce Gentry*, 1949). Republic's *Manhunt of Mystery Island* (1945) utilized a portion of the Pacific Coast Highway near Laguna Beach, where many of the exteriors for that title were filmed, while *Captain Marvel, Mysterious Dr. Satan* (1940) and a number of other serials used sites along the coast highway in the Malibu area.

Mascot utilized a variety of streets and highways for its chapter plays. Universal shot some excellent highway chase scenes. In one particularly memorable sequence, for example, a car was crashed into the railing of a Barham Blvd. bridge and, via movie magic, appeared to collapse onto the Hollywood Freeway below. But especially in later years, Universal relied heavily on stock footage, including the scene just noted, as well as the dirt roads in the hills of the studio's huge back lot.

Universal, of course, was not the only studio to rely heavily on stock footage for its chase scenes. Republic drew increasingly in later years on stock for its highway chases and related scenes. For example, an exciting car-truck chase and transfer sequence in *Government Agents vs. Phantom Legion* (1951) was lifted entirely from *Citadel of Crime* (1941), a little George Sherman gem for which exteriors had been filmed in the hills near Hemet.

In fact, the list of western and serial settings is seemingly endless. In the Los Angeles area alone, the Malibu and Laguna Beach coastline hosted many western (e.g., *Apache Rose*, 1946) and serial (*Manhunt of Mystery Island*, 1945) titles, as did Lake Elsinore and other waterways examined in this book.

In his first color feature, Roy Rogers got his man on the beach at Malibu.

Harry Lauter and Aline Towne were on the beach for
Trader Tom of the China Seas (1954), *one of Republic's last serials.*

And Bill Witney began the exciting climax to Spy Smasher (1942) *at Lake Elsinore.*

Mansions, especially the estate of Mrs. George Lewis on Hilgrove Avenue in Beverly Hills, which appeared in *Manhunt of Mystery Island* (1945), *Batman and Robin* (1949) and Roy Rogers' *Wall Street Cowboy* (1939), among many other titles, were also regular players. All helped to make westerns, serials and television productions a uniquely enjoyable experience for fans, young and old alike.

The Lewis Mansion. Photo Bison Archives

Another perspective of the mansion, in Manhunt of Mystery Island (1945).

The entrance to the Lewis Mansion was equally familiar to serial fans.   Photo Bison Archives.

Happy Trails!

The locations utilized in western features, serials and television productions not only helped to mold popular images of the American west; they also greatly enhanced viewer enjoyment of western productions. In fact, when producers relied on sound stage "exteriors," as they increasingly did in the TV era, fans invariably felt cheated.

Visits to the sites will also be an enormously rewarding experience. If you have not yet taken any movie location trips, I urge you to do so and hope that this book will help you along many "happy trails." As noted at various points in the book, several of the most used locations have fallen victim to urban and suburban sprawl. But there is much to see even at those sites. The great Iverson ranch, for example, is now largely covered with condos and mansions. But its famous Garden of the Gods formations are protected by a conservancy. Its equally famous Nyoka cliff and Lone Ranger rock also remain untouched by developers. Much of Corriganville, moreover, is now a park, despite development on one part of the ranch. Many other locations remain largely or entirely intact.

But whether you are on a location trek or simply watching your favorite productions, my hope is that this book will give you many hours of viewing enjoyment. As you visit the sites in person or on film, compare what you see with the photographs and histories contained in *Those Great Western Movie Locations*. You should not be disappointed!

Index